# THE WILL DRAFTSMAN'S HANDBOOK

# THE WILL DRAFTSMAN'S HANDBOOK

*Sixth Edition*

D M Pettitt
*MA (Oxon), Solicitor*

*edited by*

Robin E Riddett
Reader at the College of Law

LONGMAN

*First published* 1978
*Sixth Edition* 1990

*Published by*
Longman Group UK Limited
21–27 Lamb's Conduit Street
London WC1N 3NJ

*Associated Offices*

Australia, Hong Kong, Malaysia, Singapore, USA

ISBN 0 85121 7001

A CIP catalogue record for this book is available from the British Library.



Printed in Great Britain by Mackays of Chatham Plc, Chatham, Kent

# Contents

**Precedent Forms**

**Appendices**

# Preface

On reading the prefaces to the fourth and fifth editions of this book one is at once struck by the immense changes in law and practice which occurred between 1985 and March 1988. Since then, for the draftsman, the pace of change has, thankfully, declined. Nonetheless much might have occurred and may yet occur calling for radical reconsideration of, now, established practices and procedures.

The particularly ill-considered provisions included in the Finance Bill 1989 were the subject of much criticism within the profession which led to their withdrawal in June of last year. At the time, the Financial Secretary to the Treasury reserved his position by indicating he might bring forward 'a more targeted, specific measure, to counter abuse of the present facility'. This has not yet occurred. Hence for the testator and the draftsman, precatory trusts and two year discretionary trusts in wills remain a possibility in appropriate circumstances; likewise, all the provisions for 'alteration of dispositions on death with restrospective effect'—variations and disclaimers—continue to be available as important tax planning provisions.

As always this edition takes account of developments in case law; it also considers the much restricted availability of capital gains tax holdover relief on the vesting of contingent interests or the exercise of a power of appointment.

This edition, the sixth, is the first to be published without the editorship of its author. It is to be hoped that the original purpose of the book, as expressed in the preface to the first edition, continues to be achieved.

Any suggestion for the improvement of the text or the precedents will be greatly welcomed. The law is dated at 5 October 1990.

# Table of Cases

# Table of Statutes

# Table of Statutory Instruments

# Abbreviations

| | |
|---|---|
| AEA | Administration of Estates Act |
| AJA | Administration of Justice Act |
| CGT | Capital Gains Tax |
| CGTA | Capital Gains Tax Act |
| FA | Finance Act |
| ICTA | Income and Corporation Taxes Act |
| IEA | Intestates' Estates Act |
| IHT | Inheritance Tax |
| IHTA | Inheritance Tax Act |
| IT | Income Tax |
| LPA | Law of Property Act |
| SLA | Settled Land Act |
| TA | Trustee Act |
| TIA | Trustee Investment Act |
| WA | Wills Act |

# Note

The current rate of IHT is 40 per cent. The nil rate applies up to £1~~28,000~~. £150,000.

# Preliminary Notes

# A

# Introduction

The purpose of this book is to offer to the professional will draftsman, within a modest compass, the essential material from which, with suitable adaptations, he may readily prepare the draft of a will appropriate to the circumstances of most of his clients. In some cases, where the estate is very substantial and where complex trusts are envisaged, or perhaps existing trusts have to be taken into consideration, more sophisticated precedents may be required: if so, they are available elsewhere, and this book makes no claim to supersede them. In other cases, where specialised material is not called for, the standard collections of precedents will often be found inconveniently full for regular use, and sometimes not wholly apt to modern conditions. Usually, there is no real need for a will to be complex—clients understandably (and rightly) dislike complexity—and it should be possible to give effect to the wishes of most clients in reasonably simple and straightforward terms. The forms in this book are intended to help the draftsman to do so, in a convenient and economical manner.

The forms have been arranged in such a way as, it is hoped, will facilitate the selection of what is required; and in the more straightforward cases the arrangement may be found to offer what is in itself virtually an outline scheme for the draft. The process of selection should also serve to draw attention to matters on which clients, while relying very much on their advisers, ought to be asked to give specific instructions.

For the increasing number of practitioners who use word-processing techniques these forms may be of assistance in preparing material for storage which will be correspondingly simple and straightforward; and also internally compatible, in that a draft may readily be assembled from whichever of the forms are appropriate to the particular circumstances.

All the forms are accompanied by individual notes, by way of commentary on some of their more important implications. Whilst they cannot be exhaustive, it is hoped that these notes will be of some assistance to draftsmen of varying experience; but they are purely auxiliary and the forms are intended to stand on their own.

The forms are followed by a series of appendices embodying, for ready reference, some of the more important of the statutory provisions bearing on the draftsman's work.

In Appendix 9 there will be found a short series of three complete will forms. These are introduced as offering more or less standard provisions for the needs of many clients disposing of comparatively small estates; and also to illustrate the ease with which a draft may be compiled or adapted from individual forms, to meet the circumstances of any particular case.

The impact of taxation, and especially of capital taxation, is a matter of concern to many clients; and the need for careful planning of the dispositions of an estate, so as to give effect to the client's wishes in such a way as will minimise the burden of tax, imposes a considerable responsibility on the draftsman, not just to give effect to the client's instructions, but to assist the client in formulating them. Tax considerations are of great importance; but so also are a number of other considerations which may arise when instructions are taken, some of them matters of law, some of them matters of drafting, and all of them matters which may affect the way in which the will is planned and prepared. Ease of drafting depends mainly on the care with which instructions have been taken; and these instructions in turn depend on the advice which has been offered, in the light of the relevant law, and of the particular circumstances of the individual client. The Preliminary Notes which follow are concerned with various aspects of this essential preliminary process.

# B

# The Law of Intestacy: Some Comparisons

When considering the possible dispositions of a testator's estate, it is sometimes useful to consider how this would have devolved in the event of intestacy. The comparison is instructive, not only as to the effect of the relevant statutory provisions, but also as to the terms in which these are drawn. The more important of these provisions are reproduced in Appendix 1.

The following points are of particular significance:

(1) If the intestate leaves issue, the entire residuary estate[1] passes to a surviving husband or wife in so far as (exclusive of personal chattels) it does not exceed £75,000.[2] As to any excess over that amount, the estate is divided. One half is held on trust, as to income only, for the surviving spouse for life, and, subject thereto, as to capital, on the statutory trusts for issue. The income and capital of the other half are held on the statutory trusts for issue.

In the larger estates, the entitlement of a surviving spouse to capital can be increased by exercise of the right to call for the life interest to be capitalised[3] and redeemed.[4] A surviving spouse may also call[5] for appropriation of the intestate's interest in any dwelling-house in which the spouse was resident at the time of death, in or towards any absolute interest of the spouse in the estate.[6] These are valuable rights: there seems to be no obvious reason why corresponding rights should not be conferred (in appropriate cases) by will, instead of leaving the spouse to be dependent on the sympathetic exercise of whatever discretions may be given to the trustees or on a family arrangement. Forms 6–15–1 and 6–15–2 might be considered for this purpose.

(2) If the intestate leaves no issue, but other close relatives survive, the entire residuary estate passes to a surviving husband or wife in so far as it does not exceed £125,000.[2] As to any excess over that

amount, the estate is again divided, but in this case, one half of the excess passes to the surviving spouse absolutely. The other half is held absolutely for the parent or parents; or if neither survives, then upon the statutory trusts for any brothers and sisters of the whole blood. Only if there is no surviving parent, brother, sister, or issue of a deceased brother or sister, does a surviving spouse take the whole estate.

If the estate under consideration is so comparatively small that, on intestacy, it would pass entirely to a surviving wife or husband, the question may be asked: Is any purpose served by making a will? It is often said that, all other considerations apart, the real advantage of making a will is that the estate will be administered by an executor of the testator's choice. In this situation, however, the spouse, who would be the most natural choice for executor or executrix, would equally have the best right to apply for letters of administration on intestacy,[7] and although an administrator is in some circumstances at a disadvantage as compared with an executor (in that his or her appointment is not, for most purposes, retrospective), there is no practical difference where the whole estate passes to that person as sole beneficiary.

Perhaps the most convincing reason for advising that a will should be made even in such circumstances is, quite simply, that circumstances (and, in particular, the nominal values of assets) may change, and that the change may pass unnoticed. If an estate now worth less than the amount of the spouse's 'statutory legacy' were to increase above that amount in nominal value, it seems very unlikely that a well-advised testator, or testatrix, would think it right for any part of the estate to pass away from the spouse unless the increase were, in real terms, a substantial increase, or unless the spouse had (as, in particular, a husband might well have) other substantial means. The practical considerations referred to in Preliminary Note D are equally relevant here.

Although the statutory rules for intestate succession were enacted in the light of a thorough analysis of many actual wills, and so represent an attempt to arrive at something like an 'average' series of dispositions, and although, over the years, their effect has been modified by increases in the amount of a surviving spouse's 'statutory legacy',[8] it would seem to be little more than irresponsible, in modern conditions, to allow an estate to devolve (in any case where a spouse is likely to survive) on a basis so unfavourable to the spouse.[9]

Unless a *new* will is made, an intestacy or partial intestacy may also result from the effect upon an existing will of marriage, or of divorce,[10] with perhaps equally undesirable results.

---

1 Excluding assets the succession to which is regulated otherwise than by English law: *Re Collens, decd; Royal Bank of Canada (London)* v *Krogh* [1986] Ch 505.
2 Family Provision (Intestate Succession) Order 1987.
3 According to the method prescribed by the Intestate Succession (Interest and Capitalisation) Orders of 1977 and 1983.
4 Under AEA 1925, s 47A, reproduced in Appendix 1.
5 Under IEA 1952, s 5 and Sched 2, reproduced in Appendix 1.
6 On payment of equality money, if necessary: *Re Phelps* [1980] Ch 275.
7 Under the Non-Contentious Probate Rules 1987, r 22.
8 Eg, the figure where issue survive, originally £1,000, was increased in 1952 to £5,000, in 1966 to 8,750, in 1972 to £15,000, in 1977 to £25,000 and in 1981 to £40,000.
9 For the possible reform of the intestacy law see Family Law, Distribution on Intestacy: Law Commission No 187.
10 See WA 1837, ss 18 and 18A (as substituted by AJA 1982, s 18, discussed in Preliminary Note F–2).

# C

# The Law of Family Provision

Since, in those cases to which it applies, the Inheritance (Provision for Family and Dependants) Act 1975 empowers the court, in effect, to re-make the testator's will, its provisions must always be borne in mind in any case where the dispositions which the testator wishes to make do not self-evidently make 'reasonable' financial provision for any person who is a potential applicant under the Act. For convenience of reference, the Act is reproduced in Appendix 2.

The provisions of most immediate concern to the draftsman are those of ss 1, 2 and 3, which define the circumstances in which the jurisdiction of the court can arise, its powers, and the matters to which it should have regard in exercising those powers. Among subsequent provisions of the Act, perhaps the most important are those which define what property is available for financial provision (should this be ordered), those which confer special powers on the court in relation to transactions intended to defeat applications for financial provision, and those concerning the liability of personal representatives.

Since the main purpose of the Act is to put right something which has gone wrong (or may be supposed to have done so), a detailed discussion of its provisions would clearly be inappropriate in a book on will drafting. However, as the Act may also be seen as putting testators on notice of the fact that testamentary freedom has its limits, there will be cases, from time to time, where it will be part of the duty of the draftsman to offer some guidance to his client as to its effects.[1] Happily, these will be comparatively few: in concerning itself mainly with the ordinary stable marriage, this book reflects (it is hoped) what is still the norm. It will therefore suffice to mention briefly the cases where special care may be required. In terms of s 1 of the Act, these are cases where:

(*a*) the testator's marriage is not stable; or

(*b*) a former wife or husband is alive,[2] and has not remarried;[3] or

(*c*) there are children, whether of the present or of any other marriage, who are the testator's own children; or

(*d*) there are children who are treated by the testator[4] as children of the family in relation to any marriage to which the testator was ever a party; or

(*e*) there is any person for whose maintenance the testator has assumed some responsibility,[5] and who at the time of death was being wholly or partly maintained by the testator.[6]

If an application should be made under the Act by or on behalf of any such dependent, it would be the task of the court to strike a balance between the needs and resources of the applicant, and those of the various beneficiaries, and perhaps also between those of one applicant and another. The difficulty of this task lies usually in the fact that there are probably insufficient resources to provide for them all. The draftsman who is aware of a potential conflict of this kind faces precisely the same difficulty: but if with his guidance the testator has genuinely tried to do the best he can, an applicant may well be deterred.

In advising as to the effect of the Act, in relation to the wishes of his client, the draftsman may find himself called upon to attempt some estimate of the nature and extent of the provision which, in the event of an application, the court might be expected to order. Since the court is given a very wide discretion, it will be extremely difficult to make more than a very approximate estimate, even in relation to the circumstances as they are known to exist at present.[7] In this respect, it is possible to give only general guidance, by drawing attention to the fact that the Act establishes two different standards of provision.

In the case of a surviving[2] husband or wife,[8] the standard is 'such financial provision as it would be reasonable in all the circumstances of the case for a husband or wife to receive, *whether or not* that provision is required for his or her maintenance'.[9] In assessing this, the court is directed to have regard (inter alia) to the provision which the applicant might reasonably have expected to receive if the marriage had ended by divorce instead of by death.[4,10] Such provision will be likely to include a substantial transfer of capital, perhaps to the extent of making up the capital of the applicant to a third, or even half, of the total capital assets of the parties. In particular, it may involve the transfer to the applicant of some interest in the matrimonial home.

In the case of other applicants, the standard is based upon reasonable provision for *maintenance*, according to the circumstances.[11] The question is, what, on an objective view, would have been *reasonable*?[12] The provision that is to be made is to meet recurring expenses of living, of an income nature, at whatever standard of living is appropriate to the applicant.[13] However, this need not necessarily be by way of income payments: in some cases a lump sum may be appropriate.

In all cases, some further guidance as to what the court might consider reasonable is to be found in the generalised but quite detailed provisions of s 3 as to the matters to which the court is to have regard in exercising its powers under the Act.

It should also be borne in mind that although the testator's reasons for doing what he did, or refrained from doing, are not in themselves directly relevant to the question, what would have been reasonable? An oral or written statement by the testator is nevertheless admissible as evidence of fact, by virtue of s 21 of the Act. Where there are clear and specific reasons for cutting down or omitting what would otherwise have seemed to be the appropriate provision for a spouse, or any other potential applicant, a contemporaneous written and signed statement should always be placed with the will. This can provide important evidence which otherwise might not be available. Since the terms of such a statement must depend entirely on the particular circumstances, no precedent form is suggested in this book.

In such a situation, the testator may well decide to proceed as he thinks fit, and leave it to the court to make an order if so advised. If based on a careful estimate of the probabilities, this may be the only practical course to take. In some cases, however, the testator might be better advised to make some provision *beyond* what he had in mind, in the hope that an application might at least be discouraged. The facts must be faced, in the interests of the beneficiaries under the will, that even an application which has little merit may have a considerable nuisance value, and that the executors might find themselves under some pressure to compromise it.

For IHT purposes, property affected by an order under the Act is deemed to have devolved subject thereto.[14] So it does also where an order is made by consent.[15]

---

1 See, for a helpful summary, J G Ross Martyn: 'The Inheritance (Provision for Family and Dependants) Act 1975—Precautions and Pitfalls' (83 *Law Society's Gazette*, p 3571).

2 A claim on which no order has been made during the lifetime of a surviving spouse cannot be continued by his or her personal representatives: *Whytte* v *Ticehurst* [1986] Fam 64.

3 An application will be entertained only in exceptional circumstances if the parties had settled their financial affairs on divorce with legal advice: *Re Fullard* [1981] 3 WLR 743.

4 But not necessarily by both parties to the marriage: *Re Leach* [1986] Ch 226 (CA). For some of the implications of this decision see Peter Snow: 'Former Spouses Now "Children of the Family"?' (83 *Law Society's Gazette*, p 1991), suggesting in particular that a divorced wife (or husband) may be able to claim against the estate of the former spouse's deceased father or mother.

5 In terms of s 3(4); and see *Re Beaumont* [1980] Ch 444, and *Jelley* v *Iliffe* [1981] Fam 128 (CA).

6 Ie, by 'substantial contribution in money or money's worth towards the reasonable needs of that person', otherwise than for full valuable consideration (see s 1(3)). As to 'consideration', see, by way of example, *Re Wilkinson* [1978] Fam 22 and *Jelley* v *Iliffe* (above).

7 The court must take into account the facts as known at the date of the hearing (s 3(5)).

8 And also, should death occur within twelve months of decree absolute, a former wife or husband, if an application for a financial provision order or a property adjustment order has not already been made, or determined (see s 14).

9 See *Re Besterman* [1984] Ch 458, showing that the court is not limited to the concept of maintenance; and *Re Leach* (above). *Re Besterman* was considered by the Court of Appeal in *Stead* v *Stead* (1985) 15 Fam Law 154.

10 See s 1(2)(*a*), read in conjunction with s 3(2); but this is not a *maximum*; see *Re Bunning* [1984] Ch 480.

11 Section 1(2)(*b*).

12 See *Re Coventry* [1980] Ch 461, showing also that financial need (or, presumably, the absence of it) is not in itself decisive.

13 See *Re Dennis* [1981] 2 All ER 140.

14 IHTA 1984, s 146.

15 Ibid, s 146(8).

# D

# The Effects of Taxation

## D–1 Estate planning

In the planning of a will, due weight must always be given to taxation considerations, but these should never be decisive. This book is mainly concerned (as are most practitioners) with the testator who is providing for his or her immediate family. In planning a will for such a client, the first responsibility of his professional adviser is to give effect to the client's wishes in making the best possible provision for these beneficiaries. In many cases, there will be only one practicable way to do this. Only where the available resources are such as to allow a measure of choice will taxation considerations bear directly upon the planning of the will; though where choices are open, these considerations will assume great importance.

It is a fact that IHT represents a significant burden on only a comparatively small proportion of all deaths, but it does bear upon a much larger proportion of all professionally drawn wills. Accordingly, the draftsman will be ready to advise as to the bearing of taxation on the real value of the intended beneficial interests, in relation to all but the smallest of the estates with which he is concerned. Taxation bears very differently upon different estates, and upon different dispositions of the same estate. In relation to any particular disposition, while IHT considerations will usually be paramount, it may also be necessary to consider the effects of CGT, and also sometimes of IT.

Since no two cases are ever quite alike, the relevance of taxation considerations, and the weight to be attached to them, will depend entirely on the practical situation. Accordingly, in this book, taxation considerations (like any other) are seen, as far as possible, in their practical aspects. Attention is therefore drawn to particular points in the context of particular dispositions in the notes to those forms to which they may seem to be specially relevant.

It is not the purpose of this book to offer any comprehensive or systematic treatment of the law relating to IHT, CGT or IT: it would not be appropriate to do so within the compass of a book of this kind, nor is it necessary, in view of the number of standard works available for reference. However, by way of introduction to the forms, the present note is included in order to draw attention to various considerations of general importance, relating mainly to IHT and CGT, which will commonly be in view when instructions are taken, and when the draft will is prepared.

### D–2A Mitigation of tax—transfer on death: spouse exemption and nil rate of tax

In the great majority of cases, where the testator is a married man or woman, he or she will not be disposing of a sufficiently large estate for any real choice of dispositions to arise. Where this is the case, a simple will in favour of the surviving spouse will usually be also the most appropriate from the tax viewpoint, at least in the short term. Whatever the theoretical possibilities may be, it is not in practice open to the testator to take the longer view unless the combined resources of the spouses are substantial enough for there to be no short-term problem.

If it may be assumed that the first concern of the testator is to preserve for his or her spouse, so far as possible, a standard of living comparable with that at present enjoyed by the family, the real difficulty lies in estimating, in a marginal case, the amount of capital which may be expected to be required for this purpose. In relating this estimate to the probable value of the testator's estate (which in itself is usually very much of an unknown quantity), it is plainly necessary to make a generous allowance for the probability of continuing inflation, and the strong possibility of erosion of real capital values with the passage of time, particularly where the survivor is likely to outlive the testator for any considerable number of years. Many wives are younger than their husbands, and women tend on average to live longer than men. As to what allowance should be made for this contingency, it is impossible to generalise: there are too many variable and unknown factors. In particular, much will depend on the nature and likely composition of the particular estate, as well as on the view taken of prevailing and prospective social, economic and political considerations. At best, any judgment on such matters must be based to some extent on speculation. Erring, perhaps, on the side of caution, it is usually considered unwise to leave anything away from a surviving spouse unless the present value of the combined estates is at least £200,000. Usually, moreover, the capital of the fund will not be wholly income producing. The family house may account for a substantial proportion, and few widows will be likely to think of the undoubted value of their beneficial occupation as income. The actual income of the rest of the fund cannot necessarily be expected to retain its real value.

By way of contrast, a fairly modest estimate of the needs of a surviving spouse appears to be implied by the statutory provisions as to intestate succession (see Preliminary Note B) under which, where issue survive, the estate becomes divisible in so far as (disregarding personal chattels) its value exceeds £75,000, the spouse receiving that amount absolutely, but only a life interest in half the surplus. Even where no issue survive the spouse cannot expect to receive more than the first £125,000; plus one half of any excess, if there are surviving parents, brothers, sisters, nephews or nieces. While in the case of a small estate the result of these dispositions may be that where issue survive, little or no IHT may be payable on the death of either spouse, this result is obtained by confining the spouse to what may, in effect, be little more than the probable value of the matrimonial home.

Whatever the amount which, in the particular circumstances, is thought to be appropriate by way of provision for a surviving spouse, the short-term effect of the spouse exemption, as to that amount, is to postpone any liability for IHT until the death of the spouse. The whole of the testator's capital is thereby made available, without reduction, during the lifetime of the spouse and, in addition, the spouse is enabled, if sufficient funds are available, to make lifetime transfers within the usual annual and other lifetime exemptions, without any liability at all for IHT.

Hitherto, where the spouse exemption has been fully utilised, it has been seen as a potentially adverse consideration, that when the property passing through the estate of a surviving spouse was eventually taxed, as part of the estate passing on his or her death, its aggregation with the free estate of the spouse, or perhaps with settled property in which the spouse was interested, might have led to a higher rate of tax being incurred than the property in question would have attracted on its own. Under the system of graduated rates of tax which has hitherto prevailed, for purposes of Estate Duty, Capital Transfer Tax and IHT alike, this was a consideration of real importance, and it has always been one of the purposes of estate planning to avoid, so far as possible, the aggregation of values in the same taxable estate, in order to avoid the resultant inflation of the effective rate of tax chargeable on each constituent part.

The introduction of a flat rate of charge to IHT, by FA 1988, s 136, has the effect of removing this difficulty. Accordingly, it can now be said that, in general terms, not only is there no fiscal penalty attaching to the gift of an estate to the testator's surviving spouse within the IHT spouse exemption; but indeed there is a positive fiscal incentive to take full advantage of that exemption, in that any liability for payment of tax is thereby postponed, without any risk that a higher rate of tax will be incurred on the survivor's death as a result.

This generalisation must, however, be qualified in one important respect. In principle, albeit they might become aggregated in the hands of the survivor, the estates of husband and wife are regarded for IHT purposes as separate estates, each entitled to its own exemptions and reliefs. Accordingly, in principle, the benefit of the nil rate band, or (as it were) threshold exemption, is available in relation to transfers by each spouse, whether during their lives or on death. However, in relation to the death of the first of the spouses to die, the benefit of the nil rate can attach only to property on which tax is chargeable at that time; or, in terms of this discussion, on property which is left outside the spouse exemption. Therefore, if the whole estate of the first to die is left to or in trust for the survivor, there can be only one application of the nil rate: in the estate of the survivor. If, on the first death, part of the estate had been left to children, or otherwise outside the spouse exemption, then the nil rate would have been applicable on the first death, in relation to that property; and again on the second death, in relation to the estate of the survivor. Accordingly, if the children benefit under each will, the net value of their combined entitlements will then be greater than it would have been if their entitlements had arisen only under the will of the survivor. However, the estate available in the meantime for the support of the survivor will naturally have been reduced in value by the amount given to the children under the will of the first to die.

The conclusion is therefore that the full benefit of the nil rate can be obtained in each estate if each will gives to or in trust for children, or other non-exempt beneficiaries, an amount up to the nil rate band at the time of death (as in Form 5–3 in this book); residue being given to or in trust for the spouse if he or she is the survivor, and otherwise to the children. If in the circumstances it is not practicable or desirable to give such an amount to the children, the benefit of the nil rate of tax can still be secured, to a lesser extent, by giving such amount as may be appropriate in the circumstances.

Where lifetime transfers have already been made and are not exempt, or only potentially exempt (see Preliminary Note D–2B), the amount of the non-exempt gift by will should not exceed the unused balance of the nil rate of tax: Form 5–3 anticipates this.

Formerly, when tax was chargeable at progressive rates, similar considerations applied in relation to the possible application of lower rates of tax in one estate in comparison with higher rates in the other. Since under that system the overall burden of tax was minimised where the taxable dispositions by each spouse were as nearly as possible equal, it was a general principle of estate planning that the spouses should be placed in a position to make transfers as nearly equal as possible by arranging the ownership of their combined estates in such a way that the values of their estates should themselves be as nearly equal as possible.

In this respect also, the introduction of a uniform, flat rate of tax results in a welcome simplification. It is no longer necessary to advise that estates should be equalised on fiscal grounds alone, except to such extent as may be necessary to obtain the benefit of the nil rate of tax in each estate. To this extent, of course it is still important that each should in fact possess a separate estate, and dispose of it separately; or as much so as possible without detriment to the survivor. Shared ownership of the family house usually goes a long way towards this (but see further at Preliminary Note D–7): for this purpose, the house should be held by the spouses as tenants in common and not as joint tenants. Any lifetime transfers between the spouses which facilitate any of these arrangements will be made within the spouse exemption in the ordinary way: as long as they are not made under any explicit agreement or arrangement, there should be no danger that the Inland Revenue would invoke the anti-avoidance rules against 'associated operations'.

In order to obtain the full benefit of the nil rate of tax in each estate, therefore, it is sufficient for the wills of both spouses to be drawn in reciprocal terms, so that a non-exempt gift to children (or others) will take effect on the first death. For many testators, this will be the only acceptable way to make such provision. Although the effect is, unavoidably, that the amount in question will cease to be available for the support of the survivor (unless possibly made so by way of a 'mini' discretionary trust, as under Form 5–4 in this book), that amount will at least have been available to the spouses during their joint lives, when perhaps they may have been reliant upon it. However, if the amount of the resources available to the spouses exceeds what is necessary for their support, the opportunity is opened for them to consider making transfers inter vivos, either within the standard IHT exemptions or, beyond these, by way of potentially exempt transfers. If this can be done, the benefit may be considerable. Transfers which are exempt at the time when they are made, or which become so during the lifetime of the transferor, will not form part of the estate of the transferor at his or her death and will therefore not be subject to IHT at all. Further, the benefit of the nil rate of tax will continue to be available upon death, except only to such extent as it may have been taken up by any lifetime transfer which was a chargeable transfer.

It is, in general, the policy of the IHT legislation to encourage lifetime gifts (and especially the transfer inter vivos of business and agricultural assets); and these should therefore be considered whenever the available resources permit.

## D–2B Mitigation of tax—lifetime transfers: exempt and potentially exempt transfers

For most testators, the opportunity to make lifetime gifts will arise most often (if at all), within the standard exemptions. These are familiar, but, perhaps for lack of professional advice, may not always be used as fully as they could be. This would be unfortunate, for the amount of an exempt transfer will bear no IHT at all; even though the death of the transferor should occur within seven years afterwards, and even though the transferor should have reserved some benefit to himself.

Accordingly, whenever any question of estate planning comes

under review, it will be appropriate to verify, at the outset, that the available exemptions (under IHTA 1984, as variously amended) have been utilised as fully as possible. In this context, the annual exemption (under s 19), with its option to carry forward an unused balance to the following year, and the exemptions for gifts in consideration of marriage (under s 22) will be particularly in view. Also of considerable importance, and sometimes overlooked, are the provisions whereby (under s 11) 'dispositions for the maintenance of family' are, not in terms exempt, but in fact removed from the scope of the tax altogether: these include (within the meaning of s 11) provision for the maintenance, education or training of children; and reasonable provision for the care or maintenance of a 'dependent relative' of the transferor, including his or her mother or mother-in-law if widowed, separated or divorced, and of any relative of either spouse who is incapacitated by old age or infirmity. Other relieving provisions of which it will be important to take the fullest advantage, are the valuation reliefs (under ss 103–24) in respect of business and agricultural property. However, where a transfer of such property is potentially exempt (below), it may be important to appreciate that (under ss 113A and B and 124A and B, as inserted by FA 1986, Sched 19, paras 21 and 22) relief will only be available on the death of the transferor within seven years if the conditions for relief still continue to be satisfied at that time; however, relief will not be lost by reason of a disposal of the property if similar qualifying property is acquired within twelve months.

For taxpayers disposing of surplus assets beyond the scope of the general exemptions, the opportunity exists to make absolute or (in certain cases) settled gifts, which may qualify for exemption from IHT to an unlimited extent, if made within the requirements for potentially exempt transfers in FA 1986, s 101 and Sched 19, as extended by F(No 2)A 1987, s 96 and Sched 7. These provisions are reproduced in Appendix 7. They were introduced with the stated intention of allowing family businesses and farms to be passed on to the next generation without a possibly crippling charge to IHT. The benefit of these provisions is not, however, restricted to business assets, but is of quite general application. To qualify as potentially exempt, a transfer must in principle be one made by an individual (on or after 18 March 1986) in favour of another individual, or else into an accumulation and maintenance settlement (see Preliminary Note D–6), or a disabled trust. As a relaxation of this general principle (by the Act of 1987), a transfer into a settlement under which an individual has an interest in possession can qualify as potentially exempt; and so can the termination of an interest in possession, where either an individual becomes entitled to any of the settled property, or else it becomes subject to an accumulation and maintenance settlement or disabled trust.

A transfer which qualifies as potentially exempt will become so in fact if and when the transferor has survived the transfer by seven years. In the meantime, it is 'assumed' that the transfer will prove to be an exempt transfer, and accordingly no charge to tax arises when the transfer is made, nor can it have any effect on any other transfer.

A transfer into any other kind of settlement (meaning, for all practical purposes, a transfer into a discretionary trust) can never qualify as a potentially exempt transfer. As under the former law, such a transfer is chargeable as a transfer into settlement, though at half the death rate (and with the benefit of the usual exemptions and reliefs); and the settled property would thereafter be subject to the normal ten yearly charge and 'proportionate' or exit charge, under the provisions of IHTA 1984, Part III, Chapter III. By the effect of provisions in IHTA 1984, ss 54A and 54B (inserted by F(No 2)A 1987, Sched 17), an anti-avoidance charge to tax is incurred if within seven years after a potentially exempt transfer into an interest in possession trust, and during the lifetime of the original transferor, any of the settled property should become subject to discretionary trusts.

Although a transfer into a settlement on discretionary trusts will always be a chargeable transfer, it will not necessarily be a taxable transfer. In particular, it may be made within the nil rate of tax. Because of the great flexibility of such trusts, a discretionary settlement within the nil rate may sometimes be recommended for inclusion in a will, for the reasons discussed in the notes to Form 5–4. For very similar reasons, an inter vivos settlement within the nil rate may be considered. For different reasons, the introduction of short term discretionary trusts into a will may be recommended to facilitate any future variation of the dispositions of the estate, as discussed in the notes to Form 7–1.

Apart from these special applications, it is usually considered that a settlement on discretionary trusts should no longer be recommended. In general, this may be so. However, as a generalisation, it could be misleading. The flexibility which discretionary trusts provide will sometimes be important to the welfare of the beneficiaries; and this consideration may sometimes be of sufficient importance to outweigh the impact of tax charges on the settled property. Indeed, although these tax charges are generally considered to be onerous, the fact is that if estimates are made, they may sometimes seem less so, on the longer view, than those which would be likely to arise over a similar period under other dispositions. Where it is material, this question is one for consideration in relation to the actual circumstances, and with an open mind.

Where a potentially exempt transfer has been made, and the transferor dies within seven years thereafter, the transfer is then treated as a chargeable transfer; but with only partly retrospective effect. Tax is charged by reference to values at the date when the transfer was actually made; but is computed by reference to the rate (or rates) of tax chargeable at the date of the transferor's death. In the context of this and other provisions discussed in this book, the introduction of a uniform flat rate of tax in place of a progressive scale of rates may be expected to give rise, transitionally, to some anomalies.

On a transfer becoming chargeable, the usual exemptions and reliefs would normally become available; though special provisions apply in relation to the application of the annual exemption. These and other detailed rules are to be found in FA 1986, Sched 19 reproduced in Appendix 7. The contingent liability to tax in respect of a potentially exempt transfer may usually be covered by insurance without undue expense. Not only does this protect the beneficiary, but it may also provide a valuable and reasonable safeguard to the transferor's personal representatives, who are contingently but nevertheless personally liable to the Inland Revenue for payment of any tax unpaid by the beneficiary: see Preliminary Note D–3.

Just as a transfer into or out of an interest in possession settlement can be potentially exempt, so does a corresponding charge to tax arise if the life tenant of an interest in possession settlement should die within seven years after termination of the life interest. If death occurs within seven years after the partial termination of a life interest, as where there has been an advancement of capital to a remainderman, a tax charge arises in respect of that part. It is usually possible to obtain insurance to cover any contingent liability in this respect: it will be as well if the trustees have been given express power to effect such insurance.

The favourable treatment of potentially exempt transfers is subject to an important limitation, in the shape of the anti-avoidance provisions in FA 1986, s 102 and Sched 20, printed in Appendix 8. These provisions are intended to prevent a taxpayer from obtaining exemption in respect of a gift of property from which he nevertheless continues, during his lifetime, to derive some kind of benefit; for example, by continuing to live in a house which he had given away; or, perhaps, by the use of insurance arrangements in the form of a so-called 'Inheritance Trust,' as a means to retain effective access to invested capital which he had effectively given away.

The effect of these provisions is that the estate of a transferor at his death is deemed to include any property which, immediately before his death, is (within the meaning of s 102) 'property subject to a reservation'. Any such property is thereby taxed on his death as if it were still his own. For this purpose, property is 'subject to a reservation' if 'possession and enjoyment' of the property is not 'bona fide assumed by the donee' at least seven years before the donor's death; or if at any time in that seven year period 'the property is not enjoyed to the entire exclusion, or virtually to the entire exclusion, of the donor and of any benefit to him by contract or otherwise'.

Provision is made in s 102(4) for the case where there is a gift subject to a reservation and then the reservation is later released or otherwise comes to an end. There is deemed to be a potentially exempt transfer at the time when the property ceases to be subject to the reservation. This might happen at any distance of time after the original gift was made.

Although these provisions of the 1986 Act had no counterpart in the legislation relating to Capital Transfer Tax (nor have they now any application to those transfers which are fully exempt), they do closely resemble provisions which were long established and well known in the law of Estate Duty, and embodied in FA 1894, s 2(1)(*c*). Accordingly, it may be anticipated that the considerable body of authority on the interpretation of the Estate Duty legislation will prove to be of great assistance in the construction of the provisions of the 1986 Act.

As well as setting out a number of detailed rules supplemental to s 120, Sched 20 contains relieving provisions covering two exceptional cases. First, under para 6(1)(*a*), the retention or assumption of a benefit is disregarded if full consideration is given. So, for example, the grant of a lease back of property to the donor may represent consideration, if the lease is granted on fully commercial terms. Secondly, under para 6(1)(*b*), there is an exception, as regards interests in land, where following an unforeseen change in circumstances, reasonable provision is made for the care and maintenance of a relative who has become unable to maintain himself through old age, infirmity or otherwise.

Further anti-avoidance provisions are contained in FA 1986, s 103, whereby certain debts are disallowed as deductions in valuing the estate of a deceased person for tax purposes. Debts to which s 103 applies are broadly those where the consideration for the debt consists of property derived directly or indirectly from the deceased. The enforceability of such debts as between the parties would not, of course, normally be affected by their disallowance for tax purposes; but the existence of such a debt might clearly affect the balance of the beneficial dispositions.

Because, by the effect of s 103, or otherwise in certain comparatively unusual circumstances, the possibility exists that property might be chargeable to tax both in relation to an inter vivos disposition and also in relation to the death of the disponor, s 104 empowers the Board of Inland Revenue to make regulations for avoiding such double charges. They have done so, by the Inheritance Tax (Double Charges Relief) Regulations 1987 (SI 1987 No 1130).

**D–3 Burden of tax**

The balance of the beneficial dispositions under a will may sometimes depend as much on the incidence of liabilities of the estate—and, in particular, of tax liabilities—as upon the beneficial dispositions themselves. In planning the will, therefore, it is important to make the best possible evaluation of the prospective liabilities, and of the statutory provisions as to their incidence; and, where appropriate, to consider whether the effect of those provisions may need to be varied, or compensatory dispositions made, by the terms of the will. Form 4–11 provides a framework within which this can be done.

Of no less importance is the consideration that whenever personal representatives will or may incur a liability to tax, which will be a personal liability on their part, they should be placed in a position to discharge that liability, readily, out of the estate, and with the least possible disturbance to the beneficial dispositions. This aspect of the matter assumes particular importance, and may present particular difficulties where the testator has made lifetime transfers, or might do so in the future, without the personal representatives (or perhaps even his advisers) necessarily knowing anything about them.

The primary liability of personal representatives for IHT on death arises under IHTA 1984, s 200. Under s 211, in relation to deaths on or after 26 July 1983, and subject to any contrary intention shown in the will, IHT on death for which personal representatives are liable, in respect of unsettled property in the UK which vests in them, is to be treated as part of the general testamentary and administration expenses of the estate. Further, under s 211(3), IHT paid by personal representatives which is not a testamentary expense (including, for example, IHT on jointly owned property) is repayable to them by the person in whom the property becomes vested. Although in this respect the subsection does not expressly so provide, it is clearly open to the testator to vary this provision by express provision in the will. An example of such a direction may be found in Form 6–4.

Where an estate is partly exempt, as in the case where it is disposed of partly for the benefit of a surviving husband or wife (or by some other exempt disposition), and partly for the benefit of children (or by some other non-exempt disposition), the allocation of exemptions as between different gifts must be determined by reference to rules embodied in IHTA 1984, ss 36–42, considered in Preliminary Note D–4. These rules affect not only the liability (or otherwise) to tax, but also its incidence. In particular, s 41 establishes two rules. First, no tax is to fall on any specific (ie non-residuary) gift insofar as that gift is exempt. Secondly, no tax attributable to residue is to fall on any exempt share of residue. It seems unlikely that anyone would wish to vary these particular rules; but this in fact cannot be done.

Quite apart from their primary liability for tax on the estate of the deceased, it is most important that personal representatives should be aware of the effect of IHTA 1984, s 199 (as amended), under which they are secondarily liable for any tax chargeable in respect of lifetime transfers; that is, on the value of any potentially exempt transfer which has become chargeable, or of any other chargeable transfer made within seven years of the transferor's death, and which would not have been payable if the transferor had not died within seven years after the transfer. The liability on the part of personal representatives arises, by virtue of s 204(6) (as amended), should tax remain unpaid 12 months after the death.

Like jointly owned property in which the deceased had a share (in relation to which similar difficulties can possibly arise), property comprised in an inter vivos gift by the deceased is in no way under the control of the personal representatives. Indeed, they might not even know that a gift had been made. It is also possible that an unscrupulous beneficiary might perhaps delay payment of tax for which he was liable, knowing that if the personal representatives were assessed they would have to meet the liability. It cannot be too strongly emphasised that although only secondary, the liability of personal representatives is a personal liability, to which distribution of the estate is no answer. Before distributing, therefore, personal representatives should make careful enquiries; and in some cases they might wish to protect themselves by insurance,[1] or by taking an indemnity or other appropriate security. In the present context, however, the most important point of all is that the incidence and effect of prospective liabilities to tax in relation to lifetime transfers, and the possible need for special provision to meet such liabilities, ought to be properly anticipated at the time when the transfers themselves are under consideration.

Where, in conjunction with a potentially exempt transfer, there is an agreement that the donee should bear any tax in the event of the transferor's death within seven years, it is the official view that this agreement would not bring into play the gift with reservation provisions of FA 1986, s 102: see correspondence published in 84 *Law Society's Gazette*, p 1041.

A further secondary liability is faced by personal representatives under IHTA 1984, s 204(9), in respect of unpaid tax chargeable under FA 1986, s 102, on a gift with reservation. Similar or greater difficulties may arise, in that the personal representatives may not be aware that the gift had been made; much less of the possibility of a reservation, the existence of which may be in itself a difficult question of law.

---

1 For solicitor personal representatives professional indemnity cover may be available, see *Law Society's Gazette* of 22 November 1989.

**D–4 Partial exemption**

In cases where part of the estate is left within the spouse exemption (or the charity and related exemptions) and part is not, the precise amount of tax payable in respect of the non-exempt gift, and its incidence as between the beneficiaries, is governed by the partial exemption rules in Chapter III of Part II of IHTA 1984.[1]

The immediate and practical result of these rules, so far as the will draftsman is concerned, is that normal pecuniary legacies, preceding an exempt gift of residue, will rarely attract any tax at all. Tax-free legacies of a specified amount can be given up to the amount of the unused balance of the testator's nil rate band. At the planning stage, therefore, the amount and incidence of any tax liability in respect of non-exempt gifts need enter into the draftsman's calculations only if the amount of any legacies is unusually large, or if the non-exempt gift is not a legacy but a share of residue, the balance of which is given under an exempt gift.

The most usual case is the tax-free gift made immediately to children, preceding an exempt gift of residue to the surviving spouse. Here, the point which will usually concern the draftsman is that for the purpose of calculating the amount of tax attracted by such a gift, its tax-free value to the legatee must be grossed at the appropriate rate, as explained below.

If the amount is at all substantial, however, the draftsman will also be concerned with the rules as to the incidence of tax, which take effect notwithstanding any provision in the will. These depend upon the nature of the non-exempt gift. If the gift is a 'specific' gift (ie, a gift of particular assets or a specified amount) the relative tax is payable, in effect, out of residue. In other words, it reduces the value of residue in the hands of the widow. If, however, the non-exempt gift comprises a share of residue, the relative tax is payable wholly out of the non-exempt share and does not reduce the value of the exempt share of residue. This rule is mandatory, and may lead to an unexpected result. If, for example, residue is given on trust to discharge debts and funeral and testamentary expenses, and to hold the balance in equal moieties for the widow and the children, it would be natural to suppose that IHT would be payable out of the general fund of residue, along with other liabilities, leaving a balance to be divided into two equal shares. That would be incorrect.

Despite the direction in the will, the exempt share of the widow must not suffer any of the tax, which must therefore be taken wholly from the children's share. This result has to be accepted, even if it is undesired.[2] Any attempt to achieve actual equality, by way of additional gift to the children, would be likely to lead to an increase in the amount of tax payable, and should be avoided.

In either case, the amount of tax payable depends upon the gross value of the non-exempt part of the estate; computed according to the statutory rules, the main effect of which may be shortly summarised as follows.[1]

(1) *Specific tax-free gifts.* Where the only non-exempt gifts are specific gifts (as above), on which the tax is payable out of residue, the value of such gifts, for the purpose of apportioning the value of the estate as between exempt and non-exempt gifts, must be calculated by grossing the net amount at the rate appropriate to a transfer comprising only those gifts. Hence, normal legacies within the nil rate band are grossed at the nil rate; ie, they attract no tax. Whether or not a gift bears its own tax depends upon the terms of the will or, if this is silent, on the general law.

IHT attributable to unsettled property in the UK which vests in the personal representatives is declared by IHTA 1984, s 211, to be a testamentary expense. Accordingly, the burden of IHT attributable to a gift of such property, whether it is realty or personalty, will not fall upon the specific beneficiary, unless the will directs that it should do so.

See further at Preliminary Note D–3, and also Forms 4–11 and 6–4, and notes thereto. IHT paid by personal representatives on other property is repayable to them by the person in whom the property becomes vested, unless the will directs otherwise. For an example of such a direction, see Form 6–4.

(2) *Specific gifts bearing their own tax.* In as much as the tax on such a gift falls on the legatee, the amount actually given is the gross value of the gift for the purposes of these rules.

(3) *Taxable share of residue.* Where the only non-exempt gift is a share of residue, the chargeable part of the estate is the amount apportionable to the non-exempt beneficiary or beneficiaries. If there is any preceding exempt specific gift (whether to the spouse, or to charity etc), this is first deducted.

(4) *Different chargeable gifts.* Where, in addition to tax-free specific gifts, there is also any specific gift which bears its own tax, or a non-exempt gift of a share in residue, it is again necessary to calculate the gross value of the chargeable part of the estate, on which tax is payable. In order to find the true estate rate of tax at which to gross net values, however, it is first necessary to make a preliminary calculation in order to find the true relative values of the exempt and chargeable parts of the estate. These calculations are somewhat complex. Suffice it to say here that their purpose is simply to produce the fairest overall result in relation to a will including any such combination of gifts, and that in the somewhat unlikely event of the draftsman being instructed to prepare such a will, the complexity of the calculations which may have to be made on the distribution of the estate need not deter him from so doing.

The foregoing rules may have some further significance at the planning stage, however, in that if the estate is substantial, it may be necessary to consider whether some further tax might be saved by reversing the usual order of dispositions. Thus, if a specific (exempt) gift were made to the spouse with residue (non-exempt) left to children, grossing would be avoided, in that the chargeable estate would be the actual balance remaining after deducting the exempt specific gift. Alternatively, instead of making any specific gift, the will might give residue in whatever might be thought to be appropriate shares between the children and spouse. Again, the chargeable part of the estate would be reckoned without grossing. In the further alternative, there might be a specific gift to the spouse, followed by a gift of residue in shares.

Whether the saving of tax which might result from any of these somewhat unusual dispositions would be sufficient in amount to outweigh their evident practical disadvantages can be determined only by making comparative estimates (so far as these are possible) in the light of the particular circumstances. While it is difficult to generalise, it seems unlikely that in any normal estate the benefit would be more than marginal; and probably much less than the margin of error to which all such calculations are unavoidably subject.

However, in one respect at least, the manner (or order) in which beneficial gifts are made can actually assume considerable importance. Where a partly exempt estate includes property eligible for business or agricultural relief, the incidence of such relief depends upon the provisions of FA 1986, s 105. This section substantially alters the previous rules, with results which may substantially affect the value of the relief to the beneficiaries. Under s 105, where property attracting business or agricultural relief is disposed of by way of specific gift, the relief attaches to the property itself. However, in any other case, the relief has to be allocated on a proportional basis between the exempt and chargeable parts of the estate; with the result that the benefit of the relief is realised only in part. It follows that the maximum benefit can be derived from the relief only where the business or agricultural property is the subject of a specific gift to or for the benefit of non-exempt beneficiaries. From this point of view, therefore, in the normal family situation, business or agricultural property should if possible be given to or in trust for children; any loss to a surviving spouse being compensated in some other way. It should not be given to the spouse.

1 For a straightforward explanation of these somewhat complex rules, see the Board of Inland Revenue booklet IHT 1.

2 For a contrary view of construction giving effect to the testator's obvious intention see *McCutcheon on Inheritance Tax* (3rd ed 1988) para 7–84).

## D–5 Survivorship conditions

In order to guard against the possibility that the deaths of the testator and of an intended beneficiary might occur in a common disaster, or else that a beneficiary, while actually surviving the testator, might do so for a nominal period only, it is common practice to make beneficial gifts in a will subject to a 'survivorship clause'. In one form or another, the effect of such a clause is to make any particular beneficial disposition, or perhaps all such dispositions, subject to the condition precedent that the intended beneficiary should survive the testator by some stipulated period of time, commonly 28 or 30 days. Where this is done, it is of course necessary to make further provision, by way of gift over, for the contingency that the primary beneficiary might fail to survive the period of the condition.

For tax purposes, provision is made by IHTA 1984 in relation to each of these possible situations.

The possibility of contemporaneous deaths is dealt with by s 4(2), which provides that 'where it cannot be known which of two or more persons who have died survived the other or others they shall be assumed to have died at the same instant'. The effect of this provision is that property passing on one death can never, for tax purposes, be treated as passing through the estate of another person who was not actually the survivor; that is to say even though the second person may have to be treated for purposes of the law of succession as having notionally survived the first, by virtue of being the younger. This presumption for succession purposes is embodied in the well known provisions of LPA 1925, s 184; which serves to establish the actual beneficial entitlements to the property, having regard to the occurrence of the contemporaneous deaths, in any case where its ultimate devolution has not been secured by will.

In a case where s 184 operates (necessarily in the absence of a survivorship condition), it will follow that the combined estates will devolve according to the will or intestacy of the notional survivor. In a case where, outside s 184, the beneficiary does actually survive, but for a short time only, and where likewise the interest of that beneficiary was not subject to a survivorship condition, the result will be the same. This may or may not be what the parties intended. Where they are husband and wife, in particular, it may be the case that appropriate wills have been made by each, perhaps in reciprocal terms, which will cover the position. It may nevertheless be considered less than satisfactory that either estate could devolve in any way outside the terms of the testator's own will. It may also be considered a practical inconvenience that if assets in one estate do in fact devolve as part of the other, separate grants will be required.

It may therefore be suggested as a generalisation, from the practical point of view, that if beneficial gifts are made subject to a survivorship condition, all difficulties of this kind will have been prevented. The dispositions of each estate will then depend entirely on the will of the testator concerned, whatever happens; that is to say whether in the event any intended beneficiary should unfortunately predecease, or should suffer death in a common disaster, or should survive only for a short period; or whether the beneficiary should in fact survive to take the benefit in the manner intended.

The consequences of a survivorship condition for IHT purposes are governed by s 92, according to the outcome. It is provided, in effect, that the estate is to be treated for tax purposes as if the property in question had passed directly under whatever dispositions actually take effect, having regard to the operation of the condition. It follows that, as between husband and wife, if the surviving spouse actually survives the period of the survivorship condition (not being more than six months), the spouse exemption is given in the estate of the spouse who first died, in the normal way. If, on the other hand, the spouse failed to survive that period (or at all), no spouse exemption is available in relation to either estate. It would have been otherwise if the survivorship condition had been omitted, where one spouse did actually survive the other, or for succession purposes was deemed to do so; but the practical difficulties already discussed would not have been resolved.

In the case of a gift outside the spouse exemption, to a non-exempt beneficiary, the inclusion of a survivorship condition serves to exclude the possibility of a double charge to tax, if the same property were to pass through two taxable estates. The same result would normally be achieved, however, by virtue of the relief for 'successive charges' under s 141.

### D–6 Minority and contingent interests

If, in the events which happen, residue, or any other part of the estate, is held in trust for one or more beneficiaries who are minors, or whose entitlement is contingent, the property so held will be settled property for IHT purposes;[1] and, in the case of contingent (but not vested) entitlements, for CGT purposes also.[2]

Accordingly, if the terms of the will are such that a minority or contingent interest may arise, whether in favour of the testator's own children, or of grandchildren, or of children of the testator's brothers or sisters, or indeed of anyone, it is necessary to bear in mind the special charging and relieving provisions applicable to settled property, for the purposes of each of these taxes. Although the testator is unlikely to alter the substance of his instructions on this account, the taxation implications should always be considered; and in some cases these may prompt some modification of the instructions, to ensure that tax charges are not unnecessarily incurred.

1 IHTA 1984, s 43.
2 CGTA 1979, s 51, in conjunction with s 46.

*IHT: accumulation and maintenance trusts*

For IHT purposes, if the terms of the will are such that the beneficial trusts are 'accumulation and maintenance' trusts within IHTA 1984, s 71, while tax will have been chargeable on the testator's death in the normal way, the fund will not suffer the tax charges normally imposed on discretionary trusts[1] either when a minor attains majority, or when a contingent interest vests; nor in the meantime. It is therefore important to ensure that nothing in the terms of the will can infringe the requirements of s 71. In the case of what may be termed a normal family will, under which the beneficial entitlements of children (or perhaps of grandchildren or others) are governed by s 31 of TA 1925,[2] compliance with these requirements should be virtually certain, for they are framed with this type of trust primarily in view. In any other case (and perhaps especially in relation to an inter vivos settlement, with which this book is not directly concerned), care is needed. If the requirements are not satisfied, then (in so far as no beneficiary has become entitled to an interest in possession), the settled property will be subject to the ten-year anniversary and proportionate charges imposed by IHTA 1984, Part III, Chapter III.[3] Should property cease to be property to which s 71 applies (or should the trustees make a disposition depreciating its value), in circumstances other than a beneficiary becoming beneficially entitled to it within the terms of the section, or dying before obtaining the specified age,[4] it will be subject to a flat rate exit charge.[5] The rate of charge depends on the duration of the settlement and ranges from 0.25 per cent per quarter for the first 40 quarters to an overall maximum of 30 per cent after 50 years.

The terms of s 71 are thus of such special importance that this section is reproduced in Appendix 5.

The requirements for application of the section are well known, but nevertheless call for comment.

The primary requirement embodied in s 71(1)(*a*) is that . . . 'one or more . . . beneficiaries will, on or before attaining a specified age not exceeding 25, become beneficially entitled to [the settled property] or to an interest in possession in it'.

As to the age of vesting, no difficulty should normally arise. Beneficial interests need not be absolute: an interest in possession will suffice. By virtue of s 31(1)(ii) of TA 1925,[2] a beneficiary whose interest is contingent on attaining an age greater than the age of majority will obtain the necessary interest in possession at majority, since he then becomes entitled to receive the income as of right until his entitlement to capital vests or fails. If it is desired to defer not only the vesting of capital, but also the entitlement to income,[6] the income entitlement must arise by the age of 25 at the latest, to satisfy s 71. However, this entitlement should not normally be deferred beyond the age of 21, because of the next requirement of s 71, that income not applied for maintenance or the like is to be accumulated. In the present context, accumulations cannot be directed for a period longer than 21 years after the testator's death.[7]

It has to be accepted that once an interest in possession has arisen in this way, a charge to tax would arise in the event of the death of the beneficiary[8] even if this happened before he had attained a vested interest in capital,[9] but the amount of such a liability is unlikely to be considerable, unless the estate is very large, or the beneficiary has entitlements under other trusts; and the possibility of premature death will hardly influence the choice of age for entitlement to income.

This choice may, however, be influenced by the consideration that once an entitlement to income has arisen, the effect is, for IT purposes, that the income ceases to be income of the trustees, in whose hands it was liable to the additional rate;[10] and becomes income of the beneficiary, and as such fully available to support a repayment claim against any unused personal reliefs.

There is another aspect of the first requirement of s 71 which may give rise to difficulty in certain cases. This concerns the degree of certainty that (in terms of subsection (1)(*a*)) one or more persons '*will*' become entitled, on or before attaining the specified age. That provision has been construed[11] as meaning that the subsection will not be satisfied unless it can be said that if the person or persons in question attain an age not exceeding 25 they will be *bound* to become entitled. If a settlement contains any power (whether express or incorporated by statutory provision) which is capable of exercise in such a way as could prevent such an entitlement from arising, the settlement is deprived of the protection of s 71 from the outset. The existence of a power of revocation would have this result;[11] and so would the existence of a power of appointment, unless this were exercisable only in such a way as to comply with the requirements of s 71.[12]

This may affect precedent forms in fairly common use; and, in particular, two which appear in this book. Thus, under the overriding discretionary trusts in Form 7–1 (as they stand) the powers to effect a variation of the will, which it is the purpose of the form to facilitate, could possibly be so exercised as to defeat beneficial entitlements, or property could possibly be appointed in terms outside s 71: equally, the common form power of appointment in Form 6–11 (as this stands) could possibly be exercised in such a way. Accordingly, it is suggested that these forms, and indeed a power of appointment in any form, should be adopted only in conjunction with Form 8–15, or with the addition of provisions to the like effect: Form 8–15 is intended to restrict the exercise of any such power to purposes within s 71.

Similar considerations may sometimes apply in relation to powers of advancement, in that such a power (whether it is the statutory power under s 32 of TA 1925,[2] or an express power) may properly be exercised by declaring trusts of the property advanced;[13] and trusts could be so declared in terms outside s 71. It is however settled (as the law stands)[11] that a settlement will not be excluded from s 71 merely because it contains the statutory power[14] (even if this is extended from a moiety to the whole of the beneficiary's share[11]); though presumably if an advance were actually made in such a way as could contravene the requirements of the section, an exit charge to tax under s 71(3) would be incurred. If the will substitutes an express power, as under Form 8–7 or Form 8–8–3, the position is less clear: it is suggested that these forms also should be adopted only in conjunction with Form 8–15.

The second and third requirements are contained in s 71(1)(*b*): that no interest in possession subsists in the settled property; and that the income from the settled property is to be accumulated, so far as not applied for the maintenance, education or benefit of a beneficiary.

If there is a subsisting interest in possession, the settled property is treated for IHT purposes as part of the estate of the person who enjoys that interest. So, if a testator leaves property on trust for his widow for life, and after his death for children at 25, the settled property is not held on accumulation and maintenance trusts until after the widow's death (when IHT will have been charged on the termination of her interest); and then only if any child is still under 25. Conversely, if the trust is an immediate trust for children at 25 and one of them attains that age, his share then ceases to be held on accumulation and maintenance trusts (though no IHT is chargeable[4]); but the shares of any younger children continue to be so. If a child is born into the class, diminishing the shares of those already in being, a charge to IHT will arise in respect of the diminution in value of the share of any who has already attained an interest in possession;[8] though it seems unlikely that any tax would normally be payable, unless the estate is very large.

The second requirement of s 71(1)(*b*), as to accumulation of surplus income, is automatically satisfied in any case to which s 31 of the TA 1925 is applicable, since that section expressly requires it. However, accumulations under s 31 cease at 18, and so if a later vesting age is required, either the beneficiary must be allowed to take an interest in possession at that age, under s 31(1)(ii), or else the application of s 31 (including the duty to accumulate) must be extended by substituting a later age for the age of 18, as in Form 8–7, para (iii). As explained above, the substituted age should not be greater than 21. If the age at which capital vests is later than 21, beneficiaries should nevertheless be allowed to take interests in possession by 21. If, for some reason, accumulations are dealt with by express provision, and not by reference to s 31, this provision must impose a *direction* to accumulate surplus income: a mere power to accumulate is not sufficient.

The last condition for the establishment of accumulation and maintenance trusts is in s 71(2), and is in the alternative. Either not more than 25 years must have elapsed since the creation of the settlement or since the statutory requirements became satisfied (s 71(2)(*a*)), or else all the persons who are or have been beneficiaries are or were grandchildren of a common grandparent; or children, widows or widowers of such a person who has died before becoming entitled (s 71(2)(*b*)). While limiting accumulation and maintenance trusts to a single generation, this second alternative allows (inter alia) the usual substitutional gift in favour of children of a deceased child. The terms of the trust should not, however, be framed for the benefit of a mixed class of children and issue (or simply of issue) as original beneficiaries. For this purpose, children include illegitimate children, adopted children and stepchildren.

Reference is made in Note D–9 to the opportunity which arises under certain conditions, to vary the dispositions of a will after death, without penalty in terms of IHT or CGT.[15]

Subject to the reservation that (unless entirely in their favour) a variation affecting the rights of minor and possible unborn beneficiaries must be sanctioned by the court, there is no reason in principle why accumulation and maintenance trusts should not be declared retrospectively by way of variation of the will. It should, however, be borne in mind that for IT purposes, a variation can be caught by the 'settlement' provisions of ICTA 1988, ss 660–685, so that a parent making a variation in favour of children could find that he or she was assessable to IT (at all rates) on some or all of the income arising. If a similar disposition in favour of the children had been included in the will itself, these provisions could not apply. The income would have been income of their trustees for IT purposes, and so while it would have attracted the additional rate in the hands of the trustees, it would have been available to support a repayment claim against unused personal allowances of the children, in so far as it was applied for their benefit and not accumulated.

---

1 Specifically, on 'relevant property' within the meaning of IHTA 1984, s 58. It will be in view that these tax charges have not been in any way mitigated in the transition from Capital Transfer Tax to IHT; and in particular the favourable treatment of potentially exempt transfers has no application to discretionary trusts.

2 Reproduced in Appendix 4.

3 These tax charges may not necessarily prove unduly burdensome, and in some circumstances might be considered an acceptable price for the greater flexibility of a true discretionary trust. In other circumstances, the limited use of a discretionary trust might well be considered: see Preliminary Note D–2B, passim, and Forms 5–4 and 7–1, and notes thereto.

4 Section 71(4).

5 Section 71(3), in conjunction with s 70(2).

6 Paragraph (iii) of Form 8–7 will effect this: should s 31 be excluded altogether, the entitlement to income should be preserved.

7 LPA 1925, ss 164–165.

8 Not, of course, under s 71, but under ss 51–53.

9 The exemption in s 71(4)(*b*) only prevents a charge under s 71(3).

10 Under ICTA 1988, s 686. The surcharge is also avoided where beneficial interests are not contingent but vested.

11 See *Lord Inglewood* v *IRC* [1983] 1 WLR 366 (CA).

12 For published views of the Inland Revenue see *Law Society's Gazette* of 11 June 1975 [1975] BTR 436 and 8 October 1975 [1975] BTR 437; and Statement of Practice of 19 January 1976 [1976] BTR 406.

13 *Pilkington* v *IRC* [1964] AC 612.

14 As was already the view of the Inland Revenue; see [1975] BTR 437.

15 See also Form 7–1, which provides alternative machinery.

### *CGT: vesting of contingent interests*

For CGT purposes, as has been noticed, property held in trust for beneficiaries whose entitlement is contingent is settled property;

though property held for minors who would be absolutely entitled but for their minority is not. Accordingly, when a contingent entitlement vests, and a beneficiary becomes absolutely entitled as against the trustees, there is a notional disposal and re-acquisition of that property at its current market value;[1] and any resulting gain (after deduction of the relevant acquisition costs and any available indexation allowance, and also the trustees' annual exemption, if unused) is chargeable against the trustees; unless the absolute entitlement arises by reason of the death of a life tenant.[2] The notional re-acquisition provides a new acquisition cost for purposes of any future disposal by the beneficiary.

If desired, a gain arising from the notional disposal could, until 14 March, 1989, be held over to the beneficiary[3] (at the joint election of the trustees and the beneficiary), in which case the beneficiary's acquisition cost is reduced by the amount of the held-over gain; which is therefore postponed, but still prospectively taxable on any future disposal by the beneficiary. The FA 1989, while not affecting the principles of liability where a beneficiary becomes absolutely entitled against the trustees, severely restricts the occasions where holdover relief is available. Apart from cases involving business assets (where, broadly, gains may still be held over) in effect, in this context, only gains arising on the vesting of contingent entitlement at the age of 18 may be held over; since if only an interest in possession arises at that time the later vesting of the capital will not attract relief. If, typically, a testator wishes to provide that capital should vest beyond the end of the accumulation period, he should be advised that the notional disposal then occurring will not attract holdover relief.

The result of these provisions is that, in terms of CGT, a contingent interest is treated unfavourably as compared with a vested interest. This fact may prompt the question whether it may be desirable to modify the traditional view that the beneficial interests of children ought to be contingent upon attaining whatever may be considered to be the age of responsibility, thereby also avoiding the risk that a share might pass as part of the beneficiary's estate in the event of premature death. This view undoubtedly reflects what most testators would consider to be in the best interests of their children. Need this natural preference be disturbed? When it is considered that if the children are young, the trust might continue for an extended period, and that in an estate of any size, substantial gains might accrue before an absolute entitlement arises, it is clear that a substantial tax liability might be involved if beneficial interests are contingent. However, there are three mitigating factors.

First, although allowed at only half the rate available to individuals, the annual exemption allows trustees to realise tax-free gains (where these exist) on a regular basis during the life of the trust, so reducing the build-up of gains at the time of distribution.

Secondly, revision of the base date and the indexation allowance should go a long way towards eliminating purely inflationary gains on future disposals.

Thirdly, the possibility of holding over gains at distribution to the beneficiary, while it provides no exemption, does at least allow a deferment of liability, which is valuable.

An absolute beneficiary, holding the same investments for the same period, would have anticipated the future taxation of similar unrealised gains; though with this difference, that he would have enjoyed the full amount of annual exemption in the meantime.

It is a decision for the testator to make; but in most cases the advice will probably be that despite the charge to tax on distribution, the availability of the indexation allowance and the possibility of holdover relief may sufficiently mitigate the burden of CGT to leave the contingent interest as an acceptable form of disposition, where this is preferred (as almost invariably it is preferred) on personal grounds.

A charge to CGT may similarly arise where, by the exercising of a power of appointment or advancement, new trusts are declared in respect of settled property in such a way as to constitute a new settlement.[4] The prospect of this CGT charge in addition to the probable IHT charge (upon the settled property ceasing to be held on accumulation and maintenance trusts) would normally discourage the trustees from making a re-settlement. The inclusion in the will of a clause in terms of Form 8–15 is intended to avoid an additional charge to IHT by preventing any re-settlement outside the requirements for an accumulation and maintenance settlement; it should also serve, in most cases, to prevent a re-settlement from incurring a charge to CGT.

1 CGTA 1979, s 54 and FA 1981, s 87.
2 CGTA 1979, s 56 (as amended).
3 FA 1982, s 82.

4 Whether or not a re-settlement has this result depends upon the particular circumstances: see (inter alia) *Roome* v *Edwards* [1982] AC 279 (HL); and Inland Revenue Statement of Practice SP 7/84, which replaced a 1981 Statement, the Revenue wishing to add a mention of the decision in *Bond* v *Pickford* [1983] STC 517. In that case the Court of Appeal explained that the nature of the powers which the trustees purported to exercise must be examined, for these may not authorise the removal of assets from the original settlement; and in general, that the parties' intention has to be determined objectively.

### *IT: treatment of income where beneficial interests are contingent or vested*

Contingent interests are generally supposed to be treated unfavourably for purposes of IT; in that income in the hands of trustees for persons contingently entitled to capital is taxable not only at basic rate but also, under ICTA 1988, s 686, at the additional rate. If the beneficial interest had been vested, the same income would have been taxed at basic rate only, though (where appropriate) it would have fallen to be grossed up as part of the total income of the beneficiary for purposes of the higher rate of tax.

In reality, however, income attributable to a contingent interest will effectively bear the additional rate of tax only to the extent that the income exceeds the beneficiary's unused personal allowance, or is accumulated. Income applied towards the beneficiary's maintenance is available to support a repayment claim on his behalf covering the additional rate tax. Accordingly, where trust income is needed, and applied, for maintenance (as in very many cases it is), the additional rate tax will commonly be recoverable. The only disadvantage will lie in the fact that the trustees will have suffered the tax in the first place; and that some administrative expense will have been incurred.

The position may be different in cases where a surplus of income arises, whether because the trust income is greater in amount than the current needs of the beneficiaries, or perhaps because other funds are available for their maintenance. Any such surplus, when accumulated, will represent new capital formed out of income which has been taxed at the basic and additional rates; and the tax so suffered will be irrecoverable.

However, two points may be made. First, although the accumulated income has suffered basic and additional rate IT, it will never suffer the higher rate of IT, because it will never form part of the total income of an individual beneficiary for IT purposes. Secondly, while accumulated income becomes (in effect) capitalised, the accumulations will nevertheless pass eventually from the trust without liability to IHT, so long as the requirements for an accumulation and maintenance settlement are satisfied. Investments representing the accumulations are, of course, subject, like any other, to CGT.

In relation to family trusts where there is in fact surplus income available to accumulate, these benefits (in particular the freedom from higher rate IT) may be seen as establishing an important advantage in many cases, as compared with the position where vested interests were given. Surplus income (grossed up) would have been treated, for higher rate purposes, as part of the total income of a beneficiary with a vested interest, whether applied for his benefit, or accumulated under TA 1925, s 31.[1] Where an interest is contingent, income will not bear higher rate tax, unless actually applied under s 31.[1]

It is sometimes suggested that the disparity in the treatment of vested and contingent interests can be avoided, with advantage, by the device of giving a contingent interest in capital, coupled with a vested interest in income. This can be done, quite simply, by varying the application of TA 1925, s 31,[1] in such a way as to provide that accumulations of income are to be held in trust for individual beneficiaries in any event. If the age at which contingent interests are to vest is over 18, a correspondingly higher age (but not over 25) may also be substituted for 18 for purposes of the statutory entitlement to income under s 31(1)(ii): see above, under the heading 'IHT: accumulation and maintenance trusts'. That approach has not been adopted in any of the forms in this edition. The author is not convinced that an overall advantage will necessarily result, and believes that the position must be carefully evaluated (in those comparatively few cases where the question is relevant) in relation to the particular circumstances. In such a case, in addition to the considerations outlined above, it will be in view that if a vested interest in income were given, this would amount to an interest in possession for IHT purposes. On the premature death of a beneficiary, this would result in a possible IHT charge on the full capital value of the beneficiary's share under the trust, even though his entitlement to capital might still be contingent.

---

1 Reproduced in Appendix 4.

**D–7 The family home**

It is a well known fact that the family home represents the most important asset in the estates of many, if not most, testators and potential testators. Not surprisingly, its disposal for the benefit of the family is of corresponding importance to them. It is not always appreciated, however, that in case the existing family home might not pass into the absolute ownership of a surviving spouse or where it proves unsuitable for some reason, it may be of equal or greater importance to ensure that provision is made by will to enable a new home to be acquired for the benefit of the family.

*Absolute gifts*

It may be assumed that, in most cases, testators making provision for a surviving spouse will wish the family home to pass to the spouse outright. Where residue as a whole is given to the spouse, the usual general gift of residuary realty and personalty will suffice to include the interest of an absolute owner or tenant in common of freehold or leasehold land; or that of a joint tenant, should the beneficial joint tenancy be severed during the testator's lifetime.

*Gifts in trust*

A trust will necessarily arise where the spouse is restricted to a limited interest or, more commonly, where an outright gift to the spouse is followed by an alternate gift to children or issue (in case the spouse is not living at the testator's death, or fails to survive for some stipulated period), and the interests of children or issue are themselves contingent on attaining majority, or some other age. Consideration must therefore be given, in such cases, to the most appropriate disposal of the family home, including rights of occupation, responsibility for upkeep, and the possibility of sale and of purchase elsewhere.

*Limited interest*

In those cases where a life or other limited interest is given to the spouse (whether by way of specific gift or as part of residue), the main question for consideration is whether the responsibility for maintaining the home, for deciding whether and when a sale is desirable and, in that event, what new purchase should be made, should rest with the trustees, or whether the spouse should be given the control over these matters. This is entirely a matter for the testator and express instructions ought to be taken. While it may be assumed that the trustees will have been chosen for their ability to act in the best interests of the family as a whole, it does not by any means follow that the testator would wish to see his or her spouse in the position of being dependent on their discretion in this respect despite their statutory obligation[1] to consult, and to give effect to the wishes of the life tenant, 'so far as consistent with the general interest of the trust'.

1 Under LPA 1925, s 26(3).

*Trusts for sale or settled land*

Any testator whose wishes are consulted is likely to say that he would prefer his widow (or likewise, in the case of a married woman her widower) to have the greatest possible freedom of action in these matters (to be so far as possible, as it were, mistress in her own house), as long as this would not entail any undue risk to the capital of the estate, or to the interests of the children or other ultimate beneficiaries. Unfortunately, the difficulty at once arises that whereas the machinery provided by SLA 1925, in relation to settled land, appears almost exactly to meet these requirements, by virtue of the powers which it confers on a tenant for life[1] and the position of the trustees as custodians of capital money, the machinery of the trust for sale, although almost universally adopted, cannot be said to be well adapted to those requirements, in that however the operation of the trust for sale may be modified by further provisions, the duty of the trustees is a duty to sell.[2]

The creation of a settlement, within SLA 1925, is generally held to be undesirable for purely conveyancing reasons. It is thought that inconvenience and unnecessary expense will arise from the necessity to vest the settled land in the tenant for life and, on termination of the life interest, to obtain a conveyance to the person next entitled; that difficulty may arise if and when the title to the settled land has to be deduced. There is no real need for any such apprehension. Properly understood, the machinery of SLA 1925 is extremely straightforward and convenient, and need not involve any but the most trifling expense.

In reality, the adoption of a trust for sale presents much more serious difficulties to the draftsman; to say nothing of the life tenant.

These stem from the fact that the trust for sale, considered as conveyancing machinery, is not designed for the purpose of retaining property for enjoyment in specie. Its effect is, of course, qualified by the power to postpone sale, and may be modified by express provision requiring consent to any sale, though such an express provision cannot always be relied upon. Further, whereas it is within the powers of a tenant for life of settled land to purchase elsewhere, as of right,[3] the life tenant of property held under a trust for sale has no such right, nor even have the trustees, unless it is expressly conferred upon them by some further provision (as, eg, under Form 4–8 or, more usually, Form 8–5).[4]

These considerations apart, there is no difference of substance between the two types of disposition, in that trustees for sale are enabled by statute[5] to exercise all the powers of a tenant for life and of the trustees of a settlement under SLA 1925.[6] Whatever statutory or express powers are or may be available, however, the question of substance which the thoughtful draftsman should have uppermost in his mind is, quite simply, who should exercise them? While conveyancing considerations are certainly relevant, the precise relationship between the principal beneficiary and the trustees ought to be a matter for the testator himself to consider. Most testators are ready to take trustingly the drafts of their wills in this respect, though some find the concept of the trust for sale difficult to understand: their instinct may be sound.

1 See note to Form 4–9.
2 See note to Form 6–3.
3 See note to Form 4–9.
4 By virtue of SLA, s 73(1), capital money may be 'invested or otherwise applied' in the purchase of freeholds or certain leaseholds. This power is probably not available to trustees for sale who have disposed of the land previously held under trust for sale (see *Re Wakeman* [1945] Ch 177 and *Re Wellsted* [1949] Ch 296). Although the court is empowered by TA 1925, s 57, to authorise any transaction expedient to the management of the trust, this is not a satisfactory alternative to an express power.
5 LPA 1925, s 28.
6 Including, in particular, the powers and obligations arising under ss 73 and 84.

### *Terms of occupation: IHT and CGT*

If the surviving spouse becomes absolute owner of the family home, whether as surviving joint tenant or by an absolute gift in the will, it will form part of the estate of the spouse for IHT purposes, and when the spouse dies or otherwise disposes of the beneficial interest by way of gift, its then value will accordingly attract IHT. On the other hand, any increase in value since the death of the testator will not be chargeable to CGT where the conditions for the 'owner-occupier' exemption are satisfied,[1] nor in any case upon death.[2]

If the spouse occupies as tenant for life under a settlement, the position will be exactly the same. For IHT purposes the spouse will have an interest in possession. For CGT purposes the trustees of the settlement will be entitled to the exemption because the spouse was 'entitled to occupy under the terms of the settlement'.[3]

Where the spouse enjoys a limited interest under a trust for sale, the position will depend upon the nature of that spouse's right of occupation pending sale. If the trustees are directed to allow the spouse to occupy (as in Forms 4–8 and 6–3), there will again be an interest in possession for IHT purposes and an entitlement to occupy for purposes of the CGT exemption.

If, on the other hand, the trustees are simply empowered to *permit* the spouse (or anyone else) to occupy (as in Form 8–5), the position is at first sight less clear, because as a matter of property law, the exercise of such a power by the trustees creates no more than a licence in favour of the spouse, and in principle this would seem not to create a sufficiently exclusive right to amount to an interest in possession. It is, however, the practice of the Inland Revenue to treat the exercise by trustees of such a power as giving rise to an interest in possession, if the power is wide enough to cover the creation of an exclusive or joint right of residence and is exercised with the intention of providing a particular beneficiary with a permanent home.[4] If the official practice accords with the law (which has been doubted, but is not known to have been tested), the position for IHT purposes is the same as in the previous examples. The CGT exemption remains available.[5]

It is perfectly possible to give the spouse a secure right of occupation without giving rise to an interest in possession. For instance, the trustees could be authorised to grant a lease or tenancy, and, if this were done for full consideration and without creating an assured tenancy, so that no loss to the estate resulted, IHT could be saved. Other means could be devised to achieve the same result. However, such a saving could be achieved only at a high and probably unacceptable price: the benefit of the CGT exemption would almost certainly be lost, for there would no longer be occupation 'under the terms of the settlement'.

In most cases, the benefit of the CGT exemption will be likely to outweigh the burden of IHT. Accordingly, the practical choice seems to lie between absolute ownership, a tenancy for life under a settlement and an entitlement to occupy pending sale under a trust for sale, or perhaps occupation under licence granted by the trustees. As between these possibilities, the choice can and should be governed by personal rather than tax considerations.

1 Ie, under CGTA 1979, s 101.
2 Ibid, s 49.
3 Within ibid, s 104.
4 See Inland Revenue Statement of Practice SP 10/79.
5 See *Sansom* v *Peay* [1976] 1 WLR 1073.

*Can the family home be kept out of the survivor's estate?*

In many estates, the family home is a very substantial asset; in some, the most substantial. Its value may give rise to an IHT liability on the death of the surviving spouse which, in relation to the value of the whole estate, may be most unwelcome; without it there might even be no liability at all. It is therefore natural to ask whether this prospective liability might be reduced or avoided altogether by dividing the beneficial ownership in some way between the spouse and the children. Plainly, if this could be done without detriment to the spouse, such an arrangement might provide a valuable saving, for the ultimate benefit of the children. Where there is little or no opportunity to plan for such a saving by the careful disposition of other assets, attention is directed all the more closely to the family home.

The question is, then, can the family home, or a substantial part of its value, ever be kept out of the estate of the surviving spouse?

The immediate answer is that this is certainly possible. For one thing, the property could simply be given directly to children, relying upon them to ensure that (say) a widow's occupation remains undisturbed for so long as she wishes. Another possibility, allowing her more security, would be to create a tenancy in common as between husband and wife, enabling each to dispose of the undivided share by will, to the children. The survivor, as tenant in common, has a right to occupy the entirety pending sale. The widow is then more secure, though not fully so: she cannot prevent a sale. The gift to the children could be made on terms that no step is to be taken to enforce a sale without the consent of the widow. This arrangement does provide the widow with real security, but almost certainly it also destroys the possibility of saving tax: it seems to amount to a settlement of the children's share, under which the widow has an interest in possession.

Other possibilities can be imagined, but where a lifetime transfer is contemplated, it is necessary to be alert for anything which might amount to a 'reservation', within the anti-avoidance provisions of FA 1986, s 102. These provisions do not, however, apply to gifts which are themselves exempt transfers.[1] They do not apply insofar as full consideration is given for any reserved benefit. Accordingly, part consideration might be received in the form of a lease back (on appropriate terms); but, it seems, only at the cost of loss of CGT reliefs. The general conclusion seems always to be that if the widow has security, no tax is saved, whereas if tax is saved, this will have been achieved only by placing the security of the widow to some extent at risk.

In a united family the risk to the survivor's security may seem not to be very real. This may be a dangerous assumption to make. However united the family may seem to be, the fact is that if ownership of the house is shared, that security will have been weakened. Tensions could arise in the event of re-marriage. There could be difficulties if a child died. The widow's freedom to move house might be curtailed. Difficulties might arise over repairs. There might be other unforeseen difficulties. These possible difficulties might be compounded if the testator had been married before and had two families or perhaps stepchildren to provide for. Moreover, even if IHT were saved on the value of the half share given to the children, the price of this saving would seem to be the loss of the CGT exemption on that half of any gain, either on a sale or gift of the house or when the widow dies.

With one possible exception, discussed in the note to Form 5–5, the sensible conclusion seems to be that the family home ought not to be made an instrument of tax planning.

---

1 Section 102(5): hence, for instance, a purchase by one spouse followed by conveyance to both spouses as tenants in common is officially considered not to be a gift with a reservation; albeit the death of the donor might give rise to a claim to tax on other grounds. Generally, as to gifts with reservation, see correspondence published at 83 *Law Society's Gazette*, p 3728 and *British Tax Review* 1987 No 7 at p 1018.

**D–8 The family business**

If the estate includes a business, or a substantial interest in a business, its disposal will call for careful consideration.

Possibly, though comparatively unusually, where the testator is sole proprietor, and insists upon remaining so until his death, the assets of the business may fall to be disposed of by specific gift,[1] or pass as part of residue. If anything but a simple outright gift is contemplated, considerable difficulties may arise: continuity of management must somehow be secured, and the differing needs and expectations of those members of the family who depend on the business must be reconciled and provided for. Suitable trustees must be found. They may have to be asked to accept a considerable responsibility, for which special powers would be needed. Even if they are relieved of personal responsibility, it is notoriously (and understandably) difficult to find trustees who will undertake the management or close supervision of any business unless they are themselves its beneficial owners. If such a case should arise (and it is suggested that it should not normally be allowed to arise), the nature of the provisions which would be required for the disposal of the business by will must depend so much on the particular circumstances that the draftsman would need to consult those standard works which include a wide range of forms.[2]

If there is no prospect of the business being continued after the testator's death, it will have to be wound up or disposed of. This will normally be dealt with in the ordinary course of administration unless the testator has already disposed of it during his lifetime, perhaps upon retirement.

Where there is a possibility that the business will continue because other members of the family are willing and able to manage it in the general interest, there may already be (and if not, it may well be that there should be) some degree of active participation on their part, for practical and fiscal reasons alike. In this, the most usual case, it is therefore more likely than not that the interest of the testator in his business will be that of a controlling shareholder, or senior partner. In either case, the transmission of his interest should present few if any difficulties for the draftsman.

If the business is incorporated, this will allow much flexibility in that shares can be passed on to individuals, or settled, by way of lifetime transfer or by will, at any time and in any proportions. If a controlling shareholding is left in the hands of the trustees, as part of residue, it is normally necessary only to ensure that the trustees are given sufficiently wide powers to act effectively (as, eg, in Form 8–11).

If the business has not already been incorporated, the likelihood is that it will already be managed by some kind of family partnership. If it is not, and if eventual family participation is envisaged, serious consideration should be given to the possibility of forming such a partnership, either at the present time, or as soon as circumstances allow. Where, for instance, there are children who are at present too young, they could always be admitted at a later time to a partnership formed initially between the testator and his wife. Apart from its taxation advantages, the partnership represents an even more flexible instrument for the division of ownership, functions and income within the family than does the company. The partnership agreement can and should provide not only for these matters, but also for the succession to the share of any partner who retires or dies. Where this accrues as of right to the continuing or surviving partners, under provisions which represent full consideration by each,[3] it is often possible for the interest of the testator to be passed on with little or no liability either for IHT or for CGT. The transfer of shares in a company, by contrast, will normally attract both liabilities though, as to IHT, with the benefit of the valuable relief for business property[4] and of the instalment option.[5]

Under an appropriate partnership agreement, therefore, the testator's interest in his business can be excluded from his estate, and it proper devolution secured outside the terms of his will.

1 For the special treatment for IHT purposes of a specific gift of business or agricultural property within a partly exempt estate, under FA 1986, s 105, see Preliminary Note D–4.

2 See, eg, those in *Encyclopaedia of Forms and Precedents* (4th ed), vol 23, title 'Wills' at pp 691–733.

3 By analogy with *A–G* v *Boden* [1912] KB 539.

4 Under IHTA 1984, ss 103–114, as amended by FA 1987, s 58, Sched 8.

5 Under IHTA 1984, ss 227, 228, and see amendments effected by FA 1986, Sched 19 and FA 1987, Sched 8.

### D–9 The possibility of future arrangements

In view of the many uncertainties surrounding any attempt to minimise the burden of capital taxation, it is of some comfort to those advising the testator to know that if a miscalculation should prove to have been made, or if there is a material change of circumstances, there will be opportunities to vary the dispositions of his estate before or during the period of two years following his death. For the most part, however, this will be possible only if the testator has a united family, and conflicts of interest can be avoided.

While a full discussion of the relative statutory provisions lies somewhat outside the scope of a book on will drafting, the draftsman is bound to be influenced to some extent by their existence, and accordingly a brief summary of their main features may be useful.

*Variation or disclaimer*

If within two years after the death, any of the dispositions, by will or on intestacy, of property comprised in the estate of the deceased[1] are varied, or the benefit is disclaimed, by an instrument in writing[2] made by any of the persons who benefit (or would have done so) under those dispositions, the person(s) making the instrument can elect[3], under IHTA 1984, s 142,[4] that for IHT purposes, the variation or disclaimer shall not be a transfer of value, but shall be treated as if the variation had been effected by the deceased or (as the case may be) as if the disclaimed benefit had never been conferred. However, it seems that such a re-writing of testamentary dispositions for fiscal purposes can be carried out only once.[5]

This section is applicable whether or not the administration of the estate is complete, and whether or not the property concerned has been distributed in accordance with the original dispositions; but in relation to a disclaimer, it must be borne in mind that under the general law, entitlement cannot be disclaimed after any benefit has been accepted; nor can an entitlement be disclaimed in part. The section does not apply if the variation or disclaimer is made for any consideration, other than another variation or disclaimer within the section.

A corresponding right of election is given, for CGT purposes, under s 49 of CGTA 1979.[6] The exercise (or otherwise) of this election serves principally to determine what is the acquisition cost of assets to the beneficiary.

It will depend upon the particular circumstances whether or not it is advantageous to elect for the purposes of either tax, or of both. The two elections are available independently of one another.

In a case where the deceased has failed to make a will,[7] or where a will has not been regularly reviewed, these provisions will enable the beneficiaries in effect to substitute a will in terms which the deceased might have been advised to make[8] in the light of circumstances as they were at the time of his death; or perhaps in terms which seem preferable to the beneficiaries, quite independently of any supposed wishes of the deceased.

However, it must be borne in mind that these provisions have effect only for purposes of IHT and CGT. They have no counterpart for purposes of IT. The consequences of this may be adverse, to a greater or lesser extent.

For IT purposes a variation has no retrospective effect as regards any liability to tax on income which has already arisen.[9] Further, a person making a variation may thereby become a settlor for purposes of Part XV of ICTA 1988; and so may incur unexpected liabilities (in particular) under the provisions of ss 663–670 relating to settlements on children. It is generally believed that these consequences would not arise in the case of a disclaimer; but this is not certain; nor is a disclaimer always practicable. It is certain they would not have arisen at all if the disposition had actually been made by will.

For stamp duty purposes, even though it contains an element of voluntary disposition, a variation does not normally now attract a claim to ad valorem duty.[10]

Tax considerations apart, difficulty may arise in relation to a variation, if the desired rearrangement requires the agreement of some person who is not willing to co-operate. Difficulty may also arise if some person is unable to consent because of minority or other disability, or if those prospectively interested may include persons yet unborn. In these cases, it will be necessary to apply to the court under the Variation of Trusts Act 1958. While no doubt an order would be obtained in a proper case, this may prove costly in terms of the provision which the court may be expected to require to be made in favour of those on whose behalf consent is given.

---

1 For this purpose including a reversionary interest (or other excluded property) but not including settled property in which the deceased had an interest in possession; nor property chargeable as a gift with reservation: s 142(5) (as amended).

2 For the Revenue's requirements about the contents of this instrument, see the note in 82 *Law Society's Gazette*, p 1454.

3 By notice to the Capital Taxes Office, within six months of the instrument: personal representatives must join if additional tax becomes payable, but cannot refuse to do so unless they hold insufficient funds to discharge the additional tax. The notice must refer to the appropriate statutory provisions.
4 Reproduced in Appendix 3: different provision applied before 11 April 1978.
5 See *Russell* v *IRC* [1988] 2 All ER 405, per Knox J, affirming the official view.
6 Reproduced in Appendix 3: election is here made by notice to the Inspector of Taxes.
7 Or, perhaps, a new will; as where there has been a divorce or second marriage (cf Preliminary Notes B and F–2).
8 Having regard (inter alia) to the same estate planning considerations as are discussed in this book: see this note, *passim*, and specific points noted in the context of particular forms.
9 The provisions of ICTA 1988, ss 695–701, are applied accordingly.
10 FA 1985, s 84.

*Discretionary powers of variation conferred by will*

The foregoing provisions are widely used to rearrange beneficial entitlements where this is thought desirable, whether for purely personal reasons, or in the wider interests of good estate planning. Nevertheless, in view of the difficulties referred to above, the result may still be less favourable to beneficiaries in some cases, than if the preferred dispositions had been contained in the will itself. It is possible for most of these difficulties to be circumvented by including in the will provisions enabling the trustees to override the dispositions of the will as they stand, by means of what is in effect a special power of appointment, exercisable within the same two-year time limit as applies to variations and disclaimers, in terms of IHTA 1984, s 144.[1]

This section provides that where property comprised in a person's estate immediately before his death is settled by his will; and within two years after his death, and before any interest in possession has subsisted in the property, an event occurs on which IHT would otherwise be chargeable under the provisions relating to settlements without an interest in possession,[2] the property is exempted from any such charge, and is treated as if the will had provided that on the testator's death the property should be held as it is held after the event.

In other words, the effect of exercising this kind of power to rearrange beneficial entitlements is fully retrospective for IHT purposes.[3]

It is suggested that advantage might be taken of this important provision more generally than is, perhaps, the case. There has been some reluctance among professional advisers to do so, no doubt because a testator who confers such a power on his trustees necessarily places a very high degree of reliance upon them; and in doing so, he surrenders to some extent the power of disposing of his own estate. Certainly some testators will be deterred by these considerations, though they should be aware that even if no such power is given to their trustees, beneficiaries can and commonly do themselves enter into variations, which will equally override the testator's intentions. The kind of power under discussion is of course discretionary, and trustees may be expected to exercise it only with caution; and with the best interests of the testator's family in view.

A suggested clause intended to take advantage of this provision appears in Form 7–1, which is accompanied by some further notes. The inclusion of such a provision in the will is recommended in any case where the burden of IHT is likely to be such that action to mitigate it may be a possibility. However, because they would constitute 'related settlements' within the meaning of IHTA 1984, s 62, Form 7–1 should not normally be included in a will which also includes Form 5–4.

1 Reproduced in Appendix 3.
2 Under IHTA 1984, Chapter III, Part III.
3 There is, however, no corresponding provision for CGT purposes.

### *Other cases*

Further related provisions in IHTA 1984 deal with special cases.

Section 143 protects transfers in pursuance of a so-called 'precatory trust'. This provision is shortly discussed in the note to Form 4–4.

Sections 145 and 93 deal respectively with the right of election by a surviving spouse (under s 47A of AEA 1925) to redeem a life interest on intestacy, and with disclaimer of an interest in settled property. These provisions call for no special comment.

# E
# Some Drafting Points

### E–1 Technical drafting

As a conveyancer, the will draftsman is called upon to accept a considerable responsibility, the extent of which his client may not fully appreciate, for framing the draft in such terms as are best suited to the circumstances. Whilst it goes without saying that the draft must meet with the client's full approval in all respects, there are many aspects of the will-making process as to which the client will depend almost entirely on his professional adviser, and as to which it is therefore essentially the function of the professional adviser to take the initiative.

For the most part the matters in question will be concerned, somehow or another, with the way in which beneficial entitlements are framed, having regard both to personal considerations and also (where these are relevant) to tax considerations. Many such matters are discussed elsewhere in this book; some in more general terms in the Preliminary Notes, and others more specifically in the notes to the various forms, in their particular context.

The present note is concerned with two particular aspects of the will which are purely drafting matters, in the sense that they are auxiliary, and essentially legal in nature; albeit their practical implications are not less important than any other.

The first relates to the use of the conveyancing machinery of the trust for sale, considered in Note E–2.

The second concerns the administrative (and sometimes dispositive) powers which ought, in the particular circumstances, to be available to the trustees in the interests of good administration of the trust; and the question whether relevant statutory powers may need to be modified or excluded. Note E–3 serves to list 14 of the forms in this book which are concerned with the more important administrative powers. The notes to these forms deal with a number of specific points in their context.

### E–2 The trust for sale

Personal representatives have an inherent power of sale for administration purposes. Where, after completion of the administration, they continue to hold assets in the capacity of trustees, they have a general statutory power of sale[1] for the purposes of any application of capital money authorised by the terms of the trust or by the general law.

Whilst it is difficult to envisage any circumstances in which these powers would not suffice to enable the personal representatives or trustees to effect any necessary sale, it is the usual and long-established practice of draftsmen to subject the whole estate (other than assets comprised in any specific gift) to an express trust for sale, unless the terms of the will are such that the whole estate will necessarily be distributed immediately to one or more beneficiaries, all of whom (if more than one) are of full age and absolutely entitled.

As it is seldom possible to say with complete certainty that no minority or other deferred or contingent interest will arise (if only because there can be no certainty that any particular beneficiary will necessarily survive) many draftsmen subject residue to a trust for sale in all cases.

The main purpose of so doing is to convert the whole estate, notionally, into personalty. This serves to avoid difficulties which could otherwise arise, in certain cases, as to the incidence of debts and legacies.[2] It also avoids the possibility that, where the will creates a limited interest in residue, any land in the estate might thereby become settled land. This is usually considered undesirable, though, in certain cases, there may be practical advantages in creating such a settlement expressly.[3]

Although as a matter of drafting it is unobjectionable, and in most cases it is probably desirable, the purpose and terms of a trust for sale are sometimes misunderstood, and therefore objected to by testators, who do not contemplate any sale beyond what is absolutely necessary.

In case the draftsman is himself unsure whether a trust for sale should or should not be imposed, the following rules of thumb are suggested:

(1) Unless it is specifically intended to create a settlement of land, it can hardly ever be wrong, as a matter of drafting, to impose a trust for sale on residue.

(2) It is advisable to impose a trust for sale in any case where distribution will or may be for any reason delayed or postponed and, in particular, if there are successive beneficial interests in residue or if a minority or other contingent interest in residue will or may possibly arise.

(3) It is unnecessary to impose a trust for sale where it is certain that the whole of the estate will be distributable immediately to beneficiaries of full age with absolute interests. Even in such a case, however, a trust for sale does not preclude either a partition at the joint request of the beneficiaries or an appropriation of assets by the personal representatives with the consent of the beneficiaries (or even without such consent, if Form 8–2 is adopted). If the beneficiaries were unable to agree, the personal representatives would have power for the purposes of distribution to sell, with or without a trust for sale.

(4) Where land is likely to be included in the estate, a trust for sale will normally be declared in order to confer on the personal representatives the powers of a tenant for life and of the trustees of a settlement under SLA 1925. Where, however, it is intended that the land should be enjoyed beneficially, as in the case of a dwelling-house, the disadvantage of a trust for sale is that even if the consent of the life tenant to a sale is required, the trustees nevertheless remain under a duty to sell; and may be directed to do so (see note to Form 6–3).

1 Under TA 1925, s 16(1).
2 For a fuller explanation, see the concise and practical discussion in *Hallett's Conveyancing Precedents* (1965) at p 1029.
3 See p 41 and note to Form 4–9.

## E–3 Powers of executors and trustees

It is usually considered advisable, except in the very simplest case where the estate is to pass absolutely to a very few individuals, to confer various express powers on the executors and trustees by way of modification of or addition to their powers under the general law.[1] The purpose of these express powers being in all cases to facilitate the efficient administration of the estate, and of any trust which may arise under the will, it is very much the function of the draftsman to suggest their inclusion, and advise as to their effect. Of course, the inclusion of these, as of any other provision, requires the testator's express approval.

The forms in this book include provisions for the matters most commonly dealt with in this way, as well as some of less common application, and the purpose and effect of each is shortly explained in the notes accompanying these forms.

The subject matter of these forms is as follows:

| | |
|---|---|
| Form 8–1 | General words |
| 8–2 | Power to appropriate without consents |
| 8–3 | Power to insure without restriction |
| 8–4 | Power to invest at discretion |
| 8–5 | Power to acquire and/or improve a residence |
| 8–6 | Power to advance capital at discretion |
| 8–7 | Power to apply income for maintenance and to accumulate surplus income during minority |
| 8–8 | Power to make payments, advances and loans out of capital |
| 8–9 | Power to disregard statutory and equitable rules as to apportionment of income |
| 8–10 | Power to accept receipts for payments to or on behalf of minors |
| 8–11 | Powers in relation to companies |
| 8–12 | Power to act although personally interested; power to purchase trust property |
| 8–13 | Power to charge for professional services |
| 8–14 | Power of appointing new or additional trustees |
| 8–15 | Powers of trustees to be exercisable only within requirements for an accumulation and maintenance settlement. |

1 See note to Form 8–1.

# F

# Administration of Justice Act 1982

## F–1 Introductory

Because this is a drafting handbook and not a textbook, it has never contained any general discussion of the law of wills as such; but only some comments bearing on practical aspects of the drafting process. The practitioner is already well served by standard works of reference which are available if required.

However, the changes introduced by the Administration of Justice Act 1982[1] are of such major importance that they cannot be allowed to pass unnoticed. Accordingly, the text of the more important of the relevant provisions of the 1982 Act has been reproduced in this book, and may be found in Appendix 6. The succeeding paragraphs of this Note are intended to provide a brief introduction, directed mainly to considering how (if at all) those provisions may affect existing practice.

With two exceptions, these amendments in the law have effect in relation to *deaths* on or after 1 January 1983, irrespective of the date of the will. As the main exception to this, s 18(1), concerned with the revocation of wills by marriage, and with wills in contemplation of marriage (see Note F–2), has effect only in relation to *wills executed* on or after 1 January 1983.

The other exception concerns two groups of provisions in ss 23–26 and 27–28, which are to come into force on a day or days to be appointed. These are briefly referred to in Note F–4, but are not reproduced in Appendix 6.

---

1 For a very helpful summary, see Andrew Francis: 'Wills–the New Law' (80 *Law Society's Gazette*, p 196).

## F–2 Amendments to the Wills Act 1837

Sections 17–19 of AJA 1982 replace the former provisions in ss 9, 18 and 33 of WA 1837; and other related enactments, including in particular s 177 of LPA 1925. The 1982 Act substituted new ss 9, 18 and 33 and introduced an additional section 18A.

*Section 9 (substituted)*. The purpose of this provision is indicated in the side-heading: 'Relaxation of formal requirements for making wills'. Two changes are made.

First, in place of the former requirement that the testator should sign at the 'foot or end' of the will (with its attendant difficulties of construction), the requirement as now expressed is that 'it appears that the testator intended by his signature to give effect to the will'. Clearly, this requirement will be satisfied on the face of a professionally drawn will. So equally was the former requirement, in any case where the execution of the will was properly supervised. No change in normal practice is called for.

Secondly, it becomes permissible for a witness either to sign or else to acknowledge[1] a previous signature, in the presence of the testator and of a second witness. This new provision will save some few wills which might previously have been invalidated in unusual circumstances, as where a witness was called away before the formalities of execution were completed and witnesses did not sign afresh. Such cases need not have occurred if the witnesses had subscribed not only in the presence of the testator but also in the presence of each other. Whilst signature by witnesses in one another's presence has never been and still is not a legal requirement, it has always been the practice in the profession that they should do so, and this practice is reflected in all common form attestation clauses. Although intended to guard against dangers which seem now to have been removed, this practice will no doubt continue to be followed, not only because it is so familiar, but also to obviate any risk of inconsistency between the terms of the attestation clause, and what is actually done. Accordingly, Form 9–1 remains as it was.

*Section 18 (substituted)*. In essence, this section preserves the former law that marriage revokes a will,[2] unless the will was made in contemplation of marriage.[3] However it has been redrawn in significantly different terms, with the intention of preventing failure in those cases[4] where the contemplation of marriage did not extend to the will as a whole. Protection now extends not only to cases where it appears that the testator 'intended that the will should not be revoked by the marriage', but also to cases where such an intention appears in relation to any individual disposition[5] in the will. In the latter case, if there are other dispositions, these also take effect notwithstanding the marriage, unless it appears that the testator intended them to be revoked.

As mentioned above, this section applies only to wills made on or after 1 January 1983. Accordingly, the former law still applies in relation to any earlier will.

If it was made with professional assistance, the validity of a will made in contemplation of marriage, before 1983, ought not to be in doubt. Nevertheless, such a will ought sensibly to have been replaced by a new will, once the marriage had taken place; or, equally, if it did not. Should such a will be made now, on the basis of previously accepted precedent forms, there should equally be little room for doubt that this would show the requisite intention (in terms of the substituted s 18) that it should not be revoked by the marriage which the testator was 'expecting'. Nevertheless, in view of the more flexible terms in which the substituted s 18 is framed, and of the different statutory language now adopted, a new Form 1–2 has been introduced into this book, in terms which are intended to reflect the altered statutory provisions directly. The notes to that form draw attention to difficulties of a more practical nature which have always required consideration in relation to a will of this kind; and which still do so.

*Section 18A (inserted)*. This section extends the former law as to the effect of marriage upon a will, by providing for the possibility of divorce. Although, in that event, an existing will is not revoked, it takes effect as if any appointment of a former spouse as executor or trustee were omitted, and any devise or bequest to a former spouse lapses;[6] unless, in either case, a contrary intention appears by the will. If the former spouse was given a life interest, interests in remainder are accelerated. If an interest given to some other person in remainder was contingent upon surviving the former spouse it ceases to be subject to that contingency.

For the practitioner, the real significance of this provision lies in the fact that a client who is a party to divorce proceedings should always be advised to make a new will (preferably at an early stage), in order to avoid the possibility of a total or partial intestacy; and, where appropriate, to fill a vacancy in the executorship. No doubt, similar advice would formerly have been given (although not for quite the same reasons), also as a matter of course.

*Section 18A: Re Sinclair*. The consequences of lapse of a devise or bequest by the operation of s 18A were considered in *Re Sinclair*,[7] where a bequest to the testator's wife was followed by a direction that in the event of his wife predeceasing him or failing to survive him for a period of one month, the estate was to pass to charity. It was held by the Court of Appeal[7] (affirming the decision at first instance) that on the true construction of s 18A, if a devise or bequest to a spouse 'lapsed' by reason of divorce, it failed without qualification and irrespective of the consequences. In particular, the devise or bequest was not deemed to have failed (as might perhaps have been supposed) with the same consequences as if the former spouse had predeceased the testator. Accordingly, if in the event the former spouse happened to survive the testator, gifts in the will contingent on the former spouse having predeceased the testator must fail to take effect.

There are many precedent forms published before the decision in *Re Sinclair*, in which gifts over to children or others are in fact expressed as taking effect in the event that the spouse should predecease the testator; or fail to survive the testator's death by some further period. Where a will has been drawn in this way, the interest of the alternate beneficiary must clearly be at risk in the event of dissolution, annulment or avoidance of the testator's marriage, unless it so happens that in the event of partial intestacy, precisely similar beneficial entitlements would arise anyway; or unless the terms of the will have been reconsidered. Quite apart from the fact that the testator's probable intentions will have been frustrated, the draftsman might in such circumstances also find himself in breach of a duty of care owed to the disappointed beneficiary: see Preliminary Note I.

Accordingly, in relation to any gift over which is intended to take effect in the event of failure of a primary gift to or for the benefit of a spouse, it is necessary to express the terms of the contingency with care. If the gift to the spouse is to be absolute in the event of survival, this may usually be done quite simply (as in Forms 6–5 to 6–8, and Will 1 in Appendix 9), by stipulating that the gift over is to have effect if the spouse 'fails to take a vested interest'; an expression which must be apt to cover contingencies of any kind, including statutory 'lapse'. If the spouse is given a limited interest, it will usually be sufficient (as in Forms 6–9 to 6–11, and Will 3 in Appendix 9) to express interests in remainder as being 'subject thereto.'

Apart from the effect on beneficial entitlements, s 18A also provides that in the event of dissolution, etc, 'the will shall take effect as if any appointment of the former spouse as an executor or as the executor and trustee of the will were omitted'. If this were to happen, an administrator with the will could of course be appointed, and it seems unlikely that any serious inconvenience would result. However, the careful draftsman will wish to cover the possibility. This may be done most simply by appointing a second executor and trustee, jointly with the spouse, intending that if the entitlement of the spouse takes effect, he or she should prove alone; whereas if it does not, the surviving or continuing executor can prove as such. Form 2–1–0 is drawn in this way, although for more general reasons. Otherwise, the will can embody an alternate appointment, an example of which may be found in Form 2–1–1. Another form of alternate appointment, again with a more general purpose, is embodied in Will 1 in Appendix 9.

*Section 33 (substituted)*. Formerly, where a gift to a child or issue of the testator who predeceased was saved from lapse by the survival of issue of the original beneficiary, the gift was treated as an accretion to the original beneficiary's estate and devolved accordingly upon those entitled under the original beneficiary's will or intestacy.[8] Under the substituted s 33, it devolves instead upon the surviving issue themselves, on a stirpital basis. It does so whether the original beneficiary would have been entitled as an individual or (contrary to the former provision) as a member of a class.

Although the substituted s 33 effects a substantial alteration of the law, it will be unlikely to affect existing practice, since the inclusion in a will of an express substitutional gift in favour of the children of a deceased child is virtually common form. Such provisions were already included, at least optionally, in all the forms in this book under which children of the testator are intended to benefit. This is also done in the knowledge that, for IHT purposes, such a substitution will not infringe the conditions for an accumulation and maintenance settlement, discussed in Preliminary Note D–6.

It has been suggested[9] that the new s 33 obviates the need for any express substitutional provision. However, reliance on the statutory provision may result in failure to give effect to a testator's probable intention.

In particular:

(1) Substitutional provisions are usually made in relation to a class gift. Although presumably intended to do so, it is not clear that the statutory provision applies to the normal form of such a gift, to children (or grandchildren) 'living at my death'. Section 33(2)(*b*) depends on the predecease of 'a member of the class': but it is not natural in this context to refer in those terms to someone who could never have become a member of the class. Beneficial entitlements should depend upon the express intention of the testator, and not upon niceties of construction.

(2) If the primary entitlements under a class gift are contingent, the statutory substitution will presumably take effect subject to the same contingency. Under an express substitutional gift it is not uncommon for a lower age of vesting to be stipulated, than was required in relation to the primary entitlement. The age at which different entitlements vest ought to be considered, and not assumed.

(3) The statutory substitution can occur only where a primary beneficiary fails to survive the testator. Where beneficial interests are contingent, it is equally important to provide for substitution where a beneficiary survives the testator, but thereafter dies without having attained a vested interest.

(4) The statutory substitution precludes any possibility of benefit to a widow or widower of a deceased beneficiary; as might have arisen under the former law, on his intestacy. While it is certainly unusual for such a benefit to be conferred by express provision, this ought to be considered by the testator, even though in particular circumstances it may not be thought appropriate. It is perhaps significant that this possibility is envisaged by the conditions for an accumulation and maintenance settlement which expressly allow the substitution of 'children, widows or widowers . . .' See IHTA 1984, s 71(2)(*b*)(ii).

The better view must be that express provision should be made in all cases, in terms appropriate to the circumstances, and on the basis of express instructions.

1 So, in effect, reversing *Re Colling* [1972] 1 WLR 1440.
2 But now, as to a disposition exercising a power of appointment, only if in default of appointment the property appointed would pass to the deceased's personal representatives. This alters the former law, and has the effect of preserving not only appointments under special powers, but also some appointments under general powers.
3 Wills Act 1837, (original) s 18, in conjunction with LPA 1925, s 177.
4 Such as *Re Coleman* [1976] Ch 1, which is, in effect, reversed.
5 Section 18(4).
6 Though expressly without prejudice to any right of the former spouse to apply for financial provision: as to which see Preliminary Note C, text and footnote 3.
7 *Re Sinclair* [1985] Ch 446 (CA).
8 As in *Re Basioli* [1953] Ch 367, which is, in effect, reversed.
9 See Abbas Mithani: 'Reform of Section 33 of the Wills Act 1837' (79 *Law Society's Gazette*, p 1113).

## F–3 Rectification and interpretation of wills

*Section 20* of AJA 1982 confers jurisdiction to rectify a will, where the court is satisfied that this is so expressed that it fails to carry out the testator's intentions, in consequence either of a clerical error or of a failure to understand his instructions.[1] This provision adds to the burdens of personal representatives in that (as also in relation to possible Family Provision applications) they cannot distribute within six months from the grant except at their own risk.

*Section 21* allows evidence of the testator's intention[2] (as well as other extrinsic evidence) to be admitted in cases where any part of a will is 'meaningless', and also where there is an ambiguity; even if the ambiguity is patent, and not (as formerly) only if it were latent.

These provisions will not directly affect the practitioner in his capacity as draftsman and are therefore not further discussed in this Note. However, as a practical point, since the draftsman will usually be in possession of the best evidence as to what was in fact intended by his client, it is perhaps more important than formerly that he should make, and preserve, careful notes of his instructions, in case of some future dispute.

*Section 22* adds a new rule of construction to cover those cases where a gift to a spouse is made in terms which in themselves would indicate an absolute interest, but where the will also purports to give an interest to issue. Unless a contrary intention is shown, the spouse takes an absolute interest. Most practitioners will have faced, at some time, the need to clarify the instructions of a client who has some such mixed intention. This section, like most of those under discussion, is clearly framed with a view mainly to cases where the testator has not had the benefit of legal advice.

---

1 The article by Master ER Heward and BP Tickle: 'Rectification of Wills' (82 *Law Society's Gazette*, p 595) contains much useful information about taking proceedings.

2 See Michael Sladen: 'Evidence of Testator's Intentions' (83 *Law Society's Gazette*, p 97) discussing *Re Williams (otherwise Cook), decd; Wiles* v *Madgin* [1985] 1 WLR 905, apparently the first reported case under s 21.

## F–4 Registration of wills and international wills

It is necessary only to mention the existence of ss 23–26 of AJA 1982 containing provisions relating to the deposit and registration of the wills of living persons (the existing facilities for which are notoriously very little used); and of ss 27–28, giving effect to the 1973 Washington Convention providing a Uniform Law on the Form of International Wills, which is likely to be of importance only to a small (if increasing) minority of clients.

# G

# Family Law Reform Act 1987

## G–1 Introductory

The general purpose of the Family Law Reform Act 1987 is to remove legal disadvantages to children flowing from the consequences of birth outside marriage.

Except for s 6, the provisions of the Act referred to below came into force on 4 April 1988; s 6, brought into effect on 1 April 1989, is to be replaced by equivalent provisions to be found in the Children Act 1989, s 108(6) and (7) and Scheds 14 and 15 as from a day yet to be appointed.

## G–2 Provisions reproduced in this book

The purport of the provisions reproduced in Appendix 10 is as follows:

*Section 1.* Rules of construction as to certain statutory provisions referring to relationships and birth.

By virtue of ss 18 and 19 (below), these rules are further applied on intestacy and in relation to wills and codicils made on or after the commencement date.

*Section 6.* Provisions supplementary to the Guardianship of Minors Act 1971, ss 3, 4, and 5, relating to the right of a surviving parent to guardianship; and the power to appoint guardians by will and by order of the court.

*Section 18.* Presumptions and rules of construction relating to intestacy.

*Section 19.* Rules of construction and other provisions relating to dispositions of property, inter vivos or by will or codicil.

*Section 20*. Removal of protection previously afforded to trustees and personal representatives by the Family Law Reform Act 1969, s 17.

*Section 21*. Presumptions affecting entitlement to grants of probate and administration.

# H

# Recognition of Trusts Act 1987

## H–1 Introductory

The purpose of the Recognition of Trusts Act 1987 is to give effect to the Convention on the law applicable to trusts and on their recognition which was signed on 10 January 1986, as part of the law of the United Kingdom. The Act came into force on 1 August 1987.

## H–2 Provisions reproduced in this book

The text of the Convention, as scheduled to the Act, is reproduced in Appendix 11 as follows:

*Chapter I–Scope*. Trusts to which the Convention applies.

*Chapter II–Applicable law*. Choice of applicable law; and rules where no applicable law has been chosen.

*Chapter III–Recognition*. Implications of recognition of a trust as such.

*Chapter IV–General clauses*. Application of conflict rules of the forum and related matters.

# I

# The Draftsman and his Responsibilities

Clients look to their solicitor to make sure not only that their wills give clear and correct expression to their wishes, but also that they are effective: in other words, that they are duly executed and attested,[1] and, in particular, that they are not witnessed by any person who, or whose husband or wife, is a beneficiary under the will; and, more generally, that the intended benefit takes effect.[2]

Where the will is executed in the office or with the solicitor in attendance, there will be no difficulty in ensuring that the necessary formalities of execution are strictly complied with. These are well known and straightforward, but in the note to Form 9–1, a simple procedure is outlined, compliance with which should serve to make any error virtually impossible.

If for some exceptional reason the will has to be executed elsewhere, special care is needed[3] to ensure that the client understands what is required. The risk of error will be much reduced if the chosen witnesses are people such as bank employees who are wholly independent and who know the formalities. In all such cases, however, it is essential that the original will is *always* returned afterwards to the solicitor to be checked and to enable him to make up his draft with the date and particulars of execution. This is probably still better practice than taking a photographic copy, which may fade.

As well as the formalities of execution, the identity of the witnesses should be checked. Apart from the possibility that the testator's intentions may be frustrated if the will is witnessed by a beneficiary or spouse of a beneficiary, the solicitor may be held personally liable to the disappointed beneficiary if the client was not fully advised.

Although it was previously understood that the liability of a will draftsman was to his client alone,[4] it is now clear that in carrying out any kind of transaction, including a will, to confer a benefit on an identified third party the solicitor owes a duty to that third party to use proper care in carrying out his client's instructions, as in *Ross* v *Caunters*.[5] Indeed it may well be the case that (to cite but two instances, drawn from cases referred to in this book) such a duty could in future be held to arise in circumstances resembling, and as diverse as, those of *Re Sinclair* (see Preliminary Note F–2) and of *Re Recher's Will Trusts* (see note to Form 5–2). However, any such duty must have its limits. Thus, where a solicitor was instructed to prepare a will including a specific devise of certain property, but was later instructed to carry out a conflicting disposition of the same property inter vivos, no duty arose in favour of the prospective devisee, for the duty of the solicitor was to carry out his client's instructions.[6]

When the will has been executed, it is good practice for the previous will to be destroyed in the presence of the client and by his direction. Destruction is not necessary to revoke the previous will. Assuming the new will to contain a revocation clause (as in Form 1), the execution of the new will of itself revokes all others. It is simply a matter of convenience, to avoid possible future uncertainty or mistake if revoked wills are allowed to remain in existence.

In his own interests, the client should be encouraged to leave the original will for safe custody in the office or else at his bank. He should certainly be discouraged from keeping it at home. A copy should be supplied for his reference. If the will is not left in the office, a note of its whereabouts should be endorsed on the draft.

It will be found most helpful to keep a comprehensive register of all wills made in the office, whether originals are held or not. This may be maintained with very little trouble as a card index. Among other uses, this will serve as a reminder system to identify wills which may be due for review. This sort of reminder is an important part of the solicitor's service to his clients. How soon may a will need to be reviewed? This will depend on the individual client's circumstances, but as a generalisation it may be suggested that five years might be too soon, but that after seven years most wills begin to look distinctly out of date. Changes in the law or in the client's personal circumstances may, of course, call for special consideration.

---

1 In accordance with WA 1837, s 9 (as substituted by AJA 1982, s 17, reproduced in Appendix 6 and discussed in Preliminary Note F–2).

2 See WA 1837, s 15.
3 Notwithstanding relaxation of the formal requirements for execution in terms of WA 1837, s 9, above.
4 As in *Hall* v *Meyrick* [1957] 2 QB 455.
5 *Ross* v *Caunters* [1980] Ch 297.
6 See *Clarke* v *Bruce Lance & Co* [1988] 1 All ER 364 (CA).

2 See *Wingham*, 540.

3 Nor would the recent relaxation of the formal requirements for execution in [illegible]
WA 1837, s 9 [illegible]

4 As in [illegible] [1975] 2 QB 455.



# Precedent Forms

# 1

# Commencement

## 1–1 Introductory words, including revocation

The more traditional opening, 'This is the last Will and Testament of me . . . of . . . etc' introduces, it is suggested, an unnecessary element of solemnity into the process of will making, though it is, of course, perfectly acceptable. If the draftsman adopts it, he must also incorporate the words of revocation or, preferably, embody these in a separate clause.

Care should be taken to set out the full baptismal names and surname of the testator, since many people do not habitually use their full name. If, on enquiry, it transpires that the testator does not, it may avoid difficulty later to enquire further as to whether any property or investments may have been conveyed or registered to the testator without the use of his or her full name. If so, it will be convenient to add, after the true name, '(sometimes known as . . .)' which will facilitate the inclusion of the relevant alias in the grant of probate.

The inclusion of the testator's address and occupation or description serves no purpose other than as an aid to correct identification. However, it is usual and correct practice.

**Form 1–1**

> I [*full name, address and occupation or description*] HEREBY REVOKE all former wills and testamentary dispositions made by me AND DECLARE this to be my last will.

## 1–2 Contemplation of marriage (or re-marriage)

This form is intended to provide for the situation in which what was formerly known as a 'will in contemplation of marriage' would have been made, in reliance on s 177 of LPA 1925. That section having been replaced by provisions inserted into s 18 of WA 1837 by s 18 of AJA 1982 (see Preliminary Note F–2 and Appendix 6), it may be thought advisable to frame such a will in conformity with the new statutory language. Paragraph (1) of the present form seeks to do this.

It is (or should be) relatively unusual for such a will to be made before marriage, unless as a purely interim measure, pending execution of another will in a more permanent form once the marriage has taken place; which is of course to be advised. Unless that is the intention (and perhaps especially where an intended second marriage is in view), care is needed. Quite apart from the application of s 18, the requirements of which are easily satisfied, it is necessary to consider in such cases not only what is to happen if the marriage is prevented by the testator's death (the possibility against which such a will is presumably intended mainly to provide); but also what is to happen if the marriage does not take place for any other reason.

If the engagement were broken, the testator would be likely to make a new will, and should clearly do so. Nevertheless, as a precaution, it may be advisable to express the present will as ceasing to have effect if the marriage should not take place within whatever may be thought to be a reasonable time. This in turn makes it necessary to consider what is to happen at the end of that time. If a possible intestacy is to be avoided, it may be desired that as a stop-gap (pending the execution of a new will) the testator's previous will should be revived.

All these eventualities make for difficult and complex drafting; and, as suggested above, it will be much better if the substantive will is made after marriage, any will made in anticipation of the marriage being regarded as purely temporary, and being framed in the simplest terms possible. However, as the consequences of possible failure to make a further will must necessarily be kept in view, paragraphs (2) and (3) of the present form are included. Whilst these paragraphs can offer no more than an outline for a draft, since circumstances are various, it is hoped that they will serve as a reminder of the difficulties, and as a framework for their solution.

**Form 1–2**

(1) At the time of making this will I expect to be married to [ ] and intend that this my will (other than paragraphs (2) and (3) of this Clause) shall not be revoked by my marriage to the said [ ]

(2) If I die within the period of [ ] months from the date

hereof without having been married to the said [ ] [the following provisions of] [this my will] [shall nevertheless take effect without alteration] [shall take effect subject to the following alterations that is to say ] [shall become void to all intents and purposes] [and in that event (*as in (3) below*)]
(3) If in any circumstances my said intended marriage shall not have been solemnised within the period of [ ] months from the date hereof then at the end of that period this my will shall become void to all intents and purposes [and in that event any testamentary dispositions made by me before the date of this my will and which are revoked hereby shall then revive and have effect] [as if the same had been re-executed at the date hereof] [as if this present will had never been made]

# 2

# Executors and Trustees

### 2–1 Appointment of individuals; solicitors; bank

For the purposes of the normal family will, under which in all probability the whole estate, or at least the whole of residue, will pass to the spouse, an appointment of the spouse as executrix (or executor) will usually be dictated by convenience and will usually represent the wish of the testator (or testatrix). However, as such a will normally includes alternate beneficial dispositions in case the spouse should fail to survive, it will likewise normally include some form of alternate appointment of one or more executors and trustees. The following form is intended to embody such an appointment in the simplest possible way, by providing for a joint appointment of the spouse and some other person. It is envisaged that if the spouse takes, the other appointee would not need to prove the will, whereas if the spouse does not take, the other appointee will prove as surviving executor and may later appoint an additional trustee, should this appear desirable.

*Dissolution or annulment of marriage*

As to the effect of the Wills Act 1837, s 18A (as added by AJA 1982), and the decision in *Re Sinclair* [1985] Ch 446 (CA), see Preliminary Note F–2.

Should the testator's marriage later be dissolved or annulled, a joint appointment of executors and trustees as in Form 2–1–0 will have covered the deemed omission of any appointment of the former spouse by virtue of s 18A; as also will an alternate appointment in Form 2–1–1, should this be preferred.

**Form 2–1–0**

I APPOINT of and of (hereinafter called 'my Trustees' [which expression where the context admits includes any trustee hereof for the time being]) to be the executors and trustees of this my will [and I bequeath to each of those above-named who shall prove this will [and accept the trusteeship] the sum of £ for his or her own use and benefit absolutely] [and I declare that any of my Trustees being a Solicitor or being engaged in any other profession or business shall be entitled to charge and be paid all usual professional or other charges for business done services rendered or time spent by him or his firm on any matter connected with the administration of my estate or the trusts of this will including anything which a trustee who was not engaged in any profession or business could have done personally]

**Form 2–1–1**

I APPOINT my [said] [wife] [husband] [ ] to be the sole [executrix] [executor] of this my will but if [she] [he] is unwilling or unable to prove my will before the expiration of [ ] [weeks] [months] after my death then I APPOINT [ of ] to be [the sole] [jointly] [executor][s] and [trustee][s] of my will in [her] [his] place

Where the testator wishes to appoint a professional executor, he will usually wish to appoint his solicitor or his accountant (or both), personally, by name. In doing so, he will probably envisage that the work of the executorship and of any trust arising will be done by the firm of which the appointee is a member. If so, this should obviate any difficulty in the event of the appointee having retired from practice during the testator's lifetime. Sometimes, however, where there is no particular personal reason for appointing an individual, the testator may wish to appoint the firm as such. If so, it should be made clear that the appointment is of the partners at the date of death, as it would otherwise take effect as an appointment of the partners at the date of the will. It is also desirable to provide (if this is in fact acceptable to the testator) that the appointment should extend to any firm which at the date of death may be carrying on the practice of the firm named, though in the event of a change involving anything more than a reconstruction or amalgamation, the testator ought clearly to be invited to reconsider the position. Where a firm is appointed, it will be for the partners for the time being to decide how many and which of them should prove the will and the testator must be willing to leave this in their discretion. The only alternative is to appoint one or more individuals by name.

For convenience, the usual power to charge professional and

similar fees is included in the form of appointment. If preferred, it can be included in the clause dealing with trustees' powers (see Form 8–13–1), though as the matter of remuneration is an essential aspect of the appointment, it seems preferable to deal with both together. Neither the appointee nor any present partner should witness the will.

**Form 2–1–2**

I APPOINT the partners at the time of my death in the firm of Solicitors of (or in any other firm by which at the time its practice is then carried on) (hereinafter called 'my Trustees' [which expression where the context admits includes any trustee hereof of the time being]) to be the executors [and trustees] of this my will [and so that a sole principal or one only of such partners may act alone in the administration of my estate and of the trusts of this will] AND I DECLARE that my Trustees [other than any new trustee who is not engaged in any profession or business] shall be entitled to charge and be paid all usual professional or other charges in connection with the administration of my estate and the trusts of this will in all respects as if they were acting professionally therein for lay executors or trustees

Appointment of a bank or other trust corporation should always be made in the particular corporation's own published form, to ensure that the appointment will be acceptable. This form will always incorporate (by reference) the terms and conditions on which the appointment will be accepted by the corporation. It is necessary that these should be understood by and acceptable to the testator.

**Form 2–1–3**

I APPOINT Bank plc [*or as the case may be*] (hereinafter called 'the Bank') to be the sole executor and trustee hereof . . . [*continue in terms of the published forms of the particular bank or trust company relating to terms and conditions, remuneration and powers, according to circumstances*]

# 3

# Testamentary Guardians

### 3–1 Appointment of individuals

The power to appoint one or more testamentary guardians of children is not always exercised.

If the other parent survives, he or she is normally the statutory guardian of any child, either alone or jointly with any guardian appointed by the deceased parent.[1] Normally, therefore, where a spouse survives, the appointment of another guardian is unlikely to serve any useful purpose, except in case of serious disability of the spouse or perhaps where there are children of a previous marriage whose interests it is for any reason thought necessary to safeguard in this way.

An appointment is more likely to be envisaged as a safeguard in case of the death of the spouse and as taking effect only in that event. Although there is an express statutory power for the father or the mother of a child to appoint any person to be the guardian of the child after the father's or the mother's death,[2] it is not certain whether, as a matter of strict law, such an appointment can be made to take effect after the death of a parent who in fact survives the testator. Such reversionary appointments are sometimes made and are thought to have some value in that, even if not effective in law, they provide useful evidence as to the wishes of the testator which, in case the matter came before a court, the court would be entitled to take into account in making its own appointment.

In all cases, the court has a full and overriding discretion as to the appointment and removal of guardians.[3] Consequently, the inclusion of a testamentary appointment in the will serves mainly to avoid embarrassment and possible disputes as between members of the family and, in case a dispute should arise, to assist the court in determining what is the most suitable appointment to make.

If there are young children, the joint appointment of a married couple (if practicable) would clearly be desirable.

If a trust arises in favour of the children, or may do so, it might be convenient to appoint the guardian(s) to act also as trustee(s), unless the trusteeship seems likely to call for special expertise.

---

1 Guardianship of Minors Act 1971, s 3; to be amended by (and reproduced in Sched 1 to) Family Law Reform Act 1987: see Preliminary Note G.
2 Ibid, s 4.
3 Ibid, ss 5, 6, 7 et seq.

**Form 3–1**

I APPOINT [and jointly] to be the guardian[s] [jointly with] [after the death of] my [said] wife of any of my children who has not attained the age of eighteen at the time of [my] [her] death

# 4

# Specific Gifts

## Personal Chattels

### 4–1 Chattels generally, by statutory or alternative definitions

*Absolute gift*

It is most desirable, in all cases where the whole estate is not certain to pass absolutely to a single beneficiary, that the testator's personal chattels should be disposed of specifically. Great inconvenience may result if the terms of the will are such that these may be sold, or may become subject to any kind of trust (cf the proviso to AEA 1925, s 33(1), under which personal chattels are normally excepted from the statutory trust for sale on intestacy).

*Definition*

Although enacted for a different purpose, it is usual to adopt the definition in the AEA 1925, s 55(1)(x) and Form 4–1–1 does so. It is, however, important that the draftsman should consider whether this definition is in fact appropriate to the circumstances, particularly as to what is excluded. The terms of the statutory definition are contained in Appendix 1. Anything not self-evidently included in that definition (such as, for example, gold coins, or a boat and tackle) which are intended to pass with personal chattels, should be added expressly to the gift. Anything which might be within the definition, but which is not intended to pass with personal chattels, should be otherwise expressly disposed of. Express instructions should always be taken as to the testator's wishes with regard to any items of substantial value.

Form 4–1–2 offers a much simplified alternative definition, in more general terms, which it is thought should be effective to include everything which the normal testator would think of as part of his personal effects. Such a formula is perhaps more in keeping with modern conditions and does not require reference to anything outside the will for explanation to the testator.

*Shared gifts*

Usually, a gift of personal chattels will be made to a surviving spouse. Where this is not the case, and the gift is to be shared between two or more beneficiaries, some provision should be made as to the basis of division in order to avoid disputes and, possibly, an undesirable sale. For a simple formula, see Form 4–2–2, which is readily adaptable.

*Tax*

If the gift is to a surviving spouse, it is as such exempt from IHT. In other cases, a gift of personal chattels, like any other specific gift of personalty, is in effect free from IHT[1] which, as a testamentary expense, is normally payable primarily out of the general personal estate. Accordingly, it is not the practice of draftsmen to express specific gifts of personalty as being 'free of tax'.

1 Because, by definition, specific legacies are not payable out of the general estate (either real or personal) and so could never have become liable to bear any part of the tax on real estate under the rule in *Re Spencer Cooper* [1908] 1 Ch 130 and *Re Owers* [1941] Ch 17. For the present position as to this, see note to Forms 5–1 etc.

**Form 4–1–1**

I GIVE to [my] [said] [wife ] [ ] absolutely [all] [such of] my personal chattels as defined by section 55(1)(x) of the Administration of Estates Act 1925 [as are not hereby or by any codicil hereto otherwise specifically disposed of] [and also any motor car belonging to me even though used wholly or partly for business purposes] [and also my ] [but not my ]

**Form 4–1–2**

I GIVE to absolutely [all] [such of] my chattels and effects of personal domestic or household use or ornament [as are not hereby or by any codicil hereto otherwise specifically disposed of] [excepting money and securities for money] [and excepting any chattels and effects used solely for business purposes] [but including any chattels or effects of personal use which may also be used partly for the purposes of any business or employment] [and also my ] [but not my ]

## 4–2 Particular chattels: jewellery; household effects; legatee's choice

*Identification*

It goes without saying that the description of anything given specifically should not only be full enough to distinguish it from all other things of the same kind but also not so full as to risk failure of identification because of some error of detail. Descriptions of jewellery, in particular, may present difficulties of this kind: reference to the description in an insurance valuation may be of assistance.

*Substitutions*

As to descriptions of property, a will speaks from death,[1] and is therefore construed, prima facie, by reference to the testator's possessions at the time of death. However, in relation to a specific legacy, the essence of which is that the testator intended to give a particular designated thing, the gift can take effect only if the estate of the testator included that thing at the time of death: otherwise, the gift is adeemed. Even if, having parted with the thing given, the testator should later have acquired a similar thing, the substitute cannot pass under the original gift[2] unless the terms of the gift are wide enough to include such a substitute. Whether a gift is specific is a matter of construction: as a generalisation, any gift of a particular thing prefaced by the word 'my' is likely to be so held and gifts of particular chattels are therefore usually so framed. In the case of chattels, it will not usually be necessary, or practicable, to make provision for possible substitutions. By way of comparison and contrast, see the suggested provisions in relation to specific gifts of shareholdings and houses in Forms 4–6 and 4–7.

1 WA 1837, s 24.
2 As to application of WA 1837, s 24, see *Jarman on Wills* (8th ed), pp 419 and 426.

*Shared gifts: basis of division*

Form 4–2–2 adopts what is thought to be the most straightforward basis for division in specie between beneficiaries, whereby recourse to the executors is required only in so far as the beneficiaries may be unable to agree.

*Right of selection*

Sometimes it is desired to give to one beneficiary the first choice of the testator's effects, or of some particular category, any not so chosen going elsewhere. Form 4–2–3 seeks to do this as simply as possible. It can be further simplified where the property not chosen passes to the beneficiary entitled to those personal chattels not specifically disposed of. A time limit for the selection should be imposed for practical reasons.

*Expenses*

Since the expenses of putting a legatee into possession of his legacy (including the cost of insurance) fall on the legatee,[1] in the absence of provision to the contrary, it will usually be desired to transfer this burden to the general estate. Form 4–2–2 does so.

Where chattels are to be selected, the title of the beneficiary derives from the selection, and expenses *up to that time* do fall on the estate.[2]

1 See *Re Leach* [1923] 1 Ch 161.
2 *Re Collins' Will Trusts* [1971] 1 WLR 37.

*Tax*

See note to Forms 4–1–1 and 4–1–2.

**Form 4–2–1**

I GIVE the following specific legacies absolutely:

(i) To [my] [God-daughter] [ ] my two-stone diamond ring
(ii) To [my] [daughter] [ ] and to [ ] [the wife of my son ] [in equal shares] all the [jewellery] [and furs] which belonged to my late wife

**Form 4–2–2**

I GIVE absolutely and in equal shares to my [grand] children living at my death all my household furniture furnishings and effects to be divided among them as they shall agree but so that in default of such agreement the division shall be made by my Trustees in their absolute discretion [and without any obligation upon my Trustees to obtain any professional valuation] [save at the joint expense of my said [grand] children] and shall be final and binding upon all my said [grand] children [AND I DIRECT that all costs and expenses of packing carriage and insurance incurred for the purpose of giving effect to this gift shall be paid out of the residue of my estate]

**Form 4–2–3**

I GIVE to [ ] absolutely such of my [ ] as [he] [she] may select [within three months after my death] [and subject thereto I give the same to [ ] absolutely]

## 4–3 Incorporation of memorandum or list

Where a testator wishes to give a number of legacies (usually small specific legacies), it is not uncommon for these to be set out in a separate memorandum or list which it is proposed to incorporate into the will by reference, instead of repeating the contents verbatim in the will.

Although such a list may be validly incorporated in this way, and in due course admitted to probate as part of the will (provided all the requirements described in the note to Form 6–14 can be shown to have been fully satisfied), this practice involves risks and, therefore, the use of Form 4–3 is not recommended except in case of urgency or in other special circumstances.

If this form is used, care should be taken to ensure that the list is clearly identifiable and is properly signed and dated. This is to assist in its identification, to avoid separation of the list from the will, as a precaution against accidental loss, and to avoid any possibility that, in ignorance of the law, the testator might later attempt to substitute a different list.

**Form 4–3**

I GIVE to such as are living at my death of the several people named in a list [dated 19 ] [bearing even date with but] prepared and signed by me [before executing this my will] such items of [my personal chattels] [my household furniture furnishings and effects] [my jewellery furs and articles of personal use and ornament] as are respectively described therein opposite to their respective names

## 4–4 Precatory trust

Testators sometimes wish to delegate or defer decisions as to who is to benefit under a gift, by making the gift to a particular legatee, coupled with the expression of a wish or hope that the legatee will apply the gift either to some particular purpose or at his own discretion.

If the terms of a gift of this kind are such as to show an intention to create a trust, then it may take effect in equity as a half-secret trust. With such trusts, however, the present note is not concerned, because no testator would be well advised to create such a trust intentionally, in any but very exceptional circumstances.

In order to avoid any possibility of doing so by inadvertence, it is usual and necessary to provide expressly, in making a gift of the kind under consideration, that this is not intended to create any trust or obligation. The term 'precatory trust', commonly used to describe such a gift, is therefore misleading. It is the essence of such a gift that it takes effect as an absolute gift to the legatee who has an absolute discretion as to how, if at all, it should be applied. Naturally, such a gift should be inserted in the will only where there are explicit instructions that this is the result intended.

Because any subsequent application by the legatee in accordance with the testator's wish would otherwise be liable to attract IHT, it is specifically enacted that where a testator expresses a wish that property bequeathed by his will should be transferred by the legatee to other persons, and the legatee transfers any of the property in accordance with that wish within two years after the death, that transfer is not a transfer of value, and tax is chargeable (or not) as if the property transferred had been bequeathed by will to the transferee.[1]

This form is intended for use (being adapted as may be appropriate) where the testator wishes to give to some person (probably his or her spouse) the opportunity to re-dispose of some part of the estate within this provision, if this may result in a saving of tax. It will generally do so only if a transfer by the legatee would attract a higher rate of tax than is payable on death.

1 IHTA 1984, s 143, reproduced in Appendix 3.

**Form 4–4**

(1) I GIVE to [ ] [my Trustees] absolutely such and so many of [my personal chattels] [my stocks and shares] [the assets comprising my personal estate (other than any interest in the proceeds to arise from the sale of property held upon trust for sale)] as within the period of months after my death [he] [she] [they] may select

(2) WITHOUT PREJUDICE to the generality of the preceding paragraph of this Clause and without imposing any trust or obligation whatsoever on [the said ] [my Trustees] and

without conferring any legal equitable or other interest whatsoever on any other person I express the wish (within the meaning of section 143 of the Inheritance Tax Act 1984 or any enactment for the time being amending or replacing that section) that [the said ] [my Trustees] should select such only of [my personal chattels] [my stocks and shares] [the assets comprising my personal estate] as may be described in any memorandum left by me which shall come to [his] [her] [their] knowledge within the said period of months after my death expressing my wishes as to the disposal or distribution thereof respectively and that [the said ] [my Trustees] should make such transfer or transfers as may be necessary for the purpose of giving effect to such my wishes PROVIDED ALWAYS that no such memorandum or expression of my wishes shall have or be deemed to have any testamentary effect nor shall create nor be deemed to create any trust right liability or obligation whatsoever nor shall [the said ] [my Trustees] be in any way answerable or accountable to any person whomsoever in relation to anything done omitted or suffered by [him] [her] [them] in relation to anything whatsoever contained in or implied or alleged to be implied by either of the paragraphs of this Clause or any part or parts thereof respectively

### 4–5 Choses in action: words of bequest; life policy; bank account; building society account; local authority bond

In wills disposing of the smaller estates, it is sometimes desired to include what is in essence a pecuniary legacy, but is in form a specific legacy, in as much as the amount is to be the balance at the time of death in a particular bank or savings account or, perhaps, the proceeds of a life policy. Forms 4–5–2 et seq give effect to a variety of gifts of this kind and may readily be adapted.

The testator should, however, consider whether a pecuniary legacy of a stated amount might not be more satisfactory, in the interests of certainty. There is also the danger that a specific gift might be adeemed if the particular account is closed in the testator's lifetime or that the amount of the eventual benefit to the legatee might be substantially less or more than the testator expected at the time of making the will.

Although not really of direct concern to the draftsman, it is perhaps as well to bear in mind the statutory provisions[1] by which investors in national savings investments,[2] and trustee savings banks, friendly societies and industrial and provident societies may direct payment to be made, in the event of death, by way of nomination, to a named person. Nominations are not testamentary documents, and are not revoked by a later will and there is therefore some danger that they may be overlooked. In the case of post office investments, there is no limit to the amount which may be nominated: in other cases, the maximum amount is £5,000.[3]

1 National Savings Bank Act 1971, s 8; Trustee Savings Bank Act 1981, s 27; Friendly Societies Act 1974, ss 66, 67; Industrial and Provident Societies Act 1965, ss 23, 24; Credit Unions Act 1979, s 4, Sched 1, para 12; and various regulations thereunder.

2 Except National Savings Certificates.

3 Administration of Estates (Small Payments) (Increase of Limit) Order 1984 (SI 1984 No 539).

**Form 4–5–1**

I BEQUEATH to absolutely

**Form 4–5–2**

the full benefit of a Policy of Assurance dated the 19 and effected by me on my own life with the Company and all moneys (including any bonus) to become payable thereunder [but free from liability for any charge or other incumbrance thereon which (if there be any such at the time of my death) shall be discharged from my residuary estate]

**Form 4–5–3**

the balance (including accrued and current interest if any) standing at the time of my death to my credit on [my] [any] [current] or [deposit] account with [the Branch of] Bank plc [to which I may be solely and beneficially entitled]

**Form 4–5–4**

all money [including accrued] [and current] [interest] standing to my credit at the time of my death on [Share Account number ] [any share deposit or other investment account] with the Building Society [or any other Building Society to which its engagements may hereafter be transferred]

**Form 4–5–5**

all moneys for the time being secured by a Bond dated the 19 and numbered effected by me with the [County] [District] Council or by any Bond of the said Council for the time being subsisting whether directly or indirectly by way of renewal or replacement thereof PROVIDED ALWAYS that if the said Council shall be unwilling to transfer the said Bond then its nominal value [as at the time of my death] shall be paid out of my residuary estate in satisfaction of this gift.

## 4–6 Stocks and shares

It is comparatively unusual for a testator to make a specific gift of a particular holding of quoted shares or stock to an individual legatee. Such a gift is more likely to be envisaged where the testator is disposing of shares in a family or other unquoted company, probably in favour of some person already associated with the business of the company who may not necessarily be entitled to the residue of the estate.

In either case, it must be appreciated that if a particular holding is specifically disposed of by will or if the testator's holding(s) for the time being in a particular company are so disposed of, and at the time of death the testator does not possess such a holding, the gift will be adeemed. If so, the legatee will not be entitled to any substitute holding, unless the terms of the gift are wide enough to include it. Such a substitution may commonly occur, in the case of equity shares, where there is any kind of take-over or amalgamation or even where there is merely a reconstruction. In the case of fixed interest securities, redemption may occur, with or without conversion into other securities or equity shares.

Even where the testator still possesses the particular holding at the time of death, difficulty may arise if this has been specified too exactly because a gift of a particular number of shares or amount of stock will be strictly construed and will pass only that number of shares or amount of stock, even though the holding so described in the will may subsequently have been enlarged (whether by any bonus[1] or rights issue, or equally by gift, inheritance or purchase).

There are so many ways in which the composition of such an investment may change that it is not easy to cover all eventualities. This form should be found sufficiently wide to safeguard the legatee in most foreseeable circumstances but it should be used with some caution, and should be adapted as may be appropriate.

It is particularly important, in relation to a gift of this kind (assuming it to be of substantial value), that the will should be kept under regular review, and the testator should be so warned.

1 See, for a particularly hard case, *Re Tetsall* [1961] 1 WLR 938.

**Form 4–6**

I GIVE absolutely to all [shares] [stocks] [debentures] [debenture stock] [loan stock] [and other interests or rights (if any)] to which at the time of my death I may be beneficially entitled in the capital of plc/Limited [or in the capital or assets of any other company or corporation or in the public funds to which at the time of my death I may have become beneficially entitled whether directly or indirectly (except by purchase in the open market) either in right of or by way of substitution for any previous beneficial interest in the capital of the said plc/Limited]

## Interests in Land

### 4–7 Private residence: absolute

This form provides for an absolute gift of the matrimonial home (or of the testator's interest, where the parties are tenants in common), which it is sometimes desired to make, where the residue is left in trust, or for any other reason does not pass absolutely to the surviving spouse.

Where such a gift is made, it may be desired that this should be contingent upon the spouse surviving for a minimum period (see note 'Vesting' to Form 6–5). It will usually be advisable to impose such a condition in any case where this would have been advisable in relation to an absolute gift of residue, in as much as the matrimonial home will commonly be the most important and possibly the most valuable single asset in the estate.

Like any other specific gift, this gift carries the risk of possible ademption in the event of the testator moving house after the date of the will. Should this happen, the safest course (in view of the particular importance of this gift) would be to make a codicil, substituting the new house. However, as this may be overlooked, it seems most desirable that the original gift should, if possible, be framed in terms wide enough to extend to whatever is the matrimonial home at the date of death. In this respect, the only difficulties are purely drafting difficulties. In the first place, the phrase 'house or flat' may be too narrow, in as much as people sometimes live in accommodation which is neither. If this seems a possibility in the particular case, the cautious draftsman may prefer the expression 'dwelling-house', though it is difficult to be sure that even this expression would extend to, for instance, a houseboat or a caravan. Secondly, in case the testator may have more than one residence, it is necessary to establish which is meant. To facilitate this, the expression 'only or main residence' is borrowed from the legislation relating to CGT. It is considered that the meaning should be clear without further definition. For an alternative form of words see Form 6–3.

It will usually be considered right[1] to provide expressly that the gift is to be free of any mortgage or charge which may be subsisting at the time of death, thereby displacing AEA 1925, s 35. The effect of such provision on the value of residue should be carefully estimated, if, as has been presupposed, the beneficial interests are different.

1 See note to Form 4–11.

**Form 4–7**

I give absolutely to my [said] [wife] [husband] [if] [and only if] [she] [he] [survives me by twenty-eight clear days] [my] [freehold] [leasehold] [dwelling-house] [house] [flat] known as [all my share and interest of and in the] [freehold] [leasehold] [dwelling-house] [flat] known as and the proceeds of sale thereof [or such other [dwelling-house] house or flat (if any) as may be the only or main residence of myself and my said [wife] [husband] at the time of my death] [free from any mortgage or charge affecting the same at the time of my death which shall be discharged from the residue of my estate]

## 4–8 Private residence: settled, under trust for sale

Where, because of the value of the estate or some other special reason, the testator wishes to leave residue in trust for a surviving spouse for life only, it is for consideration whether the family home (if the testator is sole owner) or the testator's share in it (if the parties are tenants in common) should be dealt with as part of the residuary trust fund, or dealt with specifically.

In many such cases, it will be thought better not to restrict the spouse to a limited interest in the house but to leave this to the spouse absolutely, as in form 4–7. This frees the spouse from any dependence on the trustees which, even though mitigated by provisions such as those in Forms 6–3 and 8–5, is contrary to what many testators would wish.

Alternatively, with a view to giving to the spouse a very wide freedom of action while still preserving the capital represented by the house as an asset of the estate, the house could be settled on the spouse as tenant for life under SLA 1925, as under Form 4–9.

If neither of the foregoing alternatives is acceptable, it may be desired to declare trusts in respect of the house separate from those of residue, whereby the spouse is given a life interest under a trust for sale but (as in Forms 6–3 and 8–5, referred to above) is protected by provisions requiring consent to any sale, allowing a right of occupation pending sale, and permitting a purchase elsewhere from the proceeds of any sale. Form 4–8 embodies such provision. See generally the notes to Form 6–3 andPreliminary Note D–7, where the IHT and CGT implications of various possible arrangements as to occupation are discussed.

Apart from optional variations of detail, the effect of Form 4–8 is similar to the effect of Forms 6–3 and 8–5 (read in conjunction with Form 6–2) (see notes to these forms). The advantage of dealing with the house separately from the rest of the estate is simply that, as a matter of drafting, all provisions relating to the house are incorporated into one clause. This may also be of assistance in directing attention to the matters which, in the interest of the spouse, ought to receive careful consideration.

Although Form 4–8 can be adapted to include the contents of the house in the trust, this is not normally recommended.

**Form 4–8**

(1) I GIVE to my Trustees my [freehold] [leasehold] [dwelling-house] [house] [flat] known as          [or such other [dwelling-house] house or flat as may be the only or main residence of myself and my [said] [wife] [husband] at the time of my death] [and all furniture furnishings and effects of household use or ornament therein not otherwise specifically disposed of by this my will or any codicil hereto] UPON TRUST [with the consent of my said [wife] [husband] during [her] [his] life] to sell the same (but with full power to postpone sale without being liable for any loss) and to hold the net rents and profits (if any) until sale and the net income from the proceeds of sale in trust for my said [wife] [husband] during [her] [his] life and after [her] [his] death my Trustees shall hold the said [dwelling-house] [house] [flat] or other [dwelling-house] house or flat for the time being held by them upon the trusts of this gift or the net proceeds of sale or the investments for the time being representing the same [and the said furniture furnishings and effects] UPON the TRUSTS [and with and subject to the powers and provisions] hereinafter declared concerning my residuary estate.

(2) Pending sale of the said [dwelling-house] [house] [flat] and if the same be sold then pending sale of any other such [dwelling-house] house or flat for the time being held by my Trustees upon the trusts of this gift they shall allow my said [wife] [husband] to occupy the same [and to use the said furniture furnishings and effects] for so long as [she] [he] shall wish to do so Upon such terms and conditions as in their absolute discretion my Trustees shall from time to time think fit to require as to the payment of [rent] taxes and other outgoings in respect thereof and as to the insurance and repair thereof And so that in the like discretion if my Trustees shall from time to time think fit to do so they shall have power (but shall not be under any obligation) to discharge any of the last mentioned liabilities or any part thereof out of the income or capital (or partly out of the income and partly out of the capital) of my residuary estate in priority over any beneficial interest therein

(3) My Trustees shall have power at the request of my said [wife] [husband] to apply the whole or any part of the proceeds of any sale under the trusts of this gift in or towards the purchase of another [dwelling-house] house or flat [Provided that such purchase can be recommended to my Trustees by a professionally qualified surveyor and valuer] [if in their absolute discretion my Trustees shall think fit to do so] and thereupon the same shall be held upon the trusts of this gift and with all the powers applicable thereto [And I DIRECT that if in their absolute discretion my Trustees shall think fit to do so they shall have power (but shall not be under any obligation) to apply any part of the capital of my residuary estate (not exceeding £ )] towards the cost of any such purchase as an advance by way of loan from my residuary estate upon such terms and conditions as in the like discretion my Trustees shall from time to time think fit to require]

### 4–9 Private residence: settled, under SLA 1925

For the reasons suggested in Preliminary Note D–7 (where the IHT and CGT implications of various possible arrangements as to occupation are discussed), and in the notes to Forms 4–8, 6–3 and 8–5, where (unusually) the testator wishes a surviving spouse to enjoy a limited interest in the family home, it should not necessarily be assumed that the most appropriate method of creating such an interest is to declare a trust for sale.

If a trust for sale is declared, it will be necessary to make further provision (as in those forms) for the protection of the spouse if the spouse is not to be left entirely dependent on the sympathetic exercise of their discretions by the trustees. Even these provisions, while they do afford to the spouse a secure right of occupation of the testator's existing house, unavoidably leave the spouse very much in the hands of the trustees as to any purchase which it may be desired to make if the existing house is sold. However carefully the trustees may have been selected, and however conscientiously they may be expected to carry out their duties, few testators would really wish a widow, or widower, to be able to buy a new house only if the trustees see fit to make that particular purchase.

No doubt many testators, taking that view, would wish to reconsider the position, and to give the existing house to the spouse absolutely, as in Form 4–7, even though wishing the rest of the estate to be held in trust. However, if such a testator is concerned, as such a wish implies, that the capital value of residue should be preserved, so far as possible, for the children, or other remaindermen, a settlement of the house may provide an appropriate compromise.

In case the spouse should later wish to release her interest under the settlement, it may be noted that any future transfer out of settlement would normally be a potentially exempt transfer for IHT purposes (under F(No 2)A 1987, s 96); and that the usual relief for CGT purposes (under CGTA 1979, ss 101–103) should also be available. As tenant for life under such a settlement, the spouse would enjoy all the powers of trustees for sale and, in the event of a sale would be entitled, as of right,[1] to direct the application of the proceeds to the purchase of another house while, at the same time, the original or any substitute house would remain an asset of the estate.

---

1 SLA 1925, s 75(2), in conjunction with s 73(1)(xi).

*'to my ... wife ... for life'*

It will be the duty of the executors to vest the house in the wife as tenant for life, by vesting assent. This is the only formality which will be required.

*'she paying all taxes and other outgoings'*

This will usually be considered to be a reasonable requirement. The wife, presumably, will be in receipt of the income of residue.

*'and keeping the same in good repair'*

If the estate is substantial enough to warrant a settlement, it may also be thought reasonable that the tenant for life should bear the cost of repairs out of income.[1]

1 Unless the trust instrument expressly so requires, the tenant for life is not, in general, under any duty to keep the trust property in repair (*Re Cartwright* (1889) 41 Ch D 532).

'[*fair wear and tear excepted*]'

Otherwise, this suggested limitation may be considered, though it may lead to undesirable difficulties as between the tenant for life and the trustees.[1]

1 Ie, as to the extent of the tenant for life's obligation, which such a limitation does not necessarily discharge altogether (see *Brown* v *Davies* [1958] 1 QB 117, a landlord and tenant case).

**Form 4–9**

(1) I GIVE my freehold property [dwelling-house] known as unto my [said] wife for her life she paying all taxes and other outgoings and keeping the same in good repair [fair wear and tear excepted] and insured against loss or damage by fire to the full value thereof as my Trustees shall approve And from and after the death of my said wife I GIVE the same unto absolutely

(2) I APPOINT my Trustees to be trustees for the purposes of the Settled Land Act 1925 of the settlement hereby made

(3) I DIRECT that capital money arising under the said Act may be invested or applied (in addition to the other modes of investment or application authorised by law) [with the consent of my Trustees] in any manner authorised by this my will in relation to moneys forming part of my residuary estate [but so that nothing herein contained shall be taken to exclude the application of section 73(2) of the said Act]

## 4–10 Option to acquire share, where property already settled

Form 5–5 seeks to reduce the estate of a surviving spouse (where there was already a tenancy in common) by allowing the share of the deceased spouse in the matrimonial home (up to the amount or unused balance of the nil rate band of IHT) to be appropriated into a discretionary trust. In this way, it is suggested, a saving of IHT at the death of the spouse can be realised, without detriment to the security of the spouse, whose de facto occupation (as a tenant in common) would not in practice be disturbed by the trustees.

While the testator's interest in the matrimonial home could simply have been given to the children, likewise keeping it out of the estate of the spouse, this *would* have placed the security of the spouse at risk, unless some provision were added to prevent a sale without the spouse's consent. Almost certainly, however, such a provision would give rise to a settlement for IHT purposes, thus defeating the object.

A simpler alternative seems possible. Two steps are involved. First, the testator could give the spouse an option (exercisable at any time after his death and during the spouse's lifetime) to buy the testator's share at its full value. Then, the testator's share could be left to (or in trust for) the children; necessarily subject to the option.

In the result, the testator's share is still kept out of the estate of the spouse. If the option were exercised, the estate of the spouse would not be increased; but it need never *be* exercised. The spouse has complete de facto security, because the existence of the option makes the house effectively unsaleable without her consent.

Paragraph (3) draws attention to a practical point: but in case the Inland Revenue should take the view that its effect is to include the house in the survivor's estate (even if the option is not exercised), it might better be omitted.

**Form 4–10**

(1) My said [wife] [husband] shall have the option (exercisable at any time after my death and during [her] [his] lifetime by notice in writing to my Trustees) to purchase whatever is at my death the only or main residence of myself and my said [wife] [husband] at a price equal to the full market value thereof for the time being as reduced by the value at that time of any existing beneficial interest of my said [wife] [husband] therein taking the value of that interest as a rateable proportion of the value of the whole

(2) The market value of such residence shall be such sum as may be agreed in writing between my said [wife] [husband] and my Trustees within [ ] [days] [calendar months] from the date of any notice exercising this option and in default of such agreement shall be determined by arbitration.

[(3) The purchase money pursuant to any exercise of this option shall not be payable during the lifetime of my said [wife] [husband] but shall become payable (without interest) out of [her] [his] estate within [ ] calendar months after [her] [his] death]

### 4–11 Investment property

Although it is somewhat unusual, the testator may wish to make a specific devise of realty, other than his or her own home, in favour of some person other than the residuary legatee. This form should be readily adapted to the circumstances of the case.

It is not strictly necessary to make the gift expressly subject to leases, tenancies, etc. A gift by reference simply to the description of the property will undoubtedly pass whatever estate or interest the testator may have,[1] and will undoubtedly take effect subject to all rights of third parties subsisting at the date of death. The words in the relative square brackets may therefore be omitted.

In case the property is subject (or at the time of death might have become subject) to any mortgage or charge, the testator should consider whether the gift is to take effect subject thereto (as, in the absence of a contrary intention, it would[2]), or whether any such incumbrance is to be discharged out of residue. It is strongly recommended[3] that whichever is the intention, this should be *expressed* in the will.

It is also strongly recommended that the testator should consider whether the gift is to take effect subject to, or free from, IHT. As explained in Preliminary Note D–3, IHT on a specific gift of realty in the UK is a testamentary expense, and as such is normally payable out of residue, unless the will directs otherwise. Accordingly, if the specific beneficiary is to bear the tax (as also in the case of leaseholds, and undivided shares in land held on trust for sale), the gift must be made expressly subject to tax. However, as the incidence of tax as between beneficiaries is a matter which must receive the testator's direct consideration, the will ought (as in relation to a possible mortgage) to *express* the testator's considered intention, one way or the other. Further, as to the incidence of IHT, any will made before the decision in *Re Dougal*[4] which does not expressly declare such an intention should by now have been reconsidered. This important matter should be considered against the background of the statutory rules as to the incidence of tax, and as to the liability of personal representatives, discussed in Preliminary Note D–3.

It is also most important to guard against the possibility of ademption, especially in relation to any agreement for sale, or compulsory acquisition. Assuming that, in either event, the testator would wish the devisee to receive the consideration or compensation money, paragraph (ii) so provides. It would otherwise usually pass to the residuary legatee.

---

1 Care is still needed, because the court cannot re-write the will of a testator who is under a misapprehension as to what he owns: see, for example, *Re Lewis's Will Trusts* [1985] 1 WLR 102; applying *Re Tetsall*, cited ante, p 89.
2 By virtue of AEA 1925, s 35.
3 Because s 35 allows of a contrary intention expressed by 'will deed or other document'; the *absence* of which may be difficult or impossible to establish.
4 [1981] STC 514 (and see Preliminary Note D–3).

**Form 4–11**

[(i)] I GIVE to of absolutely my [freehold] [leasehold] property known as [and comprised in Title number at HM Land Registry] [SUBJECT to and with the benefit of all leases tenancies and contractual or other rights and obligations for the time being affecting the said property or any part or parts thereof and all covenants agreements and conditions for the time being subsisting in relation thereto] [AND SUBJECT to] [but FREED AND DISCHARGED from] [any legal mortgage or equitable charge for the time being affecting the said property or any part or parts thereof] [which I DIRECT shall be discharged out of my residuary estate in exoneration of the said property] [AND SUBJECT to the due payment by the said (in exoneration of my estate of] [but] [and] [FREED AND DISCHARGED from] [all liability in respect of Inheritance Tax attributable by reason of my death to the said property or to this gift thereof] [which I DIRECT shall be discharged out of my residuary estate in exoneration of the said property]

[(ii) I DIRECT that if at the time of my death any local or public authority or any tenant or any other person whosoever shall have acquired or shall be entitled or prospectively entitled to acquire the said property or any part or parts thereof or any interest therein (whether under powers conferred by or deriving from any statute or by way of private treaty) then the said shall be entitled to receive absolutely all if any compensation or consideration money or other payment whatsoever which at the time of my death may have become receivable or which may thereafter become receivable by reason or in consequence of any such acquisition or entitlement or prospective entitlement as aforesaid]

# 5

# Pecuniary Legacies

## General (Absolute)

### 5–1 Individuals; grandchildren; nephews and nieces

These forms are concerned only with legacies to individuals. For legacies to charities, see Form 5–2.

Forms 5–1–1 and 5–1–3 envisage that, as is usual, the gift is immediate. Form 5–1–2 provides for the more unusual requirement that the legacy should be payable only after the death of a life tenant.

*Tax*

It may be thought that, as a matter of construction, the simple gift of a sum of money, with no reference to tax, would necessarily take effect as the gift of a clear sum, free of tax. As in the case of the specific legacy, this will usually be the position because any tax in respect of amounts given by way of pecuniary legacy has always been a testamentary expense in so far as the legacy is payable out of the general personal estate. It is, however, the long-standing practice of draftsmen to provide expressly that pecuniary legacies should be 'free of tax'. This is because these might become payable out of the proceeds of a sale of a mixed fund of realty and personalty. As such (in the absence of contrary intention) they would formerly have been liable (under *Re Spencer Cooper* [1908] 1 Ch 130 and *Re Owers* [1941] Ch 17) to bear a proportion of the tax on realty; which, for estate duty purposes (and as it was long supposed, for capital transfer tax purposes also), was not a testamentary expense. For IHT purposes, that position is reversed: see Preliminary Note D–3; and so a pecuniary legacy cannot now bear any tax unless expressly so directed by the will. The practice of expressing legacies to be 'free of tax' will no doubt continue. It still cannot be wrong to show the intention expressly; though if the legacy were very substantial, the incidence of tax ought to receive special consideration.

Another possible reason for providing expressly that pecuniary legacies should be free of tax is that the estate may otherwise be exempt from tax because it passes to a surviving spouse. By IHTA 1984, Part II, Chapter III, where the only non-exempt gifts in an otherwise exempt estate are tax-free legacies, the 'nil' rate band is available and, if this is not exceeded by the amount of the non-exempt legacies when added to the cumulative total of any chargeable lifetime transfers by the testator, no tax at all will be payable on the estate. Thus in most normal circumstances, the gift of normal pecuniary legacies will not give rise to any tax liability.

*Minors*

Where any legatee may be a minor at the time of death, it will be an advantage to that legatee, and will also simplify the administration of the estate, if the executors are empowered to make payment to a parent or guardian or, alternatively, to make some appropriate investment in the name of the minor legatee. National Savings investments are envisaged as the most suitable if the legacy is of a comparatively modest amount.

Without such a provision, the executors would be obliged, in most cases,[1] to retain the legacy in trust until the legatee attains majority because, in the absence of an express provision to the contrary, a minor cannot give a good receipt, either for capital or for income.

By way of example, Form 5–1–3 includes alternative provisions which should be readily adapted to the requirements of the particular testator, and should also be appropriate, with adaptation, to any other form of gift to beneficiaries who may possibly include one or more minors. It should perhaps be borne in mind that such a power, if given, may place the executor in a difficult position if, in the particular circumstances, he does not think fit to exercise it.

It is envisaged that, in any such case, the gift will be absolute and will not be subject to a condition as to attaining majority, or in any other way contingent. If the testator wishes to attach any such condition to the gift, the kind of provision under discussion will clearly be inappropriate.

For a more general provision, see Form 8–10.

---

1 It is open to the executors, alternatively, to appoint separate trustees of a legacy to a minor who is absolutely entitled, under AEA 1925, s 42, but this power is thought not to be widely used. For the provisions of that section, see Appendix 1.

**Form 5–1–1**

I GIVE the following pecuniary legacies absolutely and free of all taxes:

(i) To of the sum of £

(ii) To of or if [he] [she] does not survive me [by twenty-eight clear days] then to [his] [her] [wife] [husband] [ ] if [she] [he] survives me [by twenty-eight clear days] the sum of £

**Form 5–1–2**

I GIVE to each of my grandchildren living at the death of the survivor of myself and my [said] wife absolutely and free of all taxes the sum of £ to be paid within six months after the death of such survivor [and if not so paid to carry interest thereafter until payment at the rate of per centum per annum]

**Form 5–1–3**

I GIVE to each of my nephews and nieces [and the nephews and nieces of my late wife] living at my death the sum of £ absolutely and free of all taxes [AND I DIRECT that if at the time when his or her legacy is payable any individual legatee has not attained the age of eighteen years] [my Trustees may pay the same to his or her parent or guardian whose receipt shall be a full discharge to my Trustees] [my Trustees may in their absolute discretion] [open an account in the name of the legatee with the National Savings Bank and pay into that account the said sum of £ ] [or may] [apply the said sum of £ in the purchase of National Savings Certificates in the name of the legatee] [and may in the like discretion accept the receipt of the parent or guardian of the legatee for the] [Bank Book] [Certificates] [as a full discharge for that legacy]

## 5–2 Charitable

*'charitable legacies'*

As such, these legacies are free of IHT.[1] The effect of this exemption may be also to reduce the rate of tax on the rest of the estate, as compared with what it would have been if the amount of any such legacies were added to the amount otherwise taxable.

It is the duty of the draftsman to verify the existence and name of the charity.[2]

1 See IHTA 1984, s 23.
2 See *Re Recher's Will Trusts* [1972] Ch 526, at 544 per Brightman J.

*'general charitable purposes'*

Unless the testator has a particular application of his legacy in view (in which case it should be set out) these general words serve at once to ensure the application of the legacy to the charitable objects of the legatee, and to ensure that the exemption from IHT arises.

*'full power to expend capital'*

It is thought that a simple pecuniary legacy for charitable purposes would normally be construed as enabling the charity to expend the whole amount and not as requiring that the legacy be invested as a capital fund, the income of which might alone be expendable. However, if the amount of the legacy is substantial, it may be desirable to consult the testator's wishes, and to make them explicit.

*'my Trustees shall not be concerned'*

Though sometimes included ex abundanti cautela, it is thought that these words are only declaratory and therefore serve no real purpose.

*'the receipt of the person appearing'*

These words ensure that the trustees are not put upon any enquiry as to the authority of any person giving a receipt on behalf of the charity.

**Form 5–2**

I GIVE the following charitable legacies absolutely:
(1) To of the sum of £
[etc]
[in each case for the general charitable purposes of the legatee] [and with full power to expend capital as well as income for such purposes] [and so that my Trustees shall not be concerned to see to the application thereof] [AND I DIRECT that the receipt of the person appearing to my Trustees to be the Treasurer or other proper officer for the time being of each of the above named legatees shall be a full discharge to my Trustees for the legacy given to that legatee]

## TAX-SAVING (ABSOLUTE OR SETTLED)

### 5–3 Immediate gift in trust for children (or grandchildren) within nil rate band of IHT

This form may be used where it is considered possible and desirable to divide the estate with a view to mitigating IHT (as discussed in Preliminary Note D–2), by setting aside for the immediate benefit of the children an appropriate amount up to the current nil rate band for IHT, so as to utilise this as fully as possible, and also reduce the taxable estate of the spouse at his or her death.

The same result could be achieved by dividing residue into shares, but it seems desirable that the children's fund should comprise a definite amount and this is most conveniently done by means of a legacy in trust.

The trustees are given the same extended powers as are applicable to residue. It is envisaged that the spouse would normally be a trustee.

Residue itself will be given to the spouse either absolutely or in trust, according to circumstances, with gift over or remainder to the children.

Where a substitutional gift is intended, in case a child should die prematurely, leaving a surviving child or children this should preferably be made by express provision, as here; and not left to the operation of s 33 (as substituted) of WA 1837: see Preliminary Note F–2.

To ensure compliance with the requirements for an accumulation and maintenance settlement (as to which see Preliminary Note D–6), the substitution should be limited to children of the deceased child, and should not extend to issue; though the widow or widower of a deceased child may likewise benefit.

See also, comparatively, Form 5–4.

**Form 5–3**

(1) I GIVE to my trustees [the sum of        thousand pounds] [such a sum as can be transferred on my death without being chargeable to Inheritance Tax (disregarding any exemption or relief) at any rate above the nil rate of tax] [or one equal        part of my residuary estate (hereinafter defined) whichever is the less] UPON TRUST for such of my children living at my death as shall attain the age of [eighteen] [        ] years [or marry under that age]

and if more than one in equal shares absolutely PROVIDED ALWAYS that if any child of mine shall die in my lifetime leaving a child or children living at my death who shall attain the age of [eighteen] [ ] years [or marry under that age] such last-mentioned child or children shall take by substitution and if more than one in equal shares the share of this gift which such deceased child of mine would have taken if he or she had survived to attain a vested interest

(2) In relation to the trusts of this gift my Trustees shall have all such and the like powers and discretions hereinafter conferred upon them or otherwise applicable in relation to my residuary estate as are for the time being capable of being exercised in relation to this gift

## 5–4 Discretionary trust, within nil rate band of IHT for spouse, children and others; and subject thereto, on the trusts of residue

This form may be considered as an alternative to Form 5–3. Its purpose is likewise to save IHT (where the estate is large enough) by making a non-exempt gift which will take up the testator's nil rate band of IHT (or balance of it) and also reduce the chargeable estate and the effective rate of IHT when the spouse dies.

Form 5–3 does this very simply, by making a direct gift to the children. Necessarily, however, the spouse can have no access to the income or capital of the amount so given. If when the testator dies it is found that the residue of the estate is insufficient for the needs of the spouse, a difficult position may arise. If the children are of age and consent, the will can be varied in favour of the spouse. If they are not, there can be no certainty that the court would consent[1] to a variation which must in law be seen as being to some extent against their interest. The only alternative might be a family provision application.[2] It is easy to say that the will ought not to include such a gift unless the estate is amply sufficient to support it, but the unexpected may sometimes happen. If, therefore, the gift to children can be made in such a way as not to deprive the spouse of recourse to the funds given, should this be necessary, this will not only provide a valuable insurance against changes in circumstances in marginal cases, it will also extend the opportunities for obtaining the IHT saving in relation to estates which would not otherwise be thought large enough to divide.

One possibility might be to couple a gift in terms of Form 5–3 with a discretionary power, based perhaps on one or other part of Form 8–8, for the trustees to pay capital to the spouse. The latter form would here need to be made applicable not to residue (or not only to residue) but (also) to the children's legacy fund. This may suffice to meet the possible needs of the spouse for capital, but not income.

If it is desirable to go so far, it seems preferable to take the idea a stage further, giving the trustees a full discretion as to capital and income alike. By establishing such a discretionary trust, as under this form, the testator can make a gift to the children utilising his nil rate band for IHT, while at the same time effectively postponing their enjoyment until the death of the spouse, without thereby rendering the fund chargeable to IHT at the death of the spouse, as part of the spouse's estate. During the lifetime of the spouse the trustees can, of course, appoint as much or as little of the income or capital of the fund to the spouse as they think fit. It will normally be in contemplation that the spouse will in fact receive all or most of the income, but probably not any of the capital, unless this is needed for some special purpose. As always where wide discretions are conferred, it will be advisable for the testator to assist the trustees by leaving with the will a letter explaining his intentions in these or other appropriate terms.

The trust fund is, of course, settled property for IHT purposes; and as there is no interest in possession[3] (with the result that the fund does not form part of the estate of the spouse, save in so far as capital is actually appointed to the spouse[4]), and as the conditions for an accumulation and maintenance settlement are not satisfied, the fund is 'relevant property' for the purposes of IHTA 1984, Part III, Chapter III. However, if and so long as the value of the trust fund, and the other circumstances, are such that no tax above the nil rate is attracted, the fund may be held, in effect, without liability to IHT throughout the life of the trust, and until after final distribution. The reason is that although the normal charges to tax on a settlement with no interest in possession are not avoided, no actual liability to tax is incurred while the amount of any particular chargeable transfer remains within the nil rate band.

Accordingly, as long as the amount of the testator's nil rate band is not exceeded, IHT will not be payable at his death; provided that the balance of the estate is left (as it should be) either to the spouse, or possibly within some other relevant exemption; and provided also that no other settlement is created by the will, because of the possible effect of the anti-avoidance rules concerning 'related property'.

Subsequently, IHT will not become payable under the ten-yearly charge, or at the time of final distribution, provided that the value of the trust fund at any relevant date is still not such as to attract any liability to tax above the nil rate at the time.

Should values increase over and above the rate of inflation (that is to say, in real terms), charges to IHT would arise at any ten-yearly anniversary[5] (if the trust continues so long); and on a proportional basis,[6] when the trust comes to an end, or if meanwhile capital is appointed out to any of the beneficiaries.[4] Even if this were to happen (and it could do so only if there were an increase in real values), the amount of any such liabilities to tax may be expected to be less than the liability which would have been incurred if the same property had been left to pass through the estate of the spouse at death.

It may, however, be seen as a disadvantage that charges to CGT are likely to be incurred whenever absolute entitlements to capital arise;[7] that is to say, whenever capital assets are appointed out of settlement to beneficiaries (if they are); and, more significantly, when the trust comes to an end. At that time, the amount of unrealised gains within the fund may be considerable. Once again, however, the effect of the CGT indexation allowance will be that only real gains are in fact vulnerable; and the build-up of such gains may well have been reduced during the life of the trust by disposals within the trustees' annual exemption. In so far as gains are chargeable at the time of distribution, the liability may be postponed by election,[8] with their concurrence, to hold over such gains to the beneficiaries.

If the estate will not include enough invested capital to set up a settled legacy fund, in terms of this form, it may still be possible, and advantageous, for that fund to comprise or include the matrimonial home, or the testator's interest in the matrimonial home, up to the value of the nil rate band for IHT. In a larger estate, it may likewise be beneficial to settle the matrimonial home, or the testator's interest in it, so as to free invested capital which would then pass as residue, absolutely to the surviving spouse. It may be better for the spouse to hold realisable investments than a house which, in reality, it will not usually be wished to realise. For these purposes, suggested additional subclauses are given in Form 5–5, and further explained in the note to that form. Form 4–10 suggests a different approach.

It will be advisable to confer the power to appoint new trustees (as in Form 8–14) on the spouse.

As a drafting point, where a substitutional gift is intended in relation to the ultimate trusts, in case a child should die prematurely, leaving a surviving child or children, this should here be made by express provision. Reliance upon s 33 (as substituted) of WA 1837 would be inappropriate: see Preliminary Note F–2.

Because they would constitute 'related settlements' within the meaning of IHTA 1984, s 62; Form 5–4 should not normally be included in a will which also includes Form 7–1.

---

1 Under the Variation of Trusts Act 1958, s 1.
2 See Preliminary Note C and Appendix 2.
3 See IHTA 1984, ss 49, 50.
4 With a view to keeping capital advances out of the estate of the spouse, the will may include a power for the trustees to make loans as under Form 8–8–2. However, the Inland Revenue are understood to take the view that an interest-free loan out of settled property gives rise to an interest in possession for IHT purposes.
5 Under IHTA 1984, s 64; see also Inland Revenue Statement of Practice SP 8/86 concerning the treatment of accumulated income of discretionary trusts.
6 Under ibid, s 65.
7 Under CGTA 1979, s 54.
8 Under CGTA 1979, s 147A inserted by FA 1989.

**Form 5–4**

(1) I GIVE to my Trustees free of all taxes [the sum of thousand pounds] [such a sum as can be transferred on my death without being chargeable to Inheritance Tax (disregarding any exemption or relief) at any rate above the nil rate of tax] (which said sum and all investments and property for the time being representing the same is hereinafter referred to as 'the Settled Legacy') UPON the TRUSTS and with and subject to the powers discretions and provisions contained in the succeeding paragraphs of this Clause

(2) For so long during the period of [eighty years from my death] [twenty-one years from the death of my said] [wife] [husband] (the perpetuity period applicable hereto) as any of the persons hereinafter mentioned is living my Trustees shall have power at any time and from time to time if and whenever they shall in their absolute discretion think fit to pay or apply the whole or any part or parts of the income or of the capital or of the income and the capital of the Settled Legacy to or for the benefit of all or any one or more exclusively of the others or other of the

following persons that is to say my [said] [wife] [husband] and any of my children and any [widow widower or] child (born during the lifetime of the survivor of myself and my [said] [wife] [husband] of any child of mine who may predecease such survivor and with power during the period of twenty-one years after my death to accumulate any income of the Settled Legacy not so paid or applied and to add any such accumulations to the capital thereof

(3) As trustees of the Settled Legacy my Trustees in addition to the powers and discretions otherwise conferred upon them by law shall have all such and the like powers and discretions hereinafter conferred upon them or otherwise applicable in relation to my residuary estate as are for the time being capable of being exercised in relation to the Settled Legacy

(4) If any of my Trustees is or may become personally interested as a beneficiary in the exercise of (or omission to exercise) any or all of the powers and discretions hereby conferred upon my Trustees generally he may from time to time join in exercising that power or any such discretion as if he were not so interested and may nevertheless retain for his own use any benefit which in good faith he may derive in consequence thereof as if he were not a trustee

(5) Subject to the foregoing provisions of this Clause and to any and every exercise of the powers and discretions hereinbefore conferred upon them my Trustees shall hold the Settled Legacy UPON TRUST for such of my children living at [the expiration of twenty-eight clear days after] the death of the survivor of myself and my said [wife] [husband] as shall attain the age of [eighteen] [ ] years [or marry under that age] and if more than one in equal shares absolutely PROVIDED ALWAYS that if any child of mine shall fail to survive the survivor of myself and my said [wife] [husband] [by twenty-eight clear days] but shall leave a child or children who shall so survive such survivor as aforesaid and shall attain the age of [eighteen] [ ] years [or marry under that age] then such last mentioned child or children shall take by substitution and if more than one in equal shares the share of the Settled Legacy which such deceased child of mine would have taken if he or she had not so failed to survive as aforesaid [*OR*]

(5) Subject to the foregoing provisions of this Clause and to any and every exercise of the powers and discretions hereinbefore conferred upon or otherwise exercisable by them my Trustees shall hold the Settled Legacy Upon Such and subject to the like Trusts and with such and subject to the like powers discretions and provisions as are hereinafter declared concerning or otherwise applicable to my residuary estate and are for the time being subsisting and capable of taking effect

## 5–5 The same: supplemental provisions as to matrimonial home

This form embodies additional subclauses for use with Form 5–4, to authorise appropriation of the matrimonial home as an asset of the settled legacy, in the circumstances mentioned at the end of the note to that form. It also allows appropriation of the testator's interest, in case the parties already own the property beneficially as tenants in common; or of part of that interest, in case the value might exceed whatever is at the time the amount of the nil rate band of IHT. This amount should not be exceeded without careful consideration: see generally note to Form 5–4.

Because an appropriation of *part* of the testator's interest might not otherwise fall within the provisions of s 41 of AEA 1925 (reproduced in Appendix 1), it is further provided that such an appropriation is an authorised 'investment', and requires no consent (see ibid, s 41(1), proviso, para (v), and note to Form 8–2).

The purpose of authorising such an appropriation is to keep the matrimonial home, or a part interest in it, out of the estate of the testator's spouse for IHT purposes, but without detriment to the spouse. This seems to involve a departure from the principle which has been advocated elsewhere in this book, that the matrimonial home should not normally be made an instrument of tax planning. It is a matter of judgment in relation to the particular circumstances whether such a departure is justified.

It is in general the case that a surviving spouse will enjoy full security in the matrimonial home (or any substitute) only if she (or he) is absolute owner, or else has a legal right of occupation in conjunction with a life interest: where, in fact, the whole beneficial interest in the matrimonial home *is* included in the estate of the spouse for IHT purposes. If beneficial ownership is in any way divided between the surviving spouse and other members of the family, the security of the spouse is necessarily placed to some extent at risk. It is therefore in principle undesirable, from the point of view of the spouse, to reduce the spouse's estate by creating beneficial entitlements in the matrimonial home in favour of the children. On the other hand, it may seem to be undesirable from the point of view of the children to incur maximum IHT at the death of the spouse just because much of the value of the estate is represented by the matrimonial home, and cannot be divided.

Against this background, a discretionary trust such as is here under discussion may be seen as offering an acceptable compromise. Whatever interest in the matrimonial home is appropriated to such a trust is kept out of the estate of the spouse. At the same time, there should be no doubt that the spouse will enjoy de facto security. Although this lies in the discretion of the trustees, they will clearly understand the intention of the testator to be that, as between the spouse and the children, the needs of the spouse will in all normal circumstances be regarded as paramount. Although these priorities may seem almost to go without saying, the testator will no doubt place them informally on record, in a letter to the trustees, to accompany the will. It will also be advisable to provide in the will that the spouse is to have the power of appointing new trustees, as in Form 8–14.

In terms, of IHT and CGT, the general position, after an appropriation, will be as summarised in the note to Form 5–4.

In that note, it was pointed out that a liability to CGT must usually be expected to arise when the discretionary trust comes to an end, though this should be greatly exceeded by the IHT saving. However, where an interest in the matrimonial home is comprised in the trust, the question arises whether the CGT relief on disposal of a private residence[1] may be available to the trustees.[2] It would be so if the spouse were 'entitled to occupy under the terms of the settlement'. It has been held[3] that a sufficient entitlement for this purpose does arise where occupation is permitted by the trustees of a discretionary trust, in exercise of a power expressly conferred upon them for that purpose. As against this, the exercise of such a power by trustees is officially considered[4] to give rise, for IHT purposes, to an interest in possession.

Accordingly, this form has been drawn on the basis that no express power to permit beneficial occupation is to be given to the trustees, and that if such a power is given elsewhere in the will in relation to residue (as in Form 8–5), it should be excluded in relation to the settled legacy. As the law is at present understood, this should suffice. However, in as much as permissive occupation by the spouse necessarily rests upon the exercise by the trustees of *some* power or discretion to allow it, this might still be regarded by the Inland Revenue as giving rise to an interest in possession. In face of that possibility, the form therefore includes an optional power for the trustees to grant a lease or tenancy, which should not have that result. If at an undervalue, a liability to IHT would be incurred, but any liability is perhaps unlikely to be considerable.

See also Form 4–10, and notes thereto.

---

1 Under CGTA 1979, ss 101–103.
2 ibid, s 104.
3 In *Sansom* v *Peay* [1976] 1 WLR 1073.
4 See Preliminary Note D–7, and Inland Revenue Statement of Practice SP 10/79.

**Form 5–5**

[*For optional inclusion as part of Form 5–4*]

(6)(i) Without prejudice to the generality of their other powers my Trustees shall have power to appropriate in or towards satisfaction of the Settled Legacy the whole or any part (being either a part or share having a specified monetary value or else an aliquot part or share of the whole) of any beneficial interest to which at the time of my death I may be entitled in respect of whatever dwelling-house is at that time the only or main residence of myself and my said [wife] [husband] and for the avoidance of doubt I Declare that any such interest or part thereof so appropriated shall be deemed to be an investment authorised for the investment of money subject to the trusts of the Settled Legacy and further that no consent shall be required to such appropriation

(ii) If my Trustees make such an appropriation as aforesaid then in relation thereto and to the Settled Legacy generally the powers conferred by [paragraph      of] [Clause      ] hereof[1] shall not apply but my Trustees shall have the following powers (without prejudice as aforesaid) in relation to the Settled Legacy (exercisable as if my Trustees were an absolute beneficial owner of the money and property subject to the trusts of the Settled Legacy) that is to say:

(*a*) power to apply money subject to the trusts of the Settled Legacy in or towards the purchase [upon trust for sale but with full power to postpone sale] or in the improvement of any freehold or leasehold dwelling-house [within the United Kingdom]

[(*b*) power to contribute to the purchase of any such dwelling-house in common with any one or more of the persons referred to in paragraph (2) of this Clause upon such terms and conditions as my Trustees think fit]

[(*c*) power from time to time to borrow and to give security for the payment of money [(and to join with any of the beforementioned persons in so doing)] for the purposes of any such purchase [(or contributory purchase)] as aforesaid] [(*d*) power (to the extent of their interest) to grant and determine leases tenancies and licences to occupy in relation to any dwelling-house for the time being wholly or partly subject to the trusts of the Settled Legacy with or without rent and upon and subject to such terms and conditions as my Trustees think fit]

1 Meaning Form 8–5, or equivalent.

# 6

# Dispositions of Residue

## Trust for Sale

### 6–1 Trust for sale (general form)

See Preliminary Note E–2.

This is the form of trust for sale traditionally adopted where no life interest is created. The corresponding form traditionally adopted where residue is held for persons in succession is Form 6–2.

An alternative short form, which is suitable for general use, is Form 6–4.

Whichever form is adopted it should embody, as all these forms do, an express power to postpone sale. The statutory power to postpone sale, implied by LPA 1925, s 25, is applicable only to land. Power to postpone is exercisable by the trustees jointly and, in the absence of special circumstances (eg, the existence of a secondary or collateral object besides sale), and unless all agree to postpone, a sale must take place.

Unless expressly exonerated, the trustees would be liable for non-conversion of any unauthorised investments within a reasonable time but, if their powers of investment are unrestricted, as under Form 8–4, it is thought that the effect must be to authorise the retention of any of the testator's existing investments, so long as the trustees act honestly and with ordinary prudence. The words 'without being liable for loss' might therefore be omitted without placing any undue responsibility on the trustees. Form 6–4 does so.

This form is used to precede either an alternate gift to children in case of non-survival of a spouse otherwise absolutely entitled, or beneficial trusts for spouse and issue where the spouse is given only a limited interest.

*'my debts and funeral and testamentary expenses'*

It is usual, and good practice, to include an express declaration as to the incidence of debts and liabilities in every will, as a matter of course, even though, as here, the direction simply reflects the effect, in the particular circumstances, of the statutory rules as to the order of application of assets in discharge of liabilities[1] which have effect subject to the provisions of the will. Commonly, the general estate is the only possible fund for payment, but in any case where the incidence of liabilities might affect the entitlement of one beneficiary as against that of another, the position should be carefully considered.

Should a debt have been incurred without full consideration or in other circumstances such that it is disallowable as a deduction from the estate for IHT purposes,[2] it will be in view for administration purposes that the debt may nevertheless still take effect as a liability of the estate.

1 See, primarily, AEA 1925, s 34(3) and Sched 1, Pt II.
2 FA 1986, s 103.

**Form 6–1**

I DEVISE AND BEQUEATH all [the remainder of] my real and [the remainder of my] personal property whatsoever and wheresoever not hereby or by any codicil hereto otherwise specifically disposed of unto my Trustees UPON TRUST to sell call in and convert the same into money (with full power to postpone such sale calling in and conversion of all or any part or parts of my said real and personal property indefinitely or for so long as they may in their absolute discretion think fit without being liable for loss and notwithstanding that the same may be of a wasting speculative or reversionary nature) and after payment thereout of my debts and funeral and testamentary expenses and all legacies bequeathed hereby or by any codicil hereto to hold the balance and all parts of my said real and personal property for the time being unsold and unconverted (hereinafter called 'my residuary estate') UPON the TRUSTS and with the subject to the powers and provisions hereinafter declared and contained

## 6–2 Trust for sale (limited interest)

See Preliminary Note E–2 and also Forms 6–1 and 6–4. Form 6–1 is intended for use where no life interest arises, but where residue may be held in trust for minors.

The present form is intended for use where a life interest is created and is accordingly extended (by the provisions in square brackets) to deal with certain matters affecting the possibly divergent interests of the life tenant, interested in income, and of the remainderman, interested prospectively in capital.

In general, where these have not been declared expressly, certain intentions are imputed, in equity, to the testator with a view to holding a fair balance between the rights of those interested in income and capital respectively.[1] These presumptions may be displaced by contrary provision and it is the almost invariable practice of draftsmen to make such provision. The traditional form of such a provision is included in the square brackets in paragraph (1) of this form: a short and much simpler alternative is given in Form 8–9.

The equitable presumptions so displaced derive from the following principle authorities:

*Howe* v *Dartmouth* (1802) 7 Ves 137: whereby if a high income is derived from the retention of unauthorised investments, part is capitalised to compensate the remaindermen for the implicit risk of capital loss;

*Re Earl of Chesterfield's Trusts* (1883) 24 Ch D 643: whereby, conversely, part of the eventual capital proceeds of an investment which was not itself income producing, is apportioned retrospectively to income;

*Allhusen* v *Whittell* (1867) LR 4 Eq 295: whereby payments in discharge of liabilities, before residue can be ascertained, are taken to have been made partly from capital and partly from the income deriving from such capital.

In modern conditions, the possible advantage in terms of greater fairness as between beneficiaries is usually considered not to justify the trouble and expense of making what may be difficult or at least complex calculations.

Apart from the equitable rules for apportionment as between capital and income, it may be proposed also to exclude the effect of the Apportionment Act 1870; this too being on the basis of the time and expense involved in making the appropriate calculations. Under this Act income current at the date of the testator's death is apportionable on a time basis by reference to the period to which it relates, the proportion so applicable to the period after the death being alone regarded as income of the life tenant and the balance being capitalised. This form does not exclude the Act (but see Form 8–9 which does[2]).

1 The comments in this note are much simplified. The standard works on equity should be consulted for further detail.
2 See the note to this form for the income tax effects of exclusion of these provisions.

**Form 6–2**

(1) I DEVISE AND BEQUEATH all [the remainder of] my real and [the remainder of my] personal property whatsoever and wheresoever unto my Trustees UPON TRUST to sell call in and convert the same into money with power to postpone the sale calling in and conversion thereof so long as they shall in their absolute discretion think fit without being liable for loss [and so that income of my] [real leasehold and personal] [property however constituted or invested] [(including the income of property required for the payment of debts and other payments made in due course of administration in payment whereof the proceeds of such sale calling in and conversion are hereinafter directed to be applied)] [shall as from my death be treated as income] [and that a reversionary or future interest shall not be sold prior to falling into possession unless my Trustees shall see special reason for such earlier sale] [and so that the net rents and profits of my real and leasehold property for the time being unsold after payment thereout of all outgoings which my Trustees shall consider payable out of income shall go and be applied as if the same were income of authorised investments made of the proceeds of an actual sale thereof] [and so that no property not actually producing income shall be treated as producing income]

[(2) *Here take in Form 6–3, if desired*]

[(3)] [(2)] My Trustees shall hold the net proceeds of the said sale and conversion and my ready money upon the following trusts:

(*a*) Upon trust to pay thereout all my just debts and funeral and testamentary expenses [and legacies]

(*b*) Upon trust to invest the residue after such payment in any investment hereinafter authorised (with full power to vary and transpose investments from time to time) and to stand possessed of such investments and all parts of my said real and personal property for the time being unsold (hereinafter called 'my residuary estate') Upon the trusts and with and subject to the powers and provisions hereinafter contained

## 6–3 Trust for sale: no sale of residence without consent

See notes to Form 4–8.

This form is intended for use in a case where the surviving spouse has only a limited interest in residue, and where residue includes the family home.

However unlikely it may seem that this would be sold against the wish of the spouse, the inclusion of an express declaration that it should not be so sold may be thought to provide the minimum of security to which the spouse should normally be entitled. It may also serve to protect the trustees who, in order to hold a fair balance between the life tenant and remaindermen, might in some circumstances otherwise feel obliged to sell, as for instance, where they were offered the inducement of a very high price.[1]

Similarly, the inclusion of an express declaration that the spouse may occupy the house seems desirable, even though such a right is probably implicit in the gift of a life interest. It should certainly be made explicit where, as will usually be the case, the testator does not wish the spouse to bear any of the burden of repairs.

To carry the protection of the spouse a stage further, it will usually be desirable to cover the contingency that the spouse may wish to move house, perhaps for the sake of economy, by giving an express power to the trustees to purchase elsewhere. This may conveniently be done by separate provision (see Form 8–5 and notes thereto).

Alternatively, if the testator should feel it to be undesirable for the spouse to be to any extent dependent upon the discretion of the trustees, wishing the spouse to be as nearly as possible mistress, or master, in her or his own house, the family home at the date of death may be settled on the spouse as tenant for life, as in Form 4–9.

---

1 The court has nevertheless jurisdiction under LPA 1925, s 30, on the application of any person interested, to direct a sale by trustees for sale where a necessary consent has been refused (*Re Beale's Settlement Trusts* [1932] 2 Ch 15). As to the nature of the court's discretion see, comparatively, *Re Holliday (A Bankrupt)* [1981] Ch 405 (CA).

### Form 6–3

[*For incorporation, if desired, as part of Form 6–2*]

(2) I DECLARE that no sale of my residence known as
(or other my [only or main] residence at the time of my death) shall be made during the lifetime of my [said] [wife] [husband]

> without [her] [his] consent [and that pending sale thereof my Trustees shall permit my said [wife] [husband] to occupy the same for so long as [she] [he] may so wish] [and without any liability on] [her] [his] [part for the repair or maintenance thereof]

### 6–4 Trust for sale (short alternative form)

This form incorporates provision for payment of IHT, extending to joint property and/or inter vivos gifts. See also Forms 6–1 and 6–2.

Paragraphs (1) and (3) of this form are suggested as an alternative to the much fuller traditional form exemplified in Form 6–2. Apart from the omission of the provisions as to exclusion of the equitable rules on apportionments (a short alternative form for which appears in Form 8–9) it is not thought that the effect of these paragraphs is significantly different from that of the corresponding paragraphs of Form 6–2, and they may be thought to be more readily intelligible to the testator, as well as being more economical. As to the trustees' liability for any loss in postponing sale, see note to Form 6–1.

Paragraph (2), dealing with the discharge of liabilities of the estate, is optionally extended to include provision which in certain cases the testator may wish to make for IHT.

First, as to any non-exempt gifts in the will which, by their express terms or by operation of law, exonerate the legatee or devisee from any liability to pay tax on their value,[1] it is expressly provided that such tax is to be paid out of the general estate before residue is ascertained. This provision is merely declaratory but does serve to draw attention to the possible effect on the value of residue.

Secondly, in case the testator wishes the estate to bear any tax payable (by reason of the death) by third parties (eg, in respect of property owned jointly with some person other than a spouse or, more commonly, an inter vivos gift within seven years[2] before death) payment can likewise be conveniently directed to be made out of the general estate. This is despite the fact that, strictly speaking, such tax is not primarily a liability of the estate and, in consequence, the direction for payment may really amount to a beneficial gift of the amount of the tax. As such, this may itself be taxable and, in case of deficiency of assets, may be liable to abatement.

The general words 'any transfer of value made by me during my lifetime' appearing (optionally) in paragraph (2) should be adapted as necessary to suit the circumstances. As they stand, they serve as a reminder that a liability to IHT may arise, not only in relation to any potentially exempt transfer made within seven years before the testator's death, but also in relation to gifts made at any time 'with reservation' in terms of FA 1986, s 102. The statutory rules as to the incidence of tax, and as to the liability of personal representatives, are discussed in Preliminary Note D–3.

---

1 See notes to Forms 4–11 and 5–1 and Preliminary Notes D-2B and D3.
2 IHTA 1984, s 199, as amended by FA 1986, Sched 19, para 26.

**Form 6–4**

(1) I GIVE to my Trustees all my real and personal property not otherwise specifically disposed of UPON TRUST for sale with full power to postpone sale

(2) My Trustees shall pay and discharge therefrom all my debts [(including any debt which is a charge on any property in which at the time of my death I have a beneficial interest)] and funeral and testamentary expenses and all tax payable by reason of my death [(including tax attributable to [any devise or bequest given free of tax and] [any property to which at the time of my death I may be beneficially entitled jointly with any other person] [and any tax payable by any person in respect of any transfer of value made by me during my lifetime])] and all legacies given by this my will or any codicil

(3) My Trustees shall hold the balance of my said real and personal property remaining after such payments (hereinafter called 'my residuary estate') Upon the beneficial trusts and with and subject to the powers and provisions hereinafter declared and contained

## Beneficial Trusts

### 6–5 Absolute gift to surviving spouse

*Vesting*

Although an absolute gift of residue to a surviving spouse necessarily places the subsequent destination of the testator's estate in the hands of the spouse and beyond the testator's own control, most testators making such a gift would consider the interests of their children, or others who would take in the event of the spouse's failure to survive, to be sufficiently protected by arranging for the spouse to make an appropriate will, accepting whatever risk there may be that such a will might later be altered or revoked. They would also normally accept whatever risk there may be that the spouse's enjoyment might be only comparatively short-lived.

If the deaths of husband and wife should occur to all appearances simultaneously (eg, as the result of an accident) then, for the purposes of succession of property, the younger is normally deemed to succeed the elder.[1] However, for IHT purposes, they are deemed to have died at the same instant,[2] so that the estate of the one never becomes part of the estate of the other.

It is, however, very common practice to guard against the contingency of an accident as a result of which the spouse might actually survive only for a nominal period, by stipulating that the gift is conditional upon the spouse surviving for some specified period, usually 28 days. This ensures that in the event of near-simultaneous deaths, the devolution of the testator's estate will be governed by his own will and that it will be administered by his own executors, and not as part of the estate of the spouse. See further, Preliminary Note D–5.

1 See LPA 1925, s 184 and *Hickman* v *Peacey* [1945] AC 304.
2 See IHTA 1984, ss 4(2), 54(4).

*'all my ... property ... not ... otherwise ... disposed of'*

It is very common practice to include these words in square brackets, with a view to facilitating later alterations by codicil but it is not at all necessary to do so. The other dispositions contemplated are specific devises and bequests. Pecuniary and other general legacies are normally payable out of the general estate, before residue is ascertained, and this should be expressly directed, as below.

*'subject to ... debts and ... legacies'*

It is usual to direct in this way that the liabilities of the estate and the pecuniary legacies (if any) given by the will, or by any later codicil, are all to be discharged out of the general estate[1] before residue is ascertained. This is so even where (as here) they could not in fact have been dealt with in any other way.

The tax, if any, payable on the testator's free personal estate is included in this direction, being a testamentary expense. For references to other tax liabilities, see Form 6–4. These will not normally be relevant in relation to the will here under consideration.

*'the succeeding provisions . . . shall take effect'*

If this form is used, it will be followed by Form 6–1 (trust for sale) and Form 6–6 (alternate beneficial trusts for children or issue). Separating, as it does, the primary gifts to the spouse from the alternate gift (which, it may be supposed, is not very likely to take effect), this sequence is preferred by some draftsmen as reflecting as explicitly as possible what the testator actually contemplates. In particular, the trust for sale arises only if the spouse fails to survive.

It is, however, more usual to declare a trust for sale in any event, as in Form 6–1, following this by a composite declaration of the beneficial trusts, ie, in favour of the spouse if surviving and otherwise in favour of children and issue, as in Form 6–7.

Considered purely as a matter of drafting, it is immaterial which approach is adopted, but if Form 6–5 is used, care should be taken to ensure that as the 'succeeding provisions' referred to in paragraph (2) become operative only in the event that the spouse fails to survive, these should not include any which may be required in any event (eg, a charging clause).

*'if [and only if] she survives me by twenty-eight clear days'*

The words in square brackets are not commonly found in survivorship clauses. Their purpose is to make it clear, for the avoidance of doubt, that the gift to the spouse is intended to be contingent upon the spouse surviving the specified period, and is not to be construed[2] as a vested gift subject to divesting should the spouse fail to survive that period or, in other words, that the survivorship condition is a condition precedent and not a condition subsequent. Although it seems quite clear that under a condition of either kind the effective disposition for IHT purposes[3] is that which in the event takes effect, it has been doubted whether a condition subsequent is apt to secure that if the spouse does survive, the spouse exemption[4] will apply.[5] It seems most unlikely that the exemption would be denied in such a case[6] but, in view of its importance, and in the absence of authority, the draftsman may wish to avoid the possibility.

*'fails to attain a vested interest hereunder . . .'*

See Preliminary Note F–2, as to the position in the event of divorce. Care is required if a gift over is not to fail in that event, especially if the gift is to someone who would not equally be entitled on intestacy, eg, to a charity.

---

1 As to debts which may be disallowed as a deduction for IHT purposes, see Note to Form 6–1.
2 Under the rule of construction known as the rule in *Phipps* v *Ackers* (1842) 9 Cl & Fin 583 (HL), as applied and extended in *Re Heath* [1936] Ch 259 and *Re Kilpatrick's Policies Trusts* [1966] Ch 730, and explained by Ungoed-Thomas J in *Re Penton's Settlements* [1968] 1 WLR 248; and see also *Brotherton* v *IRC* [1978] 1 WLR 610 (CA).
3 Ie, under IHTA 1984, s 92, which applies 'where ... property is held for any person *on condition that he survives another* for a specified period of not more than six months'.
4 Ie, under ibid, s 18.
5 Ie, under ibid, s 18(3), whereby the exemption is in general denied 'if the ... disposition ... takes effect on the termination after the transfer of value of any interest or period'; but not 'by reason only that the property is given to a spouse *only if* he survives the other spouse for a specified period'.
6 Having regard, in particular, to the retrospective operation of ibid, s 92.

**Form 6–5**

(1) I DEVISE AND BEQUEATH all my real and personal property whatsoever and wheresoever [not hereby or by any codicil hereto otherwise specifically disposed of] [SUBJECT to the payment of my debts and funeral and testamentary expenses] [and all legacies given hereby or by any codicil hereto] unto my [said] wife [ ] [if [and only if] she survives me by twenty-eight clear days] absolutely

(2) If my said wife fails to attain a vested interest hereunder (but not otherwise) the succeeding provisions of this my will shall take effect

[*Here follow provisions as in Forms 6–6 or 6–7 (or as may be appropriate to the circumstances); and such as may be appropriate of the provisions of Form 8; and Form 9–1*]

## 6–6 Gift over to children

This is intended for use where the primary gift in favour of a surviving spouse is made as a direct gift, as in Form 6–5, and where a trust for sale is imposed only in the event of the failure of the spouse to survive. In that event, the gift over to children (with substitution of grandchildren) follows and takes effect under the trust for sale.

*'living ... twenty-eight ... days after my death'*

Normally, the testator will intend that, if the gift over takes effect, residue will be shared between such of his children as may be living at his death, who attain majority or a stipulated age. However, where the interest of the spouse is made contingent on surviving for a period after the testator's death, some draftsmen think it a sensible precaution to prevent the parent's estate from passing through that of a deceased child by imposing a survivorship condition on the gift to the child. If so, a further gift over should perhaps be added to avoid possible intestacy.

It is thought better not to frame the gift (as in some precedents) in favour of children living at the death of the survivor of the spouses, in case this might give rise to difficulty in the event of divorce.

*'attain the age of ... years [or marry under that age]'*

The age of vesting is entirely a matter for decision by the testator. It should however be borne in mind that the longer vesting is postponed, the more important it is that the trustees should be carefully chosen and that they should be given greatest possible freedom to advance capital. The age of vesting should not normally be more than 25 to avoid incurring unnecessary IHT liabilities.[1]

For the position as to CGT, see Preliminary Note D–6.

*'provided always ...'*

Where a substitutional gift is intended, in case a child should die prematurely, leaving a surviving child or children, this should preferably be made by express provision, as here; and not left to the operation of s 33 (as substituted) of WA 1837: see Preliminary Note F–2.

To ensure compliance with the requirements for an accumulation and maintenance settlement (as to which see Preliminary Note D–6), the substitution should be limited to children of the deceased child, and should not extend to issue; though the widow or widower of a deceased child may likewise benefit.

---

1 See IHTA 1984, s 71 (reproduced in Appendix 5), and Preliminary Note D–6.

**Form 6–6**

My Trustees shall hold my residuary estate UPON TRUST for such of my children as shall be living at [the expiration of the period of twenty-eight clear days after] my death and shall attain the age of [eighteen] [ ] years [or marry under that age] and if more than one in equal shares absolutely PROVIDED

ALWAYS that if any child of mine shall have died during my lifetime or having survived me shall die without having attained a vested interest hereunder leaving a child or children living at my death then any such child or children (meaning in either case a grandchild or grandchildren of mine) as shall attain the age of [eighteen] [ ] years [or marry under that age] shall take by substitution and in equal share if more than one per stirpes the share of my residuary estate which such deceased child of mine would have taken had he or she survived and attained a vested interest

### 6–7 Spouse and children

This form is intended for use where a trust for sale is imposed in any event; the primary beneficial gift in favour of a surviving spouse and the gift over in favour of children, both taking effect under that trust for sale.

Form 6–5 will not then be appropriate; but see note thereto as to vesting of the gift in the spouse.

See also notes to Form 6–6.

**Form 6–7**

My Trustees shall hold my residuary estate upon the following trusts:

(1) UPON TRUST for my said [wife] [husband] if [and only if] [she] [he] survives me [by twenty-eight clear days] absolutely but

(2) If my said [wife] [husband] fails to attain a vested interest then UPON TRUST for such of my children ... [*continue as in Form 6–6*]

### 6–8 Gift over to issue (based on the statutory trusts)

The use of this form is suggested as offering a means of incorporating with the greatest possible brevity provisions to the same general effect as those of Forms 6–1, 6–5 and 6–6. This is done by reference to the statutory provisions applicable in relation to intestacy.

It is not however suggested for use otherwise than in case of great urgency because it is generally (and rightly) considered by draftsmen to be undesirable to incorporate any substantive provision by reference. Testators equally (and understandably) prefer documents which are complete in themselves.

For convenience of reference, the terms of the statutory provisions referred to are set out in Appendix I.

**Form 6–8**

(1) If [and only if] my said [wife] [husband] [ ] survives me [by twenty-eight clear days] I DEVISE AND BEQUEATH all my real and personal property whatsoever and wheresoever unto my said [wife] [husband] absolutely

(2) If my said [wife] [husband] fails to attain a vested interest I DEVISE AND BEQUEATH all my said property as aforesaid unto my Trustees upon such and subject to the like trusts as are declared by section 33 of the Administration of Estates Act 1925 as if I had died intestate and my Trustees shall hold my residuary estate (within the meaning of that section) upon the statutory trusts for my issue contained in section 47 of that Act but with the additional powers hereinafter contained

## 6–9 Limited interest, with remainders

This form is intended for use in conjunction with Forms 6–2, 6–3 and 6–4 and declares beneficial trusts in favour of the spouse for life, with remainder to surviving children, including the children of any child of the testator who may not have survived. Form 6–10 embodies alternative provisions to the same effect.

*'during [her] [his] life'*

Some of the older published precedents include an alternative provision determining the interest of a surviving spouse on remarriage. On purely personal grounds, few testators wish, in modern conditions, to impose such a limitation. If this were done, and if the surviving spouse did remarry, a liability to IHT on the whole trust fund would arise at that time.[1] Moreover, the exemption from CGT on the death of a life tenant[2] would not be available, though the exemption based on her occupation of a house comprised in the trust[3] should not be affected, assuming this to be then sold.

1 See IHTA 1984, s 52(1).
2 See CGTA 1979, s 56.
3 See ibid, s 104.

*'living at [my death] [the death of the survivor]'*

This form may be compared with Form 6–6 which makes immediate provision for children where a spouse fails to take an absolute interest. As in that form, the entitlement of children is here made contingent upon their attainment of a specified age, or (if desired) marriage under that age.

However, the present form is concerned with a different situation in that where there is a life interest, whatever their expectations may be, no child can become *absolutely entitled* until both parents have died, that is, normally until after the life tenant's death. The question for consideration is, what should be the nature of their entitlement (if any) in the meantime? Should a child who is living at the testator's death, and who has already attained, or subsequently attains, the stipulated age (or marries) be entitled to a *vested* reversionary interest, expectant on the death of the life tenant, or should the interests of all children of any age be made contingent upon surviving *both* parents? This form provides in the alternative for either possibility.

Because a child, living at the testator's death, might predecease the life tenant, many practitioners think it desirable that no child should have a vested interest during the life tenant's lifetime, for fear that if a child should predecease, that child's share might otherwise devolve (as a reversionary interest) under the child's will or intestacy, and not under the testator's own will. Instead, it is quite usual to give merely contingent interests adding a proviso (as in this form) by which the share of a deceased child passes by substitution to his children (if any)[1] contingently upon their attaining likewise a specified age (or marrying).

Such a substitutional gift must here be made by express provision, and not left to the operation of s 33 (as substituted) of WA 1837: see Preliminary Note F–2.

To ensure compliance with the requirements for an accumulation and maintenance settlement (as to which see Preliminary Note D–6), the substitution should be limited to children of the deceased child, and should not extend to issue; though the widow or widower of a deceased child could also benefit.

The testator should be invited to consider whether it is really in the interests of his children to make their entitlements contingent upon surviving the life tenant. It is suggested that there will normally be no serious disadvantage in giving a child an interest contingent only upon attaining an appropriate age, even if that child should die during the lifetime of a surviving spouse. On the contrary, inconvenience and sometimes real hardship may result if he is *not* allowed to have a vested interest during the lifetime of the life tenant. The uncertainty as to his entitlement may make it difficult for him to make proper provision for his own family and may prevent him from obtaining finance for some necessary purpose, for which there may perhaps be no spare capital for the trustees to advance.

As to the possibility that a child whose interest in capital is contingent might be given a vested interest in income, see Preliminary Note D–6. Whether the interests of children are capable of vesting on the first or only on the second death, IHT will be payable on the death of the surviving spouse, as on a notional transfer by the spouse.[2] It will similarly be payable if the interest of the spouse comes to an end previously.[3] Not all the exemptions for individuals are available.[4]

If a child with a vested interest dies while this is still a reversionary interest, it is excluded property[5] and no IHT is payable on it.

If on the determination of the life tenant's interest in possession the interest of any of the children is still contingent, no IHT will be payable on the vesting of that child's interest (or at any intermediate time), so long as the conditions for an 'accumulation and maintenance settlement'[6] are established, as, under the trusts declared in this form, they are.

If the interests of the children are *not* vested at the testator's death, even if the children are then of age, difficulty may be experienced in making a variation (should this be desired) of the testator's dispositions, for IHT or CGT purposes: see Preliminary Note D–9. Because of the possibility of minority and/or unborn interests arising, an application to the court[7] will be unavoidable, and although consent may be given, expensive provision for those interests may be required. This difficulty might, however, be avoided, if a discretion to vary is given to the trustees, as under Form 7–1.

No CGT will be payable when the life tenant dies,[8] but the assets will be re-valued as at that time, for purposes of any future disposal.[9] If any child (or grandchild) is still under age at that time, there will be a disposal for CGT purposes when that child becomes absolutely entitled,[10] unless the interest of that child was a vested interest at the outset[11]: under this form, it is not.

---

1 Ie, the testator's grandchildren. Some forms extend the substitution to issue of any degree, but this may not be desirable (see Form 6–10 and notes thereto).

2 See IHTA 1984, s 49(1).
3 Ibid, s 52(1).
4 Ibid, s 19(5), in conjunction with s 57.
5 Ibid, s 48(1).
6 Ie, those comprised in ibid, s 71; and see Preliminary Note D–6.
7 Under the Variation of Trusts Act 1958, s 1.
8 CGTA 1979, s 56 (as amended).
9 Ibid, s 55 (as amended).
10 Ibid, s 54 (as amended).
11 See Preliminary Note D–6.

**Form 6–9**

MY TRUSTEES shall hold my residuary estate UPON the following TRUSTS:

(1) UPON TRUST to pay the income thereof to my [said] [wife] [husband] [ ] during [her] [his] life and subject thereto

(2) UPON TRUST for [all or any of] [such of] my children [or child who] [as] shall be living at [the expiration of twenty-eight clear days after] [my death] and who shall have attained or shall attain the age of [eighteen] [ ] years [or marry under that age] and if more than one in equal shares absolutely PROVIDED ALWAYS that if any child of mine [has already died or] [shall die in my lifetime or] [shall die after my death without having attained a vested interest in my residuary estate] but shall leave a child or children living at [the expiration of twenty-eight clear days after] [my death] who shall attain the age of [eighteen] [ ] years [or marry under that age] such last-mentioned child or children shall take by substitution and if more than one in equal shares the share of my residuary estate which his her or their parent would have taken if he or she had survived to attain a vested interest

## 6–10 The same (alternative form)

See notes to Form 6–9, to which the present form is an alternative.

*'and for all or any of the issue'*

In this form, which is based closely on the 'statutory trusts' embodied in AEA 1925, s 47(1)(i) (applicable to intestacy), the provision as to substitution in case of the death of any of the testator's children during the lifetime of a surviving spouse is extended to include any of the issue of the deceased child and is not confined, as is the proviso in Form 6–9, to the deceased child's own children. The statutory provisions are reproduced in Appendix 1.

Such an extension appears to envisage what may be thought a very unlikely possibility, that the only descendants of the deceased child living at the distribution date (normally, the death of the surviving spouse) might be that child's grandchildren or (further straining credulity) more remote descendants. Thus, although many published forms of precedents provide in this way for the substitution of issue of a deceased child, this seems very unlikely to serve any real purpose.

Moreover, the substitution of issue appears to go beyond what is contemplated for the purposes of the exemption from IHT in respect of the vesting of an interest under any trust which is an 'accumulation and maintenance settlement'. In relation to substitutional entitlements, the exemption extends only to a widow, widower or child of the deceased beneficiary; though in the case of others, it does appear to be still available if the substitutional interest vests within 25 years of the death of the testator.[1]

As under the statutory trusts (and cf note to Form 6–9), the beneficial interests are given to those who are living at the death of the *testator*, and to the issue then living of any who have then predeceased, and who themselves attain the stipulated age or, perhaps, marry under that age.

Such a substitutional gift should preferably be made, as here, by express provision; and not left to the operation of s 33 (as substituted) of WA 1837: see Preliminary Note F–2.

1 See IHTA 1984, s 71(2)(*b*) (reproduced in Appendix 5).

**Form 6–10**

MY TRUSTEES shall hold my residuary estate UPON the following TRUSTS:

(1) UPON TRUST to pay the income thereof to my [said] [wife] [husband] [ ] during [her] [his] life and subject thereto

(2) UPON TRUST in equal shares if more than one for all or any of my children living at [the expiration of twenty-eight clear days after] my death [who attain the age of [eighteen] [ ] years] [or marry under that age] and for all or any of the issue living at my death [who attain the age of [eighteen] [ ] years] [or marry under that age] of any child of mine who shall have predeceased me such issue to take through all degrees according to their stocks in equal shares if more than one the share which their parent would have taken if living at my death and so that no issue shall take whose parent is living at my death and so capable of taking

**6–11 Limited interest, with special power of appointment, and gift over in remainder**

This form differs from Forms 6–9 and 6–10 in that, after the life interest in favour of a surviving spouse, residue devolves on the children as the surviving spouse may appoint or, in default of appointment, on the children equally, as under those forms.

Such a power of appointment may be useful where the children may be too young, at the time of the making of the will, for the testator to be able to judge how they may develop, or what their needs may be. It may also be useful where there is any reason to think that the needs of the children may turn out to be different and where the testator is prepared, if their needs are different, for the ultimate division to be made on the basis of needs, rather than of strict equality.

In all such cases, the purpose of conferring a power of appointment on the spouse is to preserve the greatest possible flexibility and freedom of action. By postponing any decision as to the ultimate distribution of residue, the needs of the children can be more exactly evaluated in the light of the financial situation existing at the time.

As an alternative, the testator could provide for these possibilities more simply by vesting the children's interests (as under Form 6–9) at a relatively later age (anything up to, say, 30 might be appropriate), at the same time giving the trustees extended powers to advance capital in the meantime, so leaving the trustees as judges of what is in the best interests of the children. Such a course implies that the testator has the fullest confidence in the trustees, but there is no reason why the widow should not be one. Forms 8–6 and 8–7 should then be used to extend the relevant provisions of TA 1925, ss 31 and 32, respectively. If the trustees have this element of discretion, it can be exercised after the death of the widow; a power of appointment cannot.

For the reasons explained in Preliminary Note D–6, it is important to ensure that powers of appointment are not possibly exercisable outside the requirements for an accumulation and maintenance settlement for IHT purposes. It is therefore recommended that this form should be used only in conjunction with Form 8–15, which is intended to avoid that possibility.

Where a substitutional gift is intended, in relation to the gift in default of appointment, this should preferably be made by express provision, as here, and not left to the operation of s 33 (as substituted) of WA 1837: see Preliminary Note F–2.

**Form 6–11**

MY TRUSTEES shall hold my residuary estate UPON the following TRUSTS:

(1) UPON TRUST to pay the income thereof to my said [wife] [husband] during [her] [his] life and subject thereto

(2) UPON TRUST for all such one or more exclusively of the others or other of my children [and any widow widower or child born during my lifetime] [of any child of mine who may predecease me] at such ages or times and if more than one in such shares and for such limited or absolute interests and with such provisions for their respective maintenance education advancement and benefit generally as my said [wife] [husband] shall by any deed or deeds revocable or irrevocable or by will or codicil appoint And in default of and subject to any and every such appointment and so far as no such appointment shall extend UPON TRUST for all or any of my children or child living at my death [who [being male] attain the age of [eighteen] [ ] years or [being female] [attain that age or] marry under that age] and if more than one in equal shares absolutely [PROVIDED ALWAYS that no person who shall take any share of or interest in my residuary estate under an appointment by virtue of the power hereinbefore contained shall [in default of apointment to the contrary] be entitled to any share of the unappointed part without bringing into account the share or interest appointed to him or her]

## 6–12 Absolute gift to grandchildren (immediate or deferred)

This form envisages the possible situation that the children of the testator have been provided for during his or her lifetime, or are otherwise in no need of a beneficial interest in the residue of the testator's estate, so that it is possible (and if substantial tax liabilities on the children's own deaths are in prospect, it may from that point of view be desirable) for the testator's estate to be left directly to grandchildren.

If there is a spouse for whom a prior life interest is to be provided, this will be done by paragraph (1). If there is none, or if the spouse has been otherwise sufficiently provided for, paragraph (2) will stand alone, as an immediate gift. It will be appreciated that if there is a spouse for whom it is necessary to make provision, such a disposition in favour of grandchildren is possible only if the spouse will be sufficiently provided for by a life interest and that, even if this is the case, it will be desirable if not essential in the interests of the spouse to give to the trustees a wide power to 'advance' capital to the spouse (eg, under Form 8–8).

Even so, the possible saving of tax by 'skipping' a generation in this way may be obtained only at the expense of equality of distribution. If, as in this form, the gift is to grandchildren 'living at my death', any grandchildren who might be born subsequently would be excluded from benefit. If all possible grandchildren were to share, it would be necessary to postpone distribution until the death of the last child to whom a child might possibly be born. This is plainly unrealistic, as is any intermediate provision which might be proposed. The advantage of a gift in these terms may therefore be much less than appears at first sight, unless it is confined to the children of an individual who has already died, or unless the birth of further grandchildren is so unlikely as not to be a practical possibility.

In a gift to the testator's own children, it is common to include a substitutional gift to the children of any child of the testator who may predecease, or otherwise fail to attain a vested interest. Where the gift is to grandchildren, the intention may be to benefit only such grandchildren as are living at the relevant date, and not to substitute the issue of any who may have died. If so, it would be necessary to displace s 33 of WA 1837 (as substituted by s 19 of AJA 1982; see Preliminary Note F–2) by expressing a contrary intention. The optional Declaration at the end of this form does so. If a substitutional gift is desired, this should preferably be made by express provision and not by reliance upon the statute (see the same note); in which case the Proviso in Form 6–9 may be incorporated, mutatis mutandis. This is advisedly limited to children of a deceased grandchild, and not extended to issue, to avoid a possible breach of the requirements for an accumulation and maintenance settlement; as to which see Preliminary Note D–6.

**Form 6–12**

MY TRUSTEES shall hold my residuary estate

[(1) UPON TRUST to pay the income thereof to my [said] [wife] [husband] [ ] during [her] [his] life and subject thereto]

[(2)] UPON TRUST in equal shares absolutely for all my

grandchldren living at [my death] [who attain the age of [eighteen] [ ] years] [or marry under that age] [AND I DECLARE that the provisions of section 33 of the Wills Act 1837 (as substituted therein) shall have no application to this gift]

## 6–13 Absolute gift to nephews and nieces (immediate)

This form envisages the possible situation that the testator has no immediate family for whom to provide and that, after whatever individual legacies may be appropriate, he or she wishes residue to be shared between the children of his or her brothers and sisters. It will usually be preferred to benefit the children, rather than the brothers and sisters themselves, but, if not, the form is readily adapted.

As a matter of construction, the expression 'nephews and nieces' includes only the testator's own nephews and nieces, and not those of the testator's (late) spouse. If the latter are to be included, this should be made clear.

As this form stands, the basis of division is equality as between individuals. If a stirpital division is required (ie, on the basis of equality as between families, the share of each family being subdivided between individuals), which would be unusual, the gift may be expressed as '[in equal shares per stirpes absolutely]'.

**Form 6–13**

I GIVE all my estate both real and personal whatsoever and wheresoever [not hereby or by any Codicil hereto otherwise specifically disposed of] to my Trustees UPON TRUST to pay my debts and funeral and testamentary expenses [and any legacies bequeathed hereby or by any Codicil hereto] [and all taxes on any gift made free of tax] and to hold the residue after all such payments UPON TRUST for such of my nephews and nieces [and also such of the nephews and nieces of my] [late] [wife] [husband] as are living at my death [and attain the age of eighteen years] equally between them if more than one absolutely

## 6–14 Gift upon trusts of an existing settlement

It may sometimes happen that the intended destination of some part of the estate (or, more probably, of residue) is similar to that of the property comprised in some subsisting settlement or other trust fund. While it is usually better practice to set out on the face of a will the beneficial interests and powers taking effect under the will, so that the will is complete and self-contained, the will may in some cases be simplified by the device of incorporating the existing trusts by reference, as in this form. If this is done, the instrument referred to becomes part of the will, and a copy of it will form part of the grant of probate.

It is, however, only an existing document which can be incorporated in this way and then only in so far as its provisions are definitive and incapable of variation. More specifically, it is clear on the authorities,[1] that, in order to form part of a will, such a document must be clearly identified in the will, must actually exist at the date of the will and must be referred to in the will as being in existence at that date. If it cannot be found at the date of death, the provision for its incorporation is ineffective.[2] If the trusts of that document include a power of appointment, those trusts can be incorporated only in so far as they would take effect in default of appointment.[3]

1 See, inter alia, *Re Keen, Evershed* v *Griffiths* [1937] Ch 236, and *University College of North Wales* v *Taylor* [1908] P 140.
2 *Re Barton, Barton* v *Bourne* (1932) 48 TLR 205.
3 *Re Edwards' Will Trusts* [1948] Ch 440.

**Form 6–14**

I GIVE to my Trustees [ ] Upon such and the like trusts and with and subject to such and the like powers and provisions (if and so far as at the time of my death such trusts powers and provisions or any of them are capable of taking effect) as are declared by [Clause of] [a Settlement dated the day of 19 and made between [etc]] [the Will proved on the day of 19 of who died on the day of 19 ] [in relation to the residue of] [his] [her] [estate]

## 6–15 Limited interest of spouse, extended rights: redemption of life interest; appropriation of interest in dwelling-house

These forms are intended for use in case it may be desired to give to a surviving spouse, who has only a life interest in residue, the same absolute rights as arise in favour of the spouse where that spouse is entitled to a life interest in part of the residue of the estate of an intestate: see Preliminary Note B.

Form 6–15–1 incorporates by reference the provisions of AEA 1925, s 47A, as to redemption of a life interest. Subsection (7), which is excluded, deals with notices to the Family Division of the High Court. Section 47A is reproduced in Appendix 1.

Form 6–15–2 incorporates by reference the provisions of IEA 1952, s 5 and Sched 2, as to appropriation of the deceased's interest in a dwelling-house in which the surviving spouse was resident at the time of death, in or towards satisfaction of any absolute interest of the spouse in the estate. If it is desired to use this form, with the object of giving the matrimonial home to the spouse without real loss to the estate, this should be done in conjunction with Form 6–15–1, in order that the spouse may acquire an absolute interest against which the appropriation may be made.

The excluded paragraphs in Sched 2 to IEA 1952 deal with applications to the court which may be required in certain circumstances, under an intestacy. This schedule is reproduced in Appendix 1.

**Form 6–15–1**

> The provisions of section 47A of the Administration of Estates Act 1925 (other than subsection (7) thereof) shall apply to the life interest in my residuary estate given by this my will to my said [wife] [husband] in all respects as if that interest were a life interest in part of the residuary estate arising on my intestacy

**Form 6–15–2**

> The provisions of section 5 of the Intestates Estates Act 1952 and of the Second Schedule to that Act (other than paragraph 2 and subparagraphs (2)[1] and (3) of paragraph 3 of that Schedule) shall apply to the administration of my estate under this my will as if I had died intestate

---

1 Subparagraph (2) makes a written notification to the personal representative irrevocable. As this seems somewhat arbitrary, and could cause difficulty in relation to a possible future variation, the suggestion is made that it should be inapplicable.

# 7

# Overriding Discretionary Trusts

## 7–1 Special power of appointment, to facilitate variation of will

Since it is impossible for any testator to foresee exactly what will be the circumstances of his family or the value of his estate at the time of his death, the dispositions made by even the most carefully considered will may turn out not to have been the most suitable, either from the point of view of individual beneficiaries or (having regard to the incidence of IHT) in the interests of the estate as a whole.

This may happen if a will has not been kept under regular review. It may happen if the testator's wife (or husband) should unexpectedly have died first. It may happen if the estate of whoever is the first to die turns out to have a value substantially more or less than was anticipated. It may happen in the event of a change in the law, by which some new tax charge is imposed; or else some exemption or relief is withdrawn, or is so framed as to be unavailable in the particular circumstances; with the result that the testator (or those advising him) may not have appreciated the existence or extent of a tax liability.

It may happen, in short, whenever any of the assumptions on the basis of which the will was planned should turn out to have been falsified by events.

As discussed in Preliminary Note D–9, it is open to the beneficiaries, or any of them, to disclaim a beneficial interest, or to vary any of the dispositions of the will. For all purposes, including IHT and CGT, a disclaimer within two years after the death is treated as though the disclaimed benefit had not been conferred. If so elected, a variation within two years after the death is treated for IHT and/or CGT purposes as if it had been effected by the deceased. Where no such election is made, however, the variation will generally amount to a potentially exempt transfer for IHT purposes and/or as a disposal for CGT purposes, as in any case it would have been, but for these provisions.

These are valuable options, but they have their limitations. A disclaimer (by its nature) cannot be made once any benefit has been accepted. If made, it serves simply to accelerate the interests of those who would have been entitled if the person making it were dead. This may not be the desired result. A variation may be made even where a benefit has been accepted, and indeed even where the administration of the estate has been completed. On the other hand, it may be precluded if it depends on the agreement of some person who is not prepared to co-operate, or it may require the sanction of the court on behalf of any person who is unable to consent because of minority or other disability, or if those prospectively interested may include persons yet unborn.

With a view to avoiding this inconvenience it is sometimes suggested that the trustees should be given express powers to consent to a variation on behalf of possible minor or unborn beneficiaries. No form is given in this book for such a provision because it is thought that this might entail legal and practical difficulties, and moreover there is statutory warrant for conferring a much wider and more flexible power, as the present form seeks to do.

By virtue of IHTA 1984, s 144 (reproduced in Appendix 3, and discussed in Preliminary Note D–9), a discretionary power can be conferred on the trustees to vary any of the testator's dispositions, within two years after the death, by what is in effect an overriding power of appointment.[1] For IHT purposes the exercise of such a power is treated as though the will had provided that the property concerned should be so applied or held on the testator's death. However, because of the effect of s 144(1)(*a*), in conjunction with ibid, s 65(4), the power ought not to be exercised within three months of the death.

Such a power cannot, of course, be considered for inclusion in the will unless the testator has the fullest confidence in his trustees and is prepared to leave it entirely in their hands to act, or not, as they think best for the beneficiaries. However, there seems to be no reason why the surviving spouse should not be one of the trustees. The position of the spouse can (and should) be further safeguarded by nominating the spouse[2] as the person to appoint new and additional trustees, as under Form 8–14.

Moreover, it should always be borne in mind that (as is clearly implicit in the preamble to the present form) the remaining provisions of the will are intended to take effect unless, in their discretion, the trustees see not merely good reasons, but compelling reasons, to override them. It will be most desirable to leave with the will a letter to the trustees making this absolutely clear (though without in any way derogating from the terms of the will itself), saying in other words, that these powers are intended to be exercised only in such a way as to prevent any detriment to the interests of the beneficiaries named in the rest of the will, in case of any unforeseen change of circumstances occurring (whether or not in the testator's lifetime) after the will was made. Seen in this way, such a provision can give a most useful safeguard against the possibility of a will ever becoming altogether out of date.

In his letter to the trustees it might be as well for the testator to emphasise that it will normally be in the interests of the beneficiaries for the necessary decisions to be taken with the least possible delay. This will also be desirable for IHT and CGT reasons as mentioned below. Indeed, with or without such a power executors and trustees should always make it one of their first duties to review the terms of the will in relation to the current circumstances.

It is the purpose of this note to suggest that the inclusion in a will of provisions on the lines of this form may be very beneficial. In particular:

(1) If a discretion is given to the trustees, they will be bound to consider whether or not to exercise it, and therefore if some exercise of their powers would be in the best interests of the beneficiaries, this is unlikely to go by default. In the absence of such powers, beneficiaries will usually be advised to make an appropriate variation, but may not necessarily have the benefit of such advice.

(2) An appointment by trustees will not attract a claim to ad valorem stamp duty. A variation may sometimes do so, if the conditions of the normal exemption[3] are not satisfied; and in particular if consideration, other than another variation, is given.

(3) An appointment by trustees in favour of a child will not involve a parent in liability as 'settlor' for IT purposes. A variation by the parent might have done so; though, probably, a disclaimer would not. In other cases, where an original beneficiary would continue to be assessable to IT on estate income despite a variation, trustees can make an appointment to compensate for this.

(4) In relation to an appointment by trustees, no application to the court will be necessary in a case where any beneficiary is a minor or otherwise under disability, nor where there are possible unborn interests, under the substantive provisions of a will. A variation might involve such an application.

(5) An appointment by trustees which is seen by them to be desirable cannot be obstructed by any person whose concurrence in a variation might have been required.

These are considerable advantages. On the other hand, there are certain possible disadvantages which may attach to the exercise by trustees of a power of appointment, as compared with a variation by beneficiaries. In particular:

(1) However *much* of the estate passes in the end to the surviving spouse, the IHT exemption does not arise unless and until it does so. In order to obtain a grant the executors must therefore pay IHT in full, and subsequently reclaim the amount attributable to property passing to the spouse when that property does so pass. There appears to be no authority for claiming interest on that amount when repaid.[4] No doubt the inconvenience of this will usually be mitigated by making an interim appointment to the spouse of any property (such as a house) which will clearly pass to her (or him) in the end.[5]

(2) For IHT purposes an appointment under the power is necessarily treated as if effected at the death.[6] No right of election[7] arises, and so there is no right *not* to elect. In some cases the effective rate of IHT in the estate of the deceased might exceed the effective rate in the estate of an individual making a similar variation; particularly since where no election is made following the variation the potentially exempt transfer may never become chargeable.

(3) No right of election arises for CGT purposes either,[8] as an appointment under the power is not an 'instrument . . . made by the persons or any of the persons who benefit'. Nor does the appointee appear to be a 'legatee'.[9] On the contrary, property subject to this power is clearly 'settled property'[10] and accordingly a charge to CGT may arise wherever property is appointed to a beneficiary absolutely,[11] or if there is an appointment on new trusts.[12] However, if action is taken promptly any chargeable gain may be eliminated, or at least reduced, by virtue of the annual exempt amount available to executors and trustees respectively[13]; it would seem that it may otherwise not be held over (by election) to the beneficiary.

It has also been suggested that the benefit of the CGT election[8] might be secured, if it were provided that any exercise of the trustees' powers and discretions should be made subject to the consent of the beneficiaries, or at any rate of the widow. Such a requirement may have much to commend it on personal grounds, and is provided for as an optional variation in the preamble to Form 7–1.

For CGT purposes, it seems to be arguable that an appointment with such consent (at least if the appointment and the consent were embodied in the same 'instrument') would be a variation made, as is required[8] 'by the persons or any of the persons who benefit or would benefit under the dispositions'. However, if the prospective liability to CGT is significant, it might be safer for the trustees to allow the relevant dispositions of the will to stand, by releasing or partly releasing their powers, so enabling the beneficiary or beneficiaries concerned to vary those dispositions of their own motion.

(4) Should the power not have been exercised before the end of the administration period (which seems unlikely) income arising after that period and before exercise or expiry of the power would be liable to tax at the additional rate in the hands of the trustee; though on distribution, it would carry a correspondingly enlarged tax credit.

(5) An appointment is necessarily restricted to objects of the power. A variation may be made in favour of anyone.

While these disadvantages must be kept in view, it is of course the case that the existence of a power of appointment in no way precludes a variation by beneficiaries if, in the circumstances, this would be preferable. On the other hand, in unusual cases, the existence of the power might perhaps serve to restrain a possibly irresponsible variation; and in such circumstances, might recommend itself to the testator on this ground alone.

Since the powers and discretions conferred by this form will, if exercised, override some or all of the other provisions of the will, the latter should be adapted appropriately. The clause disposing of residue, or defining the beneficial interests in residue, should be introduced by the words 'Subject to the provisions of Clause ...' (meaning this form). Should the will include any substantial legacy (as under Form 5–3) which there is also to be power to override, that clause should be modified similarly. Should there be any provision which is not to be overriden, the preamble to this form should be modified in such a way as to show which of the 'foregoing provisions' are 'subject to the overriding powers and discretions'. However, if this form is to be used at all, it seems better that it should apply generally and not selectively.

For the reasons explained in Preliminary Note D–6, it is important to ensure that powers of this kind are not possibly exercisable outside the requirements for an accumulation and maintenance settlement for IHT purposes. It is therefore recommended that this form should be used only in conjunction with Form 8–15, which is intended to avoid that possibility.

Additionally, it will be desirable to include Form 8–10, as to the sufficiency of receipts for payments by the trustees: and also (as suggested above), Form 8–14, as to the power of appointment of new trustees.

Because they would constitute 'related settlements' within the meaning of IHTA 1984, s 62, Form 7–1 should not normally be included in a will which also includes Form 5–4.

---

1 Because such power is given to the trustees, it is open to doubt whether it may be exercised before the administration of the estate is complete when (but not before) the trusts are complete. In view of this an express provision permitting exercise of this power during the administration period should be inserted.

2 Under TA 1925, s 36.

3 Under FA 1985, s 84 (applying to instruments executed on or after 26 March 1985).

4 Ie, under IHTA 1984, s 235. The amount in question is not 'an amount paid in excess of a liability for tax' because there was, at the time of payment, a liability.

5 However, if the interest appointed is not absolute, this may be disregarded if not exceeding two years: see IHTA 1984, s 142(4).

6 Ibid, s 144(2).

7 Under ibid, s 142.

8 Under CGTA 1979, s 49(6)–(9) (reproduced in Appendix 3).

9 Within ibid, s 47(2).

10 Within ibid, s 51.

11 Within ibid, s 54.

12 See Preliminary Note D–6, text and footnote 4.

13 See CGTA 1979, s 5; FA 1982, s 80, and orders thereunder.

### Form 7–1

I DECLARE that the foregoing provisions of my will are made and the dispositions of my estate therein contained shall have effect only (if at all) subject to the overriding powers and discretions which I hereby confer upon my Trustees [but so that all such powers and discretions shall be exercisable only (if at all) with the consent of my said] [wife] [husband] [and all or any of my children who shall then have attained the age of] [eighteen] [ ] [years] that is to say:

(1) During the period of twenty-three months following my death (or so much of that period during which any part of my estate continues to be subject to the trusts and powers of my will) my Trustees shall accumulate the income of my residuary estate (or so much thereof as is not from time to time applied for the maintenance education or benefit of any person pursuant to the provisions of paragraph (2) of this Clause) and shall hold such accumulations by way of addition to the capital of my residuary estate

(2) During the period aforesaid my Trustees shall have power at any time and from time to time if and whenever they may in their absolute and uncontrolled discretion think fit to pay or apply the whole or any part or parts of the income or of the capital or of the income and the capital of my residuary estate to or for the benefit of all or any one or more exclusively of the others or other of the following persons that is to say any [said] [wife] [husband] and any of my children and any [widow widower or] child born during the lifetime of the survivor of myself and my said [wife] [husband] of any child of mine who may predecease such survivor

(3) If any of my Trustees is or may become personally interested as a beneficiary in the exercise of (or omission to exercise) any or all of the powers and discretions hereby conferred upon my Trustees generally he may from time to time join in exercising that power or any such discretion as if he were not so interested and may nevertheless retain for his own use any benefit which in good faith he may derive in consequence thereof as if he were not a trustee

(4) My Trustees may exercise any or all of the powers and discretions hereby conferred upon them at any time after my death and in particular whether or not probate of my will has been granted and whether or not the administration of my estate has (subject to any exercise of any of the said powers and discretions) been completed

(5) Notwithstanding the fiduciary nature of the powers and discretions hereby conferred on my Trustees I further DECLARE that my Trustees may at any time wholly or in part release the same but without prejudice to any payment or application of capital or income previously made by them thereunder

# 8

# Trustees: Extended and Additional Powers

## 8–1 General words

*'their powers under the general law'*

Discussion of the statutory powers of trustees is outside the scope of this book. The principal statutory provisions, to which reference may be made, are the following:

*TA 1925, ss 12–33:* general powers of trustees and personal representatives, additional to the powers conferred by the instrument, if any, creating the trust, and applicable if and so far only as a contrary intention is not expressed in, and subject to, the terms of that instrument (see ibid, s 69(2)). Sections 19, 31 and 32 are reproduced in Appendix 4.

*LPA 1925, s 28:* whereby trustees for sale of land have the powers of a tenant for life of settled land (under the SLA 1925, ss 38–72) and of the trustees of settlement (under ibid, ss 73 et seq).

*TIA 1961:* the powers conferred by which are in addition to and not in derogation from any other power of investment or postponement of conversion exercisable by a trustee or personal representative (see ibid, s 3(1)).

**Form 8–1**

My Trustees shall have the following powers in addition to their powers under the general law:

## 8–2 Power to appropriate without consents

The terms of the statutory power of appropriation, which this clause extends, are found in the AEA 1925, s 41, which is reproduced in Appendix 1.

*'without ... any such consents as are referred to in that section'*

It is usual to dispense with any consent to the exercise of the statutory power in order to avoid incurring any liability to ad valorem stamp duty, as on a conveyance on sale.[1] However, conveyance on sale duty has ceased to be chargeable on an instrument effecting any appropriation in or towards satisfaction of a general legacy of money.[2]

The personal representatives must clearly still have regard to the interests of the beneficiaries, both on general principles and also by virtue of the terms of s 41(5).

1 In view of *Jopling* v *IRC* [1940] 2 KB 282.
2 See FA 1985, s 84(4).

*'and even though ... beneficially interested'*

These words are intended to remove any doubt which might possibly arise as to whether an appropriation in his own favour might be open to objection (even though made in good faith) as amounting to the purchase by a trustee of trust property.

**Form 8–2**

Power to make any such appropriation as is authorised by section 41 of the Administration of Estates Act 1925 but without being required to obtain any such consents as are referred to in that section [and even though one or more of my Trustees may be beneficially interested in the appropriation]

### 8–3 Power to insure without restriction

The terms of the statutory power to insure, which this clause varies, are found in the TA 1925, s 19, which is reproduced in Appendix 4.

*'fire or ... any other insurable risk'*

It is considered that trustees should in all cases be enabled to insure on the normal comprehensive terms.

*'to any amount'*

It is likewise considered that trustees should in all cases be enabled to insure up to the full insurable value, whatever this may be

**Form 8–3**

Power to insure against loss or damage by fire or from any other insurable risk any property for the time being comprised in my residuary estate to any amount and to pay all premiums for any such insurance at their discretion out of the income or capital of my residuary estate and so that any money received under any such insurance shall be applicable at their discretion either in or towards making good the loss or damage in respect of which it was received or otherwise as if it were proceeds of sale of the property insured

## 8–4 Power to invest at discretion

In the absence of express powers, trustees have the powers of investment conferred by TIA 1961, and by orders under s 12 of that Act. It is generally considered that for the purposes of a normal will trust, these powers are unduly restrictive, and are administratively somewhat cumbersome to operate. Accordingly, the adoption of express powers, giving the widest possible discretion as to investment, is usually advised.

Such a discretion is not, in reality, absolute. It seems clear, in particular, that it does not relieve the trustees of their duty, under the general law, to act honestly and with ordinary prudence.[1] Hence, although it frees them from the specific requirements of the Act as to obtaining professional advice, it does not obviate the need to take such advice whenever an ordinary prudent person would do so.

Further, even the most general power would not authorise the retention of the testator's assets in a business which the trustees have no power to carry on.[2] Neither would it authorise a loan on merely personal credit.[3] Such loans are sometimes expressly authorised, envisaging the possibility of loans to beneficiaries. This is clearly inappropriate to the will under consideration, for the purposes of which the power of the trustees to advance capital under Form 8–6 will suffice. An express power to make loans is incorporated in Form 8–8–3 for use in other circumstances.

The power to invest is also commonly further extended to enable the purchase or improvement of a residence (not, as such, an investment); as in Form 8–5.

1 See, comparatively, *Knox* v *Mackinnon* (1888) 13 App Cas 753, where a doubtful investment was made at the request of an importunate beneficiary.

2 *Re Berry* [1962] Ch 97.

3 *Re Peczenik's Settlement Trusts* [1964] 1 WLR 720.

**Form 8–4**

Power to invest trust money and to vary and transpose investments from time to time with the same full and unrestricted freedom in their choice of investments as if my Trustees were a sole absolute beneficial owner

## 8–5 Power to acquire and/or improve a residence

See also Form 4–8 and notes thereto.

This form is intended for use where residue is to be held in trust, during the lifetime of a surviving spouse (or, perhaps, during the minority of children) and complements Form 6–3 (trust for sale of residue), paragaph (2) of which provides that an existing house should not be sold without the consent of the spouse, and that the spouse should have the right of occupation pending sale. The present form enables the trustees to apply capital in buying and improving a replacement. It does not require them to do so. If the spouse is to be entitled as of right to sell and to repurchase out of trust capital, a settlement of the testator's existing house should be considered: see Form 4–9 and notes thereto.

It is not sufficient to rely on Form 8–4 (extension of trustees' powers of investment), because the purchase of a house for occupation is not an investment[1] and so it is not thereby authorised.

Normally, this form will be applicable where the family home belongs absolutely to the testator or where the testator and spouse are beneficial tenants in common. Its use should however be considered even where the house will pass to the spouse as survivor under a beneficial joint tenancy as circumstances may change, and the testator may not wish the spouse to be necessarily obliged to re-purchase only from her or his own funds. By empowering the trustees to purchase, the testator is in effect enabling them to make additional capital available to the spouse, by freeing capital already in the hands of the spouse for other purposes.

1 *Re Power* [1947] Ch 572.

*'in the purchase (upon trust for sale . . .)'*

In general, land purchased by trustees for sale is held by them upon trust for sale 'unless the settlement otherwise provides'.[1] It appears that a power to purchase for use as a residence may amount to such a contrary provision (a direction so to purchase certainly does so)[2] and, therefore, a trust for sale should be expressly directed.

---

1 LPA 1925, s 32.
2 *Re Hanson* [1928] 1 Ch 96.

*'upon such terms and conditions'*

Recurring outgoings, payable out of income, will normally be the responsibility of the beneficiary in occupation and, if the estate is substantial enough for residue to be disposed of in trust, will normally be covered by the income of other parts of residue.

The cost of repairs will normally be met from income in the same way. The trustees have a statutory power to repair, at the cost of the trust fund[1] whether or not the will contains any express provision as to repairs. They are, moreover, under a duty to repair,[2] unless they have delegated their powers of management to the life tenant,[3] and have obtained from the life tenant an undertaking to repair, as a condition of the delegation.[4] Apart from any such delegation, the life tenant will not normally be under any obligation to repair at all.[5] Commonly, trust corporations stipulate that a sufficient fund should be available to provide for repairs, before accepting the trust: such a trustee should therefore be consulted in advance, at the time when the will is made and, indeed, should be invited at that time to approve generally the terms of the prospective trust.

---

1 LPA 1925, s 28, in conjunction with SLA 1925, s 102; and see *Re Gray* [1927] 1 Ch 242.
2 See *Re Hotchkys* (1886) 32 Ch D 408; *Re Howlett* [1949] Ch 767.
3 Under LPA 1925, s 29.
4 *Re Whythes* [1893] 2 Ch 369; *Re Bagot* [1894] 1 Ch 177.
5 For a useful discussion of the duty to repair, and of the incidence of the cost of repairs as between capital and income, see *The Conveyancer* (NS), vol 20, p 351.

**Form 8–5**

Power to apply trust money at any time and from time to time in the purchase (upon trust for sale but with full power to postpone sale) or in the improvement of any freehold or leasehold dwelling-house [within the United Kingdom] [in any part of the world] and to permit any such dwelling-house to be used as a residence by [my said] [wife] [husband] [and any of my said children] upon such terms and conditions as in their absolute discretion my Trustees may from time to time think fit to require

## 8–6 Power to advance capital at discretion

The terms of the statutory power of advancement, which this clause varies, are found in the TA 1925, s 32, which is reproduced in Appendix 4. It may be excluded or modified by virtue of ibid, s 69(2).

It will be seen that this form does not greatly extend the statutory power but it should be sufficient for the purposes of most wills. For wider powers which may be considered for adoption in special circumstances, see Form 8–8.

It is for consideration whether the power in Form 8–6 should be limited to one half of the beneficiary's entitlement, as under the statutory power, or whether the amount of any advances should be left wholly within the discretion of the trustees, as is more usual.

It is also for consideration whether the beneficiary advanced should be required to bring the advance into account on final distribution, as is usually stipulated.

For the reasons explained in Preliminary Note D–6, it is important to ensure that powers of this kind are not possibly exercisable outside the requirements for an accumulation and maintenance settlement for IHT purposes. It is therefore recommended that this form should be used only in conjunction with Form 8–15, which is intended to avoid that possibility.

It must of course be accepted that this may preclude an advancement by way of re-settlement, unless effected within those requirements. If it should be desired to retain the freedom to exercise the power more widely, accepting the IHT implications (which may adversely affect the entire fund, and not just the property advanced), Form 8–15 would have to be omitted.

It should also be appreciated that if assets are advanced in specie or are realised to provide cash for an advance of cash, this will be a disposal for CGT purposes and any consequential liability to tax will fall on the fund as a whole (though without leading to inequality on final distribution).

**Form 8–6**

Power at any time or times to pay or apply any capital money from my residuary estate for the advancement or benefit in such manner as my Trustees may in their absolute discretion think fit of any person or persons presumptively entitled to any share of or interest in the capital of my residuary estate Provided that the money so paid or applied for the advancement or benefit of any person shall not exceed altogether in amount [one half of] the presumptive or vested share or interest of that person in my residuary estate And Provided that if that person is or becomes absolutely and indefeasibly entitled to a share in my residuary estate [I leave it within the discretion of my Trustees whether and if so to what extent] the money so paid or applied shall be brought into account as part of such share.

## 8–7 Power to apply income for maintenance and to accumulate surplus income during minority

It is usually considered sufficient to rely on the statutory power of maintenance during a minority, conferred on executors and trustees (unless the will shows a contrary intention) by TA 1925, s 31 (reproduction in Appendix 4). This power applies where property is held in trust for a minor for any interest, vested or contingent but, in the case of a contingent interest, only if the disposition carries the intermediate income of the property. It may be excluded or modified by virtue of ibid, s 69(2).

The statutory power is therefore available where minor children become contingently entitled on failure of the spouse to take an absolute interest. It is not available (nor is it required) during the lifetime of a spouse who has a life interest in residue but it would become available on the death of that spouse if any child were then still a minor.

It will be seen that this power is subject to certain qualifications some or all of which it may sometimes be thought desirable to modify.

This form provides for any or all of the following modifications to be made:

(i) conferring an absolute discretion on the trustees as to the amount of income applicable;
(ii) removing the restriction as to the amount of income applicable, where other funds are available;
(iii) substituting a different age for purposes of s 31(1)(ii).

As to receipts for trustees' payments, see Form 8–10 and notes thereto.

**Form 8–7**

The provisions of section 31 of the Trustee Act 1925 shall apply to this my will and shall be exercisable by my Trustees with the following modifications that is to say as if

[(i) the words 'as my Trustees shall in their absolute discretion

think fit' were substituted for the words 'as may in all the circumstances be reasonable' in paragraph (i) of subsection (1) thereof] [and]
[(ii) the proviso to subsection (1) thereof had been omitted therefrom] [and]
[(iii) references to attainment of the age of [ ] years were substituted for references to attainment of the age of eighteen years wherever they occur (references to 'infancy' being likewise construed accordingly)]

## 8–8 Power to make payments, advances and loans out of capital

The statutory power of advancement (considered above in relation to Form 8–6) is necessarily confined to beneficiaries who are or will be entitled, absolutely or contingently, to a share in the capital of the trust fund, since an advance is in fact an anticipation of that entitlement.

Where the testator's spouse is given an absolute interest, the power of advancement becomes relevant only if the spouse fails to survive and if any of the children who then become entitled should be a minor. If, however, the spouse is given only a life or other limited interest with no access to any of the capital of the estate, it will often be essential and will almost always be prudent, for the testator to provide means whereby capital may be made available to the spouse in case of need. This can be done only by conferring a discretion on the trustees. If the testator finds it repugnant that the spouse should be dependent on the trustees in this way, this may be in itself a sufficient reason for giving an absolute and not a limited interest.

If a discretion is to be given, it is suggested that this should be framed in wide terms: the following examples should be readily adaptable.

A discretion in such terms really amounts, in effect, to a power of appointment. It is not, however, thought that this derogates from the existence of an interest in possession for IHT purposes.

If the power is exercised, in favour of the spouse, no IHT will be payable because for tax purposes the trust fund is treated as part of the estate of the spouse. If the power is exercised in favour of another beneficiary, there will be a notional transfer of value by the spouse which will be a potentially exempt transfer provided the conditions of IHTA 1984, s 3A are met.[1] If the power were exercised in favour of the spouse with a view to enabling the spouse to make transfers attracting use of her own lifetime exemptions, this object might not be achieved: if there were any kind of agreement or arrangement, the transactions could be attacked as 'associated operations'.[2]

If payments are actually made to a beneficiary to supplement income, or otherwise with any degree of regularity, such as to become 'annual payments' for purposes of income tax, these will be grossed up and included in the total income of the beneficiary for the purposes of excess liability, even though the payment was actually made out of the capital of the trust.[3]

This danger may be avoided if the amounts made available to the spouse, or other beneficiary, are treated as loans, repayable on death or as may be desired. It should not, however, be thought that this arrangement saves any IHT, since tax payable on the death of the spouse is computed by reference to (inter alia) the combined values of the trust fund and the free estate of the spouse.

As to receipts for trustees' payments, see Form 8–10 and notes thereto.

For the reasons explained in Preliminary Note D–6, it is important to ensure that powers of this kind are not possibly exercisable outside the requirements for an accumulation and maintenance settlement for IHT purposes. It is therefore recommended that this form should be used only in conjunction with Form 8–15, which is intended to avoid that possibility.

It must of course be accepted that this may preclude an advancement by way of re-settlement, unless effected within those requirements. If it should be desired to retain the freedom to exercise the power more widely, accepting the IHT implications (which may adversely affect the entire fund, and not just the property advanced), Form 8–15 would have to be omitted.

---

1 IHTA 1984, s 3A in conjunction with s 3(4).
2 Within ibid, s 268.
3 See *Stevenson* v *Wishart and others* [1987] 2 All ER 428.

**Form 8–8–1**

Power at any time and from time to time to pay or apply capital money from my residuary estate [to any extent] [up to a maximum of ] to my [said] wife or for her benefit as my Trustees [other than my said wife] in their absolute discretion may think fit

**Form 8–8–2**

Power at any time and from time to time to advance capital money from my residuary estate to my [said] wife by way of loan [to any extent] [up to a maximum of ] upon such terms and conditions as my Trustees [other than my said wife] in their absolute discretion may think fit [but so that my Trustees shall not be required] [to charge interest] [nor] [to take any security for repayment] [nor] [to call for any repayment by my said wife during her lifetime]

**Form 8–8–3**

Power at any time and from time to time [so long as my Trustees are at least two in number or a trust corporation] to raise and apply capital money from my residuary estate [to any extent] [up to a maximum of ] as my Trustees in their absolute discretion may think fit [for the following purposes or either of them:]

[(i) for the absolute benefit of my said wife or any person entitled or presumptively entitled to any share of or interest in the capital of my residuary estate [but so that upon the distribution of my residuary estate or any part thereof any capital so paid or applied shall be brought into account by such person]]

[(ii) by way of loan to my said wife or any person entitled or presumptively entitled to any share of or interest in the capital of my residuary estate upon such conditions as to interest and as to security for repayment and as to the time of repayment and otherwise as my Trustees may think fit [and so that my Trustees shall not be liable for any loss arising from any such loan]]

## 8–9 Power to disregard statutory and equitable rules as to apportionment of income

This form has the same effect as the traditional and much longer provisions embodied in paragraph (1) of Form 6–2 and discussed in the notes thereto but with the variation that in the present form the operation of the Apportionment Act 1870, as well as the equitable rules, is excluded.

It is thought that this accords with the intention of most testators, to whom it is more natural to regard all receipts in the nature of income accruing after the death as being income available to the life tenant as it would have been to themselves.

Even if the Act were allowed to apply, so that income current at the death would be apportionable as between the estate and the life tenant, amounts so apportioned to the estate are not thereby converted into income of the deceased for income tax purposes[1]: for such purposes, payments made after death are wholly income in the hands of the executors.

For these reasons, the Act is usually excluded. However, if the life tenant is likely to be liable to higher rate income tax, exclusion of the Act, by increasing the income of the life tenant, may also have the effect of increasing the life tenant's marginal rate of IT. If so, the Act could be allowed to apply, and a legacy given to compensate for the lost income. The amount of such a legacy would be, of course, rather a matter of guess-work.

This form is intended to exclude the Act in all its applications, that is to say, not only on the death of the testator, or of any life tenant, but also on any change in the presumptive interests of members of a class of contingent beneficiaries, by a person dropping out through failure to attain a vested interest, or by some other person being born.[2]

---

1 *IRC* v *Henderson's Executors* (1931) 16 TC 282.
2 See *Re Joel's Will Trusts* [1967] Ch 14, at p 24.

**Form 8–9**

All the income from any part of my estate which is actually received after my death [or after the time when any person] [becomes or] [ceases to be entitled] [or prospectively entitled] [to any beneficial interest in my] [residuary] [estate] shall be treated as accruing wholly after my death [or after that time as the case may be] without apportionment whatever the period in respect of which it is actually payable to the intent that the Apportionment Act 1870 and the rules of equity relating to apportionments [including those known as the rules in *Howe* v *Dartmouth* and *Allhusen* v *Whittell* in all their branches] shall for all purposes be wholly excluded in the administration of my estate and of the trusts of this my will

## 8–10 Power to accept receipts for payments to or on behalf of minors

See note 'Minors' to Form 5–1–3. The purpose of that form was to enable the executor to deal with a legacy to a minor in the best interests of the minor, and with the least possible inconvenience and delay in the administration of the estate.

Where a trust arises, so far as children are concerned, it may be thought sufficient for the trustees to rely on the statutory powers of maintenance and advancement under TA 1925, ss 31 and 32 respectively (the terms of which are reproduced in Appendix 4). If so, the trustees will have no difficulty in obtaining a good discharge for their payments. Section 31 expressly empowers trustees to pay income to the parent or guardian, if any, 'or otherwise apply' it for maintenance etc. Section 32 empowers them to 'pay or apply' capital money for a person's advancement or benefit 'in such manner as they may in their absolute discretion think fit'.

If it is desired to give the trustees extended powers of *maintenance* (or to alter the age of vesting) and this is done (as in Form 8–7) by retaining and modifying the provisions of s 31, the provisions of that section as to payment will continue to apply, and will still be adequate.

If it is desired to give extended powers of *advancement*, this could be done in the same way by retaining and modifying s 32, probably by removing proviso (*a*) in subsection (1). For this Form 8–7 can be adapted and no separate form is given. However, the shortcoming of the statutory power is not so much that it is subject to a limit (which may well be thought desirable in itself), as that it does not allow of any provision for payments to a life tenant: s 32 is concerned with advancements, and such a provision is not an advancement. Accordingly, this situation seems to be better dealt with, not by modifying s 32, but by new and express provisions, as in Form 8–8. Whenever the trustees are given express powers or discretions under which payments may be made for the benefit of minors (as, for example, under Form 8–8–3, and equally under Forms 5–4 and 7–1), express powers as to their discharge for such payments, as in this form, may be thought not merely desirable, but necessary.

If the inclusion of such a power is under consideration with a view only to relieving the trustees of the will from any special responsibility to the beneficiaries in question and, if the interests of those beneficiaries are (apart only from minority) absolute interests, it is for consideration whether this power should be omitted and the trustees left to exercise their statutory power to appoint separate trustees for the minor under AEA 1925, s 42, which is reproduced in Appendix 1.

**Form 8–10**

Power in any case where my Trustees have any obligation or discretion under the provisions of my will or under the general law to pay or apply income or capital to or for the benefit of any person who is a minor to discharge that obligation or to exercise that discretion if and whenever they think fit to do so by making payment either to the parent or guardian of the minor or else to the minor personally if the age of [sixteen] [ ] years at least and so that their respective receipts shall be a full discharge to my Trustees who shall not be required to see to the application of any income or capital so paid

## 8–11 Powers in relation to companies

As to the circumstances in which such powers may be required, see Preliminary Note D–8.

This form is intended to give a general indication as to the kind of provision which may be required and should be adapted as may be necessary in relation to the particular circumstances.

Although in the absence of any decision on similar wording it is difficult to be certain, it is thought that in most cases the terms of paragraph (1) could safely be left to stand on their own, with only the reservation that by analogy with 'beneficial owner' powers of investment,[1] it would always be expected of trustees acting under such a power that they should act honestly and with ordinary prudence.

Because trustees are otherwise accountable as such for any remuneration received by them as directors if their appointment is procured by virtue of a trust shareholding,[2] the words in square brackets should be included unless paragraph (2)(i) of the form is adopted. The wording in that subparagraph is somewhat widened with, perhaps, an excess of caution.[3]

It is thought that in general the provisions of paragraph (2) should be wide enough to cover most likely requirements. Some draftsmen adopt even more specific and detailed provisions. In the view of the present writer, the risk of possible oversight makes it safer to rely on paragraph (1) alone but, if desired, both can be used in combination.

1 See note to Form 8–4.

2 See, for instance, *Re Macadam* [1946] Ch 73; but contrast *Re Gee* [1948] Ch 284.

3 See *Re Llewellin's Will Trusts* [1949] Ch 225.

**Form 8–11**

[(1)] In relation to any company of which any shares or securities are for the time being comprised in my residuary estate and any other company which is controlled by any such company my Trustees shall have power (by voting or otherwise) to exercise all rights conferred by the ownership of such shares or securities as fully and freely as if my Trustees were the absolute beneficial owners thereof [and without being liable to account as trustees for any remuneration or benefit obtained by them directly or indirectly in consequence thereof]

[(2)] Further and in particular (and without prejudice to the generality of the foregoing) my Trustees shall have power:

(i) to procure or join in any appointment and to accept any appointment of themselves or any of them or of their nominee or nominees as directors or other officers or employees of the company or of any subsidiary company and to receive and retain for their own advantage any remuneration or other benefit arising or deriving from any such appointment or employment notwithstanding that they are trustees of my will

(ii) to procure or join in any scheme for the reconstruction or amalgamation of the company or of any subsidiary company or in any scheme or modification of rights relating to any such company or its capital or assets in every case with or without a winding up

(iii) to subscribe for any shares or securities of the company or of any other company in the exercise of the general powers of investment given by this my will

(iv) to accept any bonus shares or securities issued by the company and in their absolute discretion to determine whether any such shares are income or capital of my residuary estate

(v) to leave the management or conduct of the affairs of the company in the hands of its directors (other than themselves) without themselves being bound or required to intervene in such management or conduct

## 8–12 Power to act although personally interested; power to purchase trust property

It may sometimes be desired to relieve individual trustees, to a greater or lesser extent, from the effects of the general rule of law that a trustee may not profit from his trust. If so, this form, suitably adapted to the particular circumstances, should be found sufficient for most normal requirements. It should, however, be used with great caution.

As drafted, the form may serve either or both of two quite distinct purposes. First, it enables individual trustees to act in some matter in which, because of a separate personal interest, they might otherwise be precluded from doing so. This may be an advantage to the estate (as long as there is at least one other trustee who is disinterested) in that a beneficiary might feel unable to act as a trustee even though it would otherwise have been appropriate for him to do so. Secondly, it enables such an individual to purchase property from the estate, although this may be to his personal advantage. It would clearly be inequitable (and would also be likely to give rise to a liability to IHT) if the individual concerned were enabled to purchase at an undervalue and any safeguard in the form of a stipulation for purchase at a valuation may give rise to practical difficulties. On the whole, it seems much more sensible to leave such a transaction to be sanctioned by the other beneficiaries. If this is impossible, because of a minority or the possibility of unborn children, it is a matter for serious consideration whether in principle any such transaction should be allowed to take place at all, unless, perhaps, under the safeguard of a public auction. If there are special circumstances, as where the estate includes a business or shareholding or family farm, in which some particular beneficiary has a special interest, it is considered that this would be better dealt with by giving an option to purchase or other express provision.

**Form 8–12**

Despite any rule of law or equity to the contrary any of my Trustees acting in good faith shall be fully at liberty to enter into any transaction whatsoever concerning the management or disposition of any property for the time being comprised in my [residuary] estate and to exercise any fiduciary power or discretion notwithstanding that he may be in any way personally interested therein [and shall be fully at liberty to purchase any such property for his own account either by public auction or by private treaty] [Provided Always that in any such case there shall be at least one other of my Trustees] [to whom any such personal interest shall first have been disclosed] [and who has no personal interest in the particular transaction] [or purchase] [and Provided Further that in case of a purchase the purchase price shall not be less than the amount of a valuation made for the purpose by a suitably qualified independent valuer]

## 8–13 Power to charge for professional services

If any of the executors and trustees named in the will is a professional person, the power to charge will more usually be embodied in the appointment, as in Forms 2–1–1 and 2–1–2.

If the original appointees are not professional people but it is desired to provide for the possibility that a professional trustee might subsequently be appointed, it may be more convenient to include the power for such a trustee to charge as one of the extended powers conferred on the trustees of the will.

It will be seen that the wording of Form 8–13–1 differs from that of Form 2–1. This has no significance: the choice depends simply on personal preference.

It might be desired in some cases to provide for the possibility that those interested in the estate might wish to appoint a bank or other trust corporation to be a new or additional trustee of the will, as for instance where the testator's appointee dies or otherwise ceases to be available. While provision of this kind is seldom made in practice, it is thought that in appropriate circumstances it might be useful, in case there are minor beneficiaries who are unable to give the necessary consent to the bank's usual terms and conditions, as to charging and otherwise. Form 8–13–2 is intended to facilitate such an appointment by giving to those making the appointment a full discretion or, alternatively, requiring consent only from those beneficiaries who are of full age and have vested interests.

**Form 8–13–1**

Power for any of my Trustees who is a Solicitor [Accountant] or other person engaged in any profession or business to be so employed or act and to charge and be paid all usual professional and other charges for any business transacted or work done by him or his firm in connection with the administration and distribution of my estate or of the trusts of my will [whether or not of a professional nature] [whether or not any other person could have done the same personally]

**Form 8–13–2**

Power to make or concur in making any appointment of a trust corporation to be sole trustee or one of the trustees of my will upon such terms and conditions in all respects as may be acceptable to the corporation so appointed [and to every person of full age who has for the time being a vested interest in my residuary estate]

## 8–14 Power of appointing new or additional trustees

The power of appointing a new or additional trustee is normally vested[1] in the continuing trustees or trustee and the personal representative of the last surviving trustee.

Though it is seldom thought necessary to do so, it seems desirable that (where a life interest arises under a will) a surviving wife or husband should always have the direct right to nominate a replacement trustee, even where the wife or husband is already a trustee. This may be of particular value in relation to:

Form 5–4 (discretionary trust for widow(er) and children);
Form 6–3 and related forms (concerned with the family home);
Form 7–1 (conferring discretionary powers of variation of the will); and
Form 8–8 (concerned with payments from trust capital).

1 By TA 1925, s 36.

**Form 8–14**

The power of appointing from time to time a new or additional trustee or trustees of this my will shall be vested in my said [wife] [husband] during [her] [his] life

## 8–15 Powers of trustees to be exercisable only within requirements for an accumulation and maintenance settlement

For the reasons discussed in Preliminary Note D–6, the danger may arise in some cases that a fund held on trusts which in other respects would have satisfied the requirements for an accumulation and maintenance settlement for IHT purposes, might fail to do so because of the existence of some dispositive power of the trustees which could possibly be exercised outside those requirements. It is thought that the inclusion in the will of a clause in this form should prevent such a possibility.

Use of this form is therefore recommended in conjunction with any of Forms 6–11, 7–1, 8–6 or 8–8–3; or any other express power of advancement or appointment in the will.

As indicated in the notes to those forms, use of the present form would have the effect in some cases of precluding an advancement by way of re-settlement. If this result is considered to be undesirable, and if the IHT implications are appreciated, this form would have to be omitted; or else attached only to any other powers to which it might still be relevant.

**Form 8–15**

None of the powers and discretions conferred upon or vested in my Trustees (whether by virtue of any of the provisions of this my will or by operation of law) [or so conferred upon or vested in any other person] shall be capable of exercise in any such way as will or may directly or indirectly prevent section 71 of the Inheritance Tax Act 1984 (or any re-enactment or replacement thereof for the time being) from applying or continuing to apply to any property given or held from time to time under the trusts of this my will for the benefit of any of my said [children] [grandchildren] [nephews and nieces] [ ] which is for the time being settled property for the purposes of Inheritance Tax and in which for the time being no interest in possession subsists

# 9

# Conclusion

## 9–1 Testimonium and attestation

Two alternative forms of attestation clause are here reproduced. The second, longer, form has been traditionally used for many years but many draftsmen prefer to use the first, short, form which omits nothing of substance. It is generally more convenient to use and is, in particular, easier to memorise for use in case of emergency.

Either form affords equally good prima facie evidence of the due execution of the will in accordance with WA 1837, s 9 (as substituted by s 17 of AJA 1982), which is reproduced in Appendix 6 and discussed in Preliminary Note F–2.

The importance of adopting a sufficient attestation clause is shown by the Non-Contentious Probate Rules 1987, r 12 which is also reproduced in Appendix 6.

The forms here shown, both of which are in common use, imply that following signature of the will by the testator, both witnesses will have added their signatures, not only in the presence of the testator, but also in one another's presence. This goes beyond the requirements of s 9, but does represent the usual, and desirable, practice. If the testator and both witnesses have all signed before any of them leaves the room, there should be no risk of non-compliance with the actual requirements of the section.

The only possible difficulties in relation to the execution of a will are likely to arise where the testator is elderly, or else is seriously ill or perhaps is under partial sedation, as his capacity to make the will and to understand what he and the witnesses are doing in relation to its execution may be open to doubt.

If the will is duly executed, and appears on its face to be rational, there is a presumption of law in favour of its validity, but in case any question should arise, it is most advisable in such cases to ask the testator's doctor or other medically qualified person to act as a witness.[1] Notes should be taken on the basis of which expert evidence could later be given should this be called for. This precaution is, perhaps, unnecessary if there is no one who could possibly have any reason to question the will.

As to the formalities of execution, it is equally essential that the testator should have capacity in the sense of being mentally as well as physically 'present'. He must be fully aware of what is being done, both in relation to his own signature (especially where this is made on his behalf) and in relation to the signatures of the witnesses. In particular, it is most important that when the witnesses sign, the testator should be fully capable of seeing them and understanding what they are doing. It is not essential that he should actually see their signatures made; but he must be capable of doing so, and therefore should in fact do so.

1 This 'golden if tactless rule' has received strong judicial endorsement in *Kenward* v *Adams* (1975) *The Times*, 29 November, and in *Re Simpson* (1977) 121 SJ 224. It is perhaps possible that failure to observe it could be held to amount to professional negligence: see, comparatively, Preliminary Note I, text and footnote 5.

**Form 9–1**

IN WITNESS whereof I have hereunto set my hand this day of 19

SIGNED by the above-named

in our joint presence and then by us in [his] [hers]:

*OR*

SIGNED by the above-named

as and for [his] [her] last will in the presence of us both present together at the same time who at [his] [her] request and in [his] [her] presence and in the presence of each other have hereunto subscribed our names as witnesses:

# 10

# Codicils

## 10–1 General form

A codicil is a document which, being itself duly executed as a testamentary document, adds to or varies an existing will and/or any previous codicils.

If a will requires amendment, it is better practice, wherever possible, to prepare a new will, complete in itself. Where two or more documents have to be read together, there is an increased risk that ambiguities or other difficulties of construction may arise. This is particularly the case where, as commonly happens, the codicil is prepared hurriedly and without time for proper consideration of its effect. There is also some risk that a codicil may become separated from the will and lost; so, to prevent this, it should be endorsed on the will itself, wherever possible.

It is suggested that a will should not normally be amended by a codicil unless there is real urgency or the will is long or complex and the alteration is minor or perfectly simple (involving only the addition of a straightforward gift) or involves the substitution of one straightforward provision for another.

Some examples which may be readily adapted appear in the numbered paragraphs of this form. If not so adaptable to the particular circumstances, this form should not be used: a new will should be considered instead.

*'In all other respects I confirm my said will'*

These words, which are common form, serve to make explicit what is otherwise normally the effect of a codicil. This is to republish the will, and any previous codicils so that these will now take effect and be construed as if actually executed at the date of the present codicil.[1] This may alter the meaning from what was originally intended, and the terms of the will and any previous codicils must be carefully reconsidered with this in view. In particular, all descriptions of beneficiaries and of the subject-matter of specific gifts must be checked to ensure that these still hold good.

---

1 See WA 1837, s 34.

**Form 10–1**

I of DECLARE this to be a [FIRST] [ ] CODICIL to my WILL dated and made the day of 19

(1) WHEREAS by my said Will I have appointed [ ] and [ ] to be the executors and trustees thereof NOW I hereby REVOKE the appointment of the said [ ] and in his place I appoint [ ] to be an executor and trustee of my said Will jointly with the said [ ]

(2) I GIVE to [ ] my [ ] in addition to all gifts in [his] [her] favour contained in my said Will

(3) I REVOKE the legacy of £ given to [ ] by Clause [ ] of my said Will [and in substitution for that legacy I GIVE to him [the sum of £ ] [free of all taxes]

(4) IN ADDITION to the legacies given by my said Will I GIVE the following further legacies [free of all taxes] namely:

(5) WHEREAS [ ] one of the residuary legatees named in my said Will has since died NOW I hereby GIVE to [ ] all the share and interest in my residuary estate which was given in my said Will to the said [ ] [AND in case the said [ ] shall die in my lifetime then I give the same to [ ] [and ] [in equal shares]

[(6)] [In all other respects I confirm my said Will]
IN WITNESS whereof I have hereunto set my hand this
day of 19
SIGNED by the above-named

as a [First] [ ]
Codicil to his Will dated
the day of
19 [*continue as in*
*Form 9–1*]

# Appendices

*Appendix 1*

# Statutory Provisions relating to Intestacy

ADMINISTRATION OF ESTATES ACT 1925, ss 33, 41, 42, 46, 47, 47A, 55(1)(iiiA) and (x)

**33. Trust for sale**

(1) On the death of a person intestate as to any real or personal estate, such estate shall be held by his personal representatives:

(*a*) as to the real estate upon trust to sell the same; and

(*b*) as to the personal estate upon trust to call in sell and convert into money such part thereof as may not consist of money,

with power to postpone such sale and conversion for such a period as the personal representatives, without being liable to account, may think proper, and so that any reversionary interest be not sold until it falls into possession, unless the personal representatives see special reason for sale, and so also that, unless required for purposes of administration owing to want of other assets, personal chattels be not sold except for special reason.

(2) Out of the net money to arise from the sale and conversion of such real and personal estate (after payment of costs), and out of the ready money of the deceased (so far as not disposed of by his will, if any), the personal representative shall pay all such funeral, testamentary and administration expenses, debts and other liabilities as are properly payable thereout having regard to the rules of administration contained in this Part of this Act, and out of the residue of the said money the personal representative shall set aside a fund sufficient to provide for any pecuniary legacies bequeathed by the will (if any) of the deceased.

(3) During the minority of any beneficiary or the subsistence of any life interest and pending the distribution of the whole or any part of the estate of the deceased, the personal representatives may invest the residue of the said money, or so much thereof as may not have been distributed, in any investments for the time being authorised by statute for the investment of trust money, with power, at the discretion of the personal representatives, to change such investments for others of a like nature.

(4) The residue of the said money and any investments for the time being representing the same, including (but without prejudice to the trust for sale) any part of the estate of the deceased which may be retained unsold and is

not required for the administration purposes aforesaid, is in this Act referred to as 'the residuary estate of the intestate'.

(5) The income (including net rents and profits of real estate and chattels real after payment of rates, taxes, rent, costs of insurance, repairs and other outgoings properly attributable to income) of so much of the real and personal estate of the deceased as may not be disposed of by his will, if any, or may not be required for the administration purposes aforesaid, may, however such estate is invested, as from the death of the deceased, be treated and applied as income, and for that purpose any necessary apportionment may be made between tenant for life and remainderman.

(6) Nothing in this section affects the rights of any creditor of the deceased or the rights of the Crown in respect of death duties.

(7) Where the deceased leaves a will, this section has effect subject to the provisions contained in the will.

**41. Powers of personal representatives as to appropriation**

(1) The personal representative may appropriate any part of the real or personal estate, including choses in action, of the deceased in the actual condition or state of investment thereof at the time of appropriation in or towards satisfaction of any legacy bequeathed by the deceased, or of any other interest or share in his property, whether settled or not, as to the personal representative may seem just and reasonable, according to the respective rights of the persons interested in the property of the deceased:

Provided that:

(i) an appropriation shall not be made under this section so as to affect prejudicially any specific devise or bequest;

(ii) an appropriation of property, whether or not being an investment authorised by law or by the will, if any, of the deceased for the investment of money subject to the trust, shall not (save as hereinafter mentioned) be made under this section except with the following consents:

(*a*) when made for the benefit of a person absolutely and beneficially entitled in possession, the consent of that person;

(*b*) when made in respect of any settled legacy share or interest, the consent of either the trustee thereof, if any (not being also the personal representative), or the person who may for the time being be entitled to the income:

If the person whose consent is so required as aforesaid is an infant or is incapable by reason of mental disorder within the meaning of the Mental Health Act 1983, of managing and administering his property and affairs the consent shall be given on his behalf by his parents or parent, testamentary or other guardian . . . or receiver, or if, in the case of an infant, there is no such parent or guardian, by the court on the application of his next friend;

(iii) no consent (save of such trustee as aforesaid) shall be required on behalf of a person who may come into existence after the time of appropriation, or who cannot be found or ascertained at that time;

(iv) if no receiver is acting for a person suffering from mental disorder then, if the appropriation is of an investment authorised by law or by the will, if any, of the deceased for the investment of money subject to the trust, no consent shall be required on behalf of the said person;

(v) if, independently of the personal representative, there is no trustee of a settled legacy share or interest, and no person of full age and capacity entitled to the income thereof, no consent shall be required to an appropriation in respect of such legacy share or interest, provided that the appropriation is of an investment authorised as aforesaid.

(1A) The county court has jurisdiction under proviso (ii) to subsection (1) of this section where the estate in respect of which the application is made does not exceed in amount or value the county court limit.

(2) Any property duly appropriated under the powers conferred by this section shall thereafter be treated as an authorised investment, and may be retained or dealt with accordingly.

(3) For the purposes of such appropriation, the personal representative may ascertain and fix the value of the respective parts of the real and personal estate and the liabilities of the deceased as he may think fit, and shall for that purpose employ a duly qualified valuer in any case where such employment may be necessary; and may make any conveyance (including an assent) which may be requisite for giving effect to the appropriation.

(4) An appropriation made pursuant to this section shall bind all persons interested in the property of the deceased whose consent is not hereby made requisite.

(5) The personal representative shall, in making the appropriation, have regard to the rights of any person who may thereafter come into existence, or who cannot be found or ascertained at the time of appropriation, and of any other person whose consent is not required by this section.

(6) This section does not prejudice any other power of appropriation conferred by law or by the will (if any) of the deceased, and takes effect with any extended powers conferred by the will (if any) of the deceased, and where an appropriation is made under this section, in respect of a settled legacy, share or interest, the property appropriated shall remain subject to all trusts for sale and powers of leasing, disposition, and management or varying investments which would have been applicable thereto or to the legacy, share or interest in respect of which the appropriation is made, if no such appropriation has been made.

(7) If after any real estate has been appropriated in purported exercise of the powers conferred by this section, the person to whom it was conveyed disposes of it or any interest therein, then, in favour of a purchaser, the appropriation shall be deemed to have been made in accordance with the requirements of this section and after all requisite consents, if any, had been given.

(8) In this section, a settled legacy, share or interest includes any legacy, share or interest to which a person is not absolutely entitled in possession at the date of the appropriation, also an annuity, and 'purchaser' means a purchaser for money or money's worth.

(9) This section applies whether the deceased died intestate or not, and whether before or after the commencement of this Act, and extends to property over which a testator exercises a general power of appointment, including the statutory power to dispose of entailed interests, and authorises the setting apart of a fund to answer an annuity by means of the income of that fund or otherwise.

**42. Power to appoint trustees of infants' property**

(1) Where an infant is absolutely entitled under the will or on the intestacy of a person dying before or after the commencement of this Act (in this subsection called 'the deceased') to a devise or legacy, or to the residue of the estate of the deceased, or any share therein, and such devise, legacy, residue or share is not under the will, if any, of the deceased, devised or bequeathed to trustees for the infant, the personal representatives of the deceased may appoint a trust corporation or two or more individuals not exceeding four (whether or not including the personal representatives or one or more of the personal representatives), to be the trustee or trustees of such devise, legacy, residue or share for the infant, and to be trustees of any land devised or any land being or forming part of such residue or share for the purposes of the Settled Land Act 1925, and of the statutory provisions relating to the management of land during a minority, and may execute or do any assurance or thing requisite for vesting such devise, legacy, residue or share in the trustee or trustees so appointed.

On such appointment the personal representatives, as such, shall be discharged from all further liability in respect of such devise, legacy, residue, or share, and the same may be retained in its existing condition or state of investment, or may be converted into money, and such money may be invested in any authorised investment.

(2) Where a personal representative has before the commencement of this Act retained or sold any of such devise, legacy, residue or share, and invested the same or the proceeds thereof in any investments in which he was authorised to invest money subject to the trust, then, subject to any order of the court made before such commencement, he shall not be deemed to have incurred any liability on that account, or by reason of not having paid or transferred the money or property into court.

**46. Succession to real and personal estate on intestacy**

(1) The residuary estate of an intestate shall be distributed in the manner or be held on the trusts mentioned in this section, namely:

(i) If the intestate leaves a husband or wife, then in accordance with the following Table:

TABLE

| If the intestate— | |
|---|---|
| (1) leaves—<br>(*a*) no issue and<br>(*b*) no parent, or brother or sister of the whole blood, or issue of a brother or sister of the whole blood | the residuary estate shall be held in trust for the surviving husband or wife absolutely. |
| (2) leaves issue (whether or not persons mentioned in sub-paragraph (*b*) above also survive) | the surviving husband or wife shall take the personal chattels absolutely and, in addition, the residuary estate of the intestate (other than the personal chattels) shall stand charged with the payment of a fixed net sum,[1] free of death duties and costs, to the surviving husband or wife with interest thereon from the date of the death . . . at such rate as the Lord Chancellor may specify by order until paid or appropriated, and, subject to providing for that sum and the interest thereon, the residuary estate (other than the personal chattels) shall be held—<br>(*a*) as to one half upon trust for the surviving husband or wife during his or her life, and, subject to such life interest, on the statutory trusts for the issue of the intestate, and<br>(*b*) as to the other half, on the statutory trusts for the issue of the intestate. |
| (3) leaves one or more of the following, that is to say, a parent, a brother or sister of the whole blood, or issue of a brother or sister of the whole blood, but leaves no issue | the surviving husband or wife shall take the personal chattels absolutely and, in addition, the residuary estate of the intestate (other than the personal chattels) shall stand charged with the payment of a fixed net sum,[1] free of death duties and costs, to the surviving husband or wife with interest thereon from the date of the death . . . at such rate as the Lord Chancellor may specify by order until paid or appropriated, and, subject to providing for that sum and the interest thereon, the residuary estate (other than the personal chattels) shall be held—<br>(*a*) as to one half in trust for the surviving husband or wife absolutely, and<br>(*b*) as to the other half—<br>(i) where the intestate leaves one parent or both parents (whether or not brothers or sisters of the intestate or their issue also survive) in trust for the parent absolutely or, as the case may be, for the two parents in equal shares absolutely<br>(ii) where the intestate leaves no parent, on the statutory trusts for the brothers and sisters of the whole blood of the intestate. |

The fixed net sums referred to in paragraphs (2) and (3) of this Table shall be of the amounts provided by or under section 1 of the Family Provision Act 1966.[1]

(ii) If the intestate leaves issue but no husband or wife, the residuary estate of the intestate shall be held on the statutory trusts for the issue of the intestate;

(iii) If the intestate leaves no husband or wife and no issue but both parents, then ... the residuary estate of the intestate shall be held in trust for the father and mother in equal shares absolutely;

(iv) If the intestate leaves no husband or wife and no issue but one parent, then ... the residuary estate of the intestate shall be held in trust for the surviving father or mother absolutely;

(v) If the intestate leaves no husband or wife and no issue and no parent, then ... the residuary estate of the intestate shall be held in trust for the following persons living at the death of the intestate, and in the following order and manner, namely:

First, on the statutory trusts for the brothers and sisters of the whole blood of the intestate; but if no person takes an absolutely vested interest under such trusts; then

Secondly, on the statutory trusts for the brothers and sisters of the half blood of the intestate; but if no person takes an absolutely vested interest under such trusts; then

Thirdly, for the grandparents of the intestate and, if more than one survive the intestate, in equal shares; but if there is no member of this class; then

Fourthly, on the statutory trusts for the uncles and aunts of the intestate (being brothers or sisters of the whole blood of a parent of the intestate); but if no person takes an absolute vested interest under such trusts; then

Fifthly, on the statutory trusts for the uncles and aunts of the intestate (being brothers or sisters of the half blood of a parent of the intestate) ...

(vi) In default of any person taking an absolute interest under the foregoing provisions, the residuary estate of the intestate shall belong to the Crown or to the Duchy of Lancaster or to the Duke of Cornwall for the time being, as the case may be, as bona vacantia, and in lieu of any right to escheat.

The Crown or the said Duchy or the said Duke may (without prejudice to the powers reserved by section nine of the Civil List Act 1910, or any other powers), out of the whole or any part of the property devolving on them respectively, provide, in accordance with the existing practice, for dependants, whether kindred or not, of the intestate, and other persons for whom the intestate might reasonably have been expected to make provision.

(1A) The power to make orders under subsection (1) above shall be exercisable by statutory instrument subject to annulment in pursuance of a resolution of either House of Parliament; and any such order may be varied or revoked by a subsequent order made under the power.[2]

(2) A husband and wife shall for all purposes of distribution or division under the foregoing provisions of this section be treated as two persons.

(3) Where the intestate and the intestate's husband or wife have died in circumstances rendering it uncertain which of them survived the other and the intestate's husband or wife is by virtue of section 184 of the Law of Property Act 1925 deemed to have survived the intestate, this section shall, nevertheless, have effect as respects the intestate as if the husband or wife had not survived the intestate.

(4) The interest payable on the fixed net sum payable to a surviving husband or wife shall be primarily payable out of income.

---

1 In relation to the estate of a person dying on or after 1 June 1987, these amounts are £75,000 and £125,000 respectively (Family Provision (Intestate Succession) Order 1987 (SI 1987 No 799)).

2 This power has been exercised (see the Intestate Succession (Interest and Capitalisation) Order 1977 (SI 1977 No 1491)).

### 47. Statutory trusts in favour of issue and other classes of relatives of intestate

(1) Where under this Part of this Act the residuary estate of an intestate, or any part thereof, is directed to be held on the statutory trusts for the issue of the intestate, the same shall be held upon the following trusts, namely:

(i) In trust, in equal shares if more than one, for all or any of the children or child of the intestate, living at the death of the intestate, who attain the age of eighteen years or marry under that age, and for all or any of the issue living at the death of the intestate who attain the age of eighteen years or marry under that age of any child of the intestate who predeceases the intestate, such issue to take through all degrees, according to their stocks, in equal shares if more than one, the share which their parent would have taken if living at the death of the intestate, and so that no issue shall take whose parent is living at the death of the intestate and so capable of taking;

(ii) The statutory power of advancement, and the statutory provisions which relate to maintenance and accumulation of surplus income, shall apply, but when an infant marries such infant shall be entitled to give valid receipts for the income of the infant's share or interest;

(iii) Where the property held on the statutory trusts for issue is divisible into shares, then any money or property which, by way of advancement or on the marriage of a child of the intestate, has been paid to such child by the intestate or settled by the intestate for the benefit of such child (including any life or less interest and including property covenanted to be paid or settled) shall, subject to any contrary intention expressed or appearing from the circumstances of the case, be taken as being so paid or settled in or towards satisfaction of the share of such child or the share which such child would have taken if living at the death of the intestate, and shall be brought into account, at a valuation (the value to be reckoned as at the death of the intestate), in accordance with the requirements of the personal representatives;

(iv) The personal representatives may permit any infant contingently interested to have the use and enjoyment of any personal chattels in such manner and subject to such conditions (if any) as the personal representatives may consider reasonable, and without being liable to account for any consequential loss.

(2) If the trusts in favour of the issue of the intestate fail by reason of no child or other issue attaining absolutely vested interest—

(*a*) the residuary estate of the intestate and the income thereof and all statutory accumulations, if any, of the income thereof, or so much thereof as may not have been paid or applied under any power affecting the same, shall go, devolve and be held under the provisions of this Part of this Act as if the intestate had died without leaving issue living at the death of the intestate;

(*b*) references in this Part of this Act to the intestate 'leaving no issue' shall be construed as 'leaving no issue who attain an absolutely vested interest';

(*c*) references in this Part of this Act to the intestate 'leaving issue' or 'leaving a child or other issue' shall be construed as 'leaving issue who attain an absolutely vested interest'.

(3) Where under this Part of this Act the residuary estate of an intestate or any part thereof is directed to be held on the statutory trusts for any class of relatives of the intestate, other than issue of the intestate, the same shall be held on trusts corresponding to the statutory trusts for the issue of the intestate (other than the provision for bringing any money or property into account) as if such trusts (other than as aforesaid) were repeated with the substitution of references to the members or member of that class for references to the children or child of the intestate.

(4) References in paragraph (i) of subsection (1) of the last foregoing section to the intestate leaving, or not leaving, a member of the class consisting of brothers or sisters of the whole blood of the intestate and issue of brothers or sisters of the whole blood of the intestate shall be construed as references to the intestate leaving, or not leaving, a member of that class who attains an absolutely vested interest.

**47A. Right of surviving spouse to have his own life interest redeemed**

(1) Where a surviving husband or wife is entitled to a life interest in part of the residuary estate, and so elects, the personal representative shall purchase or redeem the life interest by paying the capital value thereof to the tenant for life, or the persons deriving title under the tenant for life, and the costs of the transaction; and thereupon the residuary estate of the intestate may be dealt with and distributed free from the life interest.

***

(3) An election under this section shall only be exercisable if at the time of the election the whole of the said part of the residuary estate consists of property in possession, but, for the purposes of this section, a life interest in property partly in possession and partly not in possession shall be treated as consisting of two separate life interests in those respective parts of the property.

(3A) The capital value shall be reckoned in such manner as the Lord Chancellor may by order direct, and an order under this subsection may include transitional provisions.

(3B) The power to make orders under subsection (3A) above shall be exercisable by statutory instrument subject to annulment in pursuance of a resolution of either House of Parliament; and any such order may be varied or revoked by a subsequent order made under the power.[1]

***

(5) An election under this section shall be exercisable only within the period of twelve months from the date on which representation with respect to the estate of the intestate is first taken out:

Provided that if the surviving husband or wife satisfies the court that the limitation to the said period of twelve months will operate unfairly—

(*a*) in consequence of the representation first taken out being probate of a will subsequently revoked on the ground that the will was invalid, or

(*b*) in consequence of a question whether a person had an interest in the estate, or as to the nature of an interest in the estate, not having been determined at the time when representation was first taken out, or

(*c*) in consequence of some other circumstances affecting the administration or distribution of the estate,

the court may extend the said period.

(6) An election under this section shall be exercisable, except where the tenant for life is the sole personal representative, by notifying the personal representative (or, where there are two or more personal representatives of

whom one is the tenant for life, all of them except the tenant for life) in writing; and a notification in writing under this subsection shall not be revocable except with the consent of the personal representative.

(7) Where the tenant for life is the sole personal representative an election under this section shall be effective unless written notice thereof is given to the Senior Registrar of the Family Division of the High Court within the period within which it must be made; and provision may be made by probate rules for keeping a record of such notices and making that record available to the public.

In this subsection the expression 'probate rules' means rules of court made under section 127 of the Supreme Court Act 1981.

(8) An election under this section by a tenant for life who is an infant shall be as valid and binding as it would be if the tenant for life were of age; but the personal representative shall, instead of paying the capital value of the life interest to the tenant for life, deal with it in the same manner as with any other part of the residuary estate to which the tenant for life is absolutely entitled.

(9) In considering for the purposes of the foregoing provisions of this section the question when representation was first taken out, a grant limited to settled land or to trust property shall be left out of account and a grant limited to real estate or to personal estate shall be left out of account unless a grant limited to the remainder of the estate has previously been made or is made at the same time.

---

1 This power has been exercised: see the Intestate Succession (Interest and Capitalisation) Order 1977 (SI 1977 No 1491), art 3.

**55. Definitions**

(1)(iiiA) 'the County Court limit', in relation to any enactment contained in this Act, means the amount for the time being specified by an Order in Council under section 145 of the County Courts Act 1984 as the county court limit for the purposes of that enactment (or, where no such Order in Council has been made, the corresponding limit specified by Order in Council under section 192 of the County Courts Act 1959);

(x) 'Personal chattels' mean carriages, horses, stable furniture and effects (not used for business purposes), motor cars and accessories (not used for business purposes), garden effects, domestic animals, plate, plated articles, linen, china, glass, books, pictures, prints, furniture, jewellery, articles of household or personal use or ornament, musical and scientific instruments and apparatus, wines, liquors and consumable stores, but do not include any chattels used at the death of the intestate [*sic*] for business purposes nor money or securities for money.

INTESTATES' ESTATES ACT 1952, s 5, SECOND SCHEDULE

**5. Rights of surviving spouse as respects the matrimonial home**

The Second Schedule to this Act shall have effect for enabling the surviving husband or wife of a person dying intestate after the commencement of this Act to acquire the matrimonial home.

## SECOND SCHEDULE

RIGHTS OF SURVIVING SPOUSE AS RESPECTS THE MATRIMONIAL HOME

**1.**—(1) Subject to the provisions of this Schedule, where the residuary estate of the intestate comprises an interest in a dwelling-house in which the surviving husband or wife was resident at the time of the intestate's death, the surviving husband or wife may require the personal representative, in exercise of the power conferred by section 41 of the principal Act (and with due regard to the requirements of that section as to valuation) to appropriate the said interest in the dwelling-house in or towards satisfaction of any absolute interest of the surviving husband or wife in the real and personal estate of the intestate.

(2) The right conferred by this paragraph shall not be exercisable where the interest is—

(*a*) a tenancy which at the date of the death of the intestate was a tenancy which would determine within the period of two years from that date; or

(*b*) a tenancy which the landlord by notice given after that date could determine within the remainder of that period.

(3) Nothing in subsection (5) of section 41 of the principal Act (which requires the personal representative, in making an appropriation to any person under that section, to have regard to the rights of others) shall prevent the personal representative from giving effect to the right conferred by this paragraph.

(4) The reference in this paragraph to an absolute interest in the real and personal estate of the intestate includes a reference to the capital value of a life interest which the surviving husband or wife has under this Act elected to have redeemed.

(5) Where part of a building was, at the date of the death of the intestate, occupied as a separate dwelling, that dwelling shall for the purposes of this Schedule be treated as a dwelling-house.

**2.** Where—

(*a*) the dwelling-house forms part of a building and an interest in the whole of the building is comprised in the residuary estate; or

(*b*) the dwelling-house is held with agricultural land and an interest in the agricultural land is comprised in the residuary estate; or (*c*) the whole or part of the dwelling-house was at the time of the intestate's death used as a hotel or lodging house; or

(*d*) a part of the dwelling-house was at the time of the intestate's death used for purposes other than domestic purposes,

the right conferred by paragraph 1 of this Schedule shall not be exercisable unless the court, on being satisfied that the exercise of that right is not likely to diminish the value of assets in the residuary estate (other than the said interest in the dwelling-house) or make them more difficult to dispose of, so orders.

**3.**—(1) The right conferred by paragraph 1 of this Schedule—

(*a*) shall not be exercisable after the expiration of twelve months from the first taking out of representation with respect to the intestate's estate;

(*b*) shall not be exercisable after the death of the surviving husband or wife;

(*c*) shall be exercisable, except where the surviving husband or wife is the sole personal representative, by notifying the personal representative (or, where there are two or more personal representatives of whom one is the surviving husband or wife, all of them except the surviving husband or wife) in writing.

(2) A notification in writing under paragraph (*c*) of the foregoing subparagraph shall not be revocable except with the consent of the personal representative; but the surviving husband or wife may require the personal representative to have the said interest in the dwelling-house valued in accordance with section 41 of the principal Act and to inform him or her of the result of that valuation before he or she decides whether to exercise the right.

(3) Subsection (9) of the section 47A added to the principal Act by section 2 of this Act shall apply for the purposes of the construction of the reference in this paragraph to the first taking out of representation, and the proviso to subsection (5) of that section shall apply for the purpose of enabling the surviving husband or wife to apply for an extension of the period of twelve months mentioned in this paragraph.

**4.**—(1) During the period of twelve months mentioned in paragraph 3 of this Schedule the personal representative shall not without the written consent of the surviving husband or wife sell or otherwise dispose of the said interest in the dwelling-house except in the course of administration owing to want of other assets.

(2) An application to the court under paragraph 2 of this Schedule may be made by the personal representative as well as by the surviving husband or wife, and if, on an application under that paragraph, the court does not order that the right conferred by paragraph 1 of this Schedule shall be exercisable by the surviving husband or wife, the court may authorise the personal representative to dispose of the said interest in the dwelling-house within the said period of twelve months.

(3) Where the court under sub-paragraph (3) of paragraph 3 of this Schedule extends the said period of twelve months, the court may direct that this paragraph shall apply in relation to the extended period as it applied in relation to the original period of twelve months.

(4) This paragraph shall not apply where the surviving husband or wife is the sole personal representative or one of two or more personal representatives.

(5) Nothing in this paragraph shall confer any right on the surviving husband or wife as against a purchaser from the personal representative.

**5.**—(1) Where the surviving husband or wife is one of two or more personal representatives, the rule that a trustee may not be a purchaser of trust property shall not prevent the surviving husband or wife from purchasing out of the estate of the intestate an interest in a dwelling-house in which the surviving husband or wife was resident at the time of the intestate's death.

(2) The power of appropriation under section 41 of the principal Act shall include power to appropriate an interest in a dwelling-house in which the surviving husband or wife was resident at the time of the intestate's death partly in satisfaction of an interest of the surviving husband or wife in the real and personal estate of the intestate and partly in return for a payment of money by the surviving husband or wife to the personal representative.

**6.**—(1) Where the surviving husband or wife is a person of unsound mind or a defective, a requirement or consent under this Schedule may be made or given on his or her behalf by the committee or receiver, if any, or, where there is no committee or receiver, by the court.

(2) A requirement or consent made or given under this Schedule by a surviving husband or wife who is an infant shall be as valid and binding as it would be if he or she were of age; and, as respects an appropriation in pursuance of paragraph 1 of this Schedule, the provisions of section 41 of the principal Act as to obtaining the consent of the infant's parent or guardian, or of the court on behalf of the infant, shall not apply.

**7.**—(1) Except where the context otherwise requires, references in this Schedule to a dwelling-house include references to any garden or portion of ground attached to and usually occupied with the dwelling-house or otherwise required for the amenity or convenience of the dwelling-house.

(2) This Schedule shall be construed as one with Part IV of the principal Act.

*Appendix 2*

# Statutory Provisions relating to Family Provision

INHERITANCE (PROVISION FOR FAMILY AND DEPENDANTS) ACT 1975

*Powers of court to order financial provision for deceased's estate*

**1. Application for financial provision from deceased's estate**

(1) Where after the commencement of this Act a person dies domiciled in England and Wales and is survived by any of the following persons:

(*a*) the wife or husband of the deceased;

(*b*) a former wife or former husband of the deceased who has not remarried;

(*c*) a child of the deceased;

(*d*) any person (not being a child of the deceased) who, in the case of any marriage to which the deceased was at any time a party, was treated by the deceased as a child of the family in relation to that marriage;

(*e*) any person (not being a person included in the foregoing paragraphs of this subsection) who immediately before the death of the deceased was being maintained, either wholly or partly, by the deceased;

that person may apply to the court for an order under section 2 of this Act on the ground that the disposition of the deceased's estate effected by his will or the law relating to intestacy, or the combination of his will and that law, is not such as to make reasonable financial provision for the applicant.

(2) In this Act 'reasonable financial provision'—

(*a*) in the case of an application made by virtue of subsection (1)(*a*) above by the husband or wife of the deceased (except where the marriage with the deceased was the subject of a decree of judicial separation and at the date of death the decree was in force and the separation was continuing), means such financial provision as it would be reasonable in all the circumstances of the case for a husband or wife to receive, whether or not that provision is required for his or her maintenance;

(*b*) in the case of any other application made by virtue of subsection (1) above, means such financial provision as it would be reasonable in all the circumstances of the case for the applicant to receive for his maintenance.

(3) For the purposes of subsection (1)(*e*) above, a person shall be treated as being maintained by the deceased, either wholly or partly, as the case may be, if the deceased, otherwise than for full valuable consideration, was making a substantial contribution in money or money's worth towards the reasonable needs of that person.

**2. Powers of court to make orders**

(1) Subject to the provisions of this Act, where an application is made for an order under this section, the court may, if it is satisfied that the disposition of the deceased's estate effected by his will or the law relating to intestacy, or the combination of his will and that law, is not such as to make reasonable financial provision for the applicant, make any one or more of the following orders:

(*a*) an order for the making of the applicant out of the net estate of the deceased of such periodical payments and for such term as may be specified in the order;
(*b*) an order for the payment to the applicant out of that estate of a lump sum of such amount as may be so specified;
(*c*) an order for the transfer to the applicant of such property comprised in that estate as may be so specified;
(*d*) an order for the settlement for the benefit of the applicant of such property comprised in that estate as may be so specified;
(*e*) an order for the acquisition out of property comprised in that estate of such property as may be so specified and for the transfer of the property so acquired to the applicant or for the settlement thereof for his benefit;
(*f*) an order varying any ante-nuptial or post-nuptial settlement (including such a settlement made by will) made on the parties to a marriage to which the deceased was one of the parties, the variation being for the benefit of the surviving party to that marriage, or any child of that marriage, or any person who was treated by the deceased as a child of the family in relation to that marriage.

(2) An order under subsection (1)(*a*) above providing for the making out of the net estate of the deceased of periodical payments may provide for—

(*a*) payments of such amount as may be specified in the order,
(*b*) payments equal to the whole of the income of the net estate or of such portion thereof as may be so specified,
(*c*) payments equal to the whole of the income of such part of the net estate as the court may direct to be set aside or appropriated for the making out of the income thereof of payments under this section,

or may provide for the amount of the payments or any of them to be determined in any other way the court thinks fit.

(3) Where an order under subsection (1)(*a*) above provides for the making of payments of an amount specified in the order, the order may direct that such part of the net estate as may be so specified shall be set aside or appropriated for the making out of the income thereof of those payments; but no larger part of the net estate shall be so set aside or appropriated than is sufficient, at the date of the order, to produce by the income thereof the amount required for the making of those payments.

(4) An order under this section may contain such consequential and supplemental provisions as the court thinks necessary or expedient for the purpose of giving effect to the order or for the purpose of securing that the order operates fairly as between one beneficiary of the estate of the deceased and another and may, in particular, but without prejudice to the generality of this subsection—

(*a*) order any person who holds any property which forms part of the net estate of the deceased to make such payment or transfer such property as may be specified in the order;

(*b*) vary the disposition of the deceased's estate effected by the will or the law relating to intestacy, or by both the will and the law relating to intestacy, in such manner as the court thinks fair and reasonable having regard to the provisions of the order and all the circumstances of the case;

(*c*) confer on the trustees of any property which is the subject of an order under this section such powers as appear to the court to be necessary or expedient.

**3. Matters to which court is to have regard in exercising powers under s 2**

(1) Where an application is made for an order under section 2 of this Act, the court shall, in determining whether the disposition of the deceased's estate effected by his will or the law relating to intestacy, or the combination of his will and that law, is such as to make reasonable financial provision for the applicant and, if the court considers that reasonable financial provision has not been made, in determining whether and in what manner it shall exercise its powers under that section, have regard to the following matters, that is to say—

(*a*) the financial resources and financial needs which the applicant has or is likely to have in the foreseeable future;

(*b*) the financial resources and financial needs which any other applicant for an order under section 2 of this Act has or is likely to have in the foreseeable future;

(*c*) the financial resources and financial needs which any beneficiary of the estate of the deceased has or is likely to have in the foreseeable future;

(*d*) any obligations and responsibilities which the deceased had towards any applicant for an order under the said section 2 or towards any beneficiary of the estate of the deceased;

(*e*) the size and nature of the net estate of the deceased;

(*f*) any physical or mental disability of any applicant for an order under the said section 2 or any beneficiary of the estate of the deceased;

(*g*) any other matter including the conduct of the applicant or any other person, which in the circumstances of the case the court may consider relevant.

(2) Without prejudice to the generality of paragraph (*g*) of subsection (1) above, where an application for an order under section 2 of this Act is made by virtue of section 1(1)(*a*) or 1(1)(*b*) of this Act, the court shall, in addition to the matters specifically mentioned in paragraphs (*a*) to (*f*) of that subsection, have regard to—

(*a*) the age of the applicant and the duration of the marriage;

(*b*) the contribution made by the applicant to the welfare of the family of the deceased, including any contribution made by looking after the home or caring for the family;

and, in the case of an application by the wife or husband of the deceased, the court shall also, unless at the date of death a decree of judicial separation was in force and the separation was continuing, have regard to the provision which the applicant might reasonably have expected to receive if on the day on which the deceased died the marriage, instead of being terminated by death, had been terminated by a decree of divorce.

(3) Without prejudice to the generality of paragraph (*g*) of subsection (1) above, where an application for an order under section 2 of this Act is made by virtue of section 1(1)(*c*) or 1(1)(*d*) of this Act, the court shall, in addition to the matters specifically mentioned in paragraphs (*a*) to (*f*) of that subsection, have regard to the manner in which the applicant was being or in which he might expect to be educated or trained, and where the application is made by virtue of section 1(1)(*d*) the court shall also have regard—

(*a*) to whether the deceased had assumed any responsibility for the applicant's maintenance and, if so, to the extent to which and the basis upon which the deceased assumed that responsibility and to the length of time for which the deceased discharged that responsibility;

(*b*) to whether in assuming and discharging that responsibility the deceased did so knowing that the applicant was not his own child;

(*c*) to the liability of any other person to maintain the applicant.

(4) Without prejudice to the generality of paragraph (*g*) of subsection (1) above, where an application for an order under section 2 of this Act is made by virtue of section 1(1)(*e*) of this Act, the court shall, in addition to the matters specifically mentioned in paragraphs (*a*) to (*f*) of that

subsection, have regard to the extent to which and the basis upon which the deceased assumed responsibility for the maintenance of the applicant and to the length of time for which the deceased discharged that responsibility.

(5) In considering the matters to which the court is required to have regard under this section, the court shall take into account the facts as known to the court at the date of the hearing.

(6) In considering the financial resources of any person for the purposes of this section the court shall take into account his earning capacity and in considering the financial needs of any person for the purposes of this section the court shall take into account his financial obligations and responsibilities.

**4. Time-limit for applications**

An application for an order under section 2 of this Act shall not, except with the permission of the court, be made after the end of the period of six months from the date on which representation with respect to the estate of the deceased is first taken out.

**5. Interim orders**

(1) Where on an application for an order under section 2 of this Act it appears to the court—

- (*a*) that the applicant is in immediate need of financial assistance, but it is not yet possible to determine what order (if any) should be made under that section; and
- (*b*) that property forming part of the net estate of the deceased is or can be made available to meet the need of the applicant;

the court may order that, subject to such conditions or restrictions, if any, as the court may impose and to any further order of the court, there shall be paid to the applicant out of the net estate of the deceased such sum or sums and (if more than one) at such intervals as the court thinks reasonable; and the court may order that, subject to the provisions of this Act, such payments are to be made until such date as the court may specify, not being later than the date on which the court either makes an order under the said section 2 or decides not to exercise its powers under that section.

(2) Subsections (2), (3) and (4) of section 2 of this Act shall apply in relation to an order under this section as they apply to an order under that section.

(3) In determining what order, if any, should be made under this section the court shall, so far as the urgency of the case admits, have regard to the same matters as those to which the court is required to have regard under section 3 of this Act.

(4) An order made under section 2 of this Act may provide that any sum paid to the applicant by virtue of this section shall be treated to such an

extent and in such a manner as may be provided by that order as having been paid on account of any payment provided for by that order.

**6. Variation, discharge etc of orders for periodical payments**

(1) Subject to the provisions of this Act, where the court has made an order under section 2(1)(*a*) of this Act (in this section referred to as 'the original order') for the making of periodical payments to any person (in this section referred to as 'the original recipient'), the court, on an application under this section, shall have power by order to vary or discharge the original order or to suspend any provision of it temporarily and to revive the operation of any provision so suspended.

(2) Without prejudice to the generality of subsection (1) above, an order made on an application for the variation of the original order may—

(*a*) provide for the making out of any relevant property of such periodical payments and for such terms as may be specified in the order to any person who has applied, or would but for section 4 of this Act be entitled to apply, for an order under section 2 of this Act (whether or not, in the case of any application, an order was made in favour of the applicant);

(*b*) provide for the payment out of any relevant property of a lump sum of such amount as may be so specified to the original recipient or to any such person as is mentioned in paragraph (*a*) above;

(*c*) provide for the transfer of the relevant property, or such part thereof as may be so specified, to the original recipient or to any such person as is so mentioned.

(3) Where the original order provides that any periodical payments payable thereunder to the original recipient are to cease on the occurrence of an event specified in the order (other than the remarriage of a former wife or former husband) or on the expiration of a period so specified, then, if, before the end of the period of six months from the date of the occurrence of that event or of the expiration of that period, an application is made for an order under this section, the court shall have power to make any order which it would have had power to make if the application had been before that date (whether in favour of the original recipient or any such person as is mentioned in subsection (2)(*a*) above and whether having effect from that date or from such later date as the court may specify).

(4) Any reference in this section to the original order shall include a reference to an order made under this section and any reference in this section to the original recipient shall include a reference to any person to whom periodical payments are required to be made by virtue of an order under this section.

(5) An application under this section may be made by any of the following persons, that is to say—

(*a*) any person who by virtue of section 1(1) of this Act has applied, or would but for section 4 of this Act be entitled to apply, for an order under section 2 of this Act,
(*b*) the personal representatives of the deceased,
(*c*) the trustees of any relevant property, and
(*d*) any beneficiary of the estate of the deceased.

(6) An order under this section may only affect—
(*a*) property the income of which is at the date of the order applicable wholly or in part for the making of periodical payments to any person who has applied for an order under this Act, or
(*b*) in the case of an application under subsection (3) above in respect of payments which have ceased to be payable on the occurrence of an event or the expiration of a period, property the income of which was so applicable immediately before the occurrence of that event or the expiration of that period, as the case may be,

and any such property as is mentioned in paragraph (*a*) or (*b*) above is in subsections (2) and (5) above referred to as 'relevant property'.

(7) In exercising the powers conferred by this section the court shall have regard to all the circumstances of the case, including any change in any of the matters to which the court was required to have regard when making the order to which the application relates.

(8) Where the court makes an order under this section, it may give such consequential directions as it thinks necessary or expedient having regard to the provisions of the order.

(9) No such order as is mentioned in sections 2(1)(*d*), (*e*), or (*f*), 9, 10 or 11 of this Act shall be made on an application under this section.

(10) For the avoidance of doubt it is hereby declared that, in relation to an order which provides for the making of periodical payments which are to cease on the occurrence of an event specified in the order (other than the remarriage of a former wife or former husband) or on the expiration of a period so specified, the power to vary an order includes power to provide for the making of periodical payments after the expiration of that period or the occurrence of that event.

**7. Payment of lump sums by instalments**

(1) An order under section 2(1)(*b*) or 6(2)(*b*) of this Act for the payment of a lump sum may provide for the payment of that sum by instalments of such amount as may be specified in the order.

(2) Where an order is made by virtue of subsection (1) above, the court shall have power, on an application made by the person to whom the lump sum is payable, by the personal representatives of the deceased or by the trustees of the property out of which the lump sum is payable, to vary that order by varying the number of instalments payable, the amount of any instalment and the date on which any instalment becomes payable.

*Property available for financial provision*

**8. Property treated as part of 'net estate'**

(1) Where a deceased person has in accordance with the provisions of any enactment nominated any person to receive any sum of money or other property on his death and that nomination is in force at the time of his death, that sum of money, after deducting therefrom any inheritance tax payable in respect thereof, or that other property, to the extent of the value thereof at the date of the death of the deceased after deducting therefrom any inheritance tax so payable, shall be treated for the purposes of this Act as part of the net estate of the deceased; but this subsection shall not render any person liable for having paid that sum or transferred that other property to the person named in the nomination in accordance with the directions given in the nomination.

(2) Where any sum of money or other property is received by any person as a donatio mortis causa made by a deceased person, that sum of money, after deducting therefrom any inheritance tax payable thereon, or that other property, to the extent of the value thereof at the date of the death of the deceased after deducting therefrom any inheritance tax so payable, shall be treated for the purposes of this Act as part of the net estate of the deceased; but this subsection shall not render any person liable for having paid that sum or transferred that other property in order to give effect to that donatio mortis causa.

(3) The amount of inheritance tax to be deducted for the purposes of this section shall not exceed the amount of that tax which has been borne by the person nominated by the deceased or, as the case may be, the person who has received a sum of money or other property as a donatio mortis causa.

**9. Property held on a joint tenancy**

(1) Where a deceased person was immediately before his death beneficially entitled to a joint tenancy of any property, then, if, before the end of the period of six months from the date on which representation with respect to the estate of the deceased was first taken out, an application is made for an order under section 2 of this Act, the court for the purpose of facilitating the making of financial provision for the applicant under this Act may order that the deceased's severable share of that property, at the value thereof immediately before his death, shall, to such extent as appears to the court to be just in all the circumstances of the case, be treated for the purposes of this Act as part of the net estate of the deceased.

(2) In determining the extent to which any severable share is to be treated as part of the net estate of the deceased by virtue of an order under subsection (1) above, the court shall have regard to any inheritance tax payable in respect of that severable share.

(3) Where an order is made under subsection (1) above, the provisions of this section shall not render any person liable for anything done by him before the order was made.

(4) For the avoidance of doubt, it is hereby declared that for the purposes of this section there may be a joint tenancy of a chose in action.

*Powers of court in relation to transactions intended to defeat applications for financial provision*

**10. Dispositions intended to defeat applications for financial provision**

(1) Where an application is made to the court for an order under section 2 of this Act, the applicant may, in the proceedings on that application, apply to the court for an order under subsection (2) below.

(2) Where on an application under subsection (1) above the court is satisfied—

(*a*) that, less than six years before the date of the death of the deceased, the deceased with the intention of defeating an application for financial provision under this Act made a disposition, and

(*b*) that full valuable consideration for that disposition was not given by the person to whom or for the benefit of whom the disposition was made (in this section referred to as 'the donee') or by any other person, and

(*c*) that the exercise of the powers conferred by this section would facilitate the making of financial provision for the applicant under this Act,

then, subject to the provisions of this section and of sections 12 and 13 of this Act, the court may order the donee (whether or not at the date of the order he holds any interest in the property disposed of to him or for his benefit by the deceased) to provide, for the purpose of the making of that financial provision, such sum of money or other property as may be specified in the order.

(3) Where an order is made under subsection (2) above as respects any disposition made by the deceased which consisted of the payment of money to or for the benefit of the donee, the amount of any sum of money or the value of any property ordered to be provided under that subsection shall not exceed the amount of the payment made by the deceased after deducting therefrom any inheritance tax borne by the donee in respect of that payment.

(4) Where an order is made under subsection (2) above as respects any disposition made by the deceased which consisted of the transfer of property (other than a sum of money) to or for the benefit of the donee, the amount of any sum of money or the value of any property ordered to be

provided under that subsection shall not exceed the value at the date of death of the deceased of the property disposed of by him to or for the benefit of the donee (or if that property has been disposed of by the person to whom it was transferred by the deceased, the value at the date of that disposal thereof) after deducting therefrom any inheritance tax borne by the donee in respect of the transfer of that property by the deceased.

(5) Where an application (in this subsection referred to as 'the original application') is made for an order under subsection (2) above in relation to any disposition, then, if on an application under this subsection by the donee or by any applicant for an order under section 2 of this Act the court is satisfied—

(*a*) that, less than six years before the date of the death of the deceased, the deceased with the intention of defeating an application for financial provision under this Act made a disposition other than the disposition which is the subject of the original application, and

(*b*) that full valuable consideration for that other disposition was not given by the person to whom or for the benefit of whom that other disposition was made or by any other person,

the court may exercise in relation to the person to whom or for the benefit of whom that other disposition was made the powers which the court would have had under subsection (2) above if the original application had been made in respect of that other disposition and the court had been satisfied as to the matters set out in paragraphs (*a*), (*b*) and (*c*) of that subsection; and where any application is made under this subsection, any reference in this section (except in subsection (2)(*b*)) to the donee shall include a reference to the person to whom or for the benefit of whom that other disposition was made.

(6) In determining whether and in what manner to exercise its powers under this section, the court shall have regard to the circumstances in which any disposition was made and any valuable consideration which was given therefor, the relationship, if any, of the donee to the deceased, the conduct and financial resources of the donee and all the other circumstances of the case.

(7) In this section 'disposition' does not include—

(*a*) any provision in a will, any such nomination as is mentioned in section 8(1) of this Act or any donatio mortis causa, or

(*b*) any appointment of property made, otherwise than by will, in the exercise of a special power of appointment,

but, subject to these exceptions, includes any payment of money (including the payment of a premium under a policy of assurance) and any conveyance, assurance, appointment or gift of property of any description, whether made by an instrument or otherwise.

(8) The provisions of this section do not apply to any disposition made before the commencement of this Act.

**11. Contracts to leave property by will**

(1) Where an application is made to a court for an order under section 2 of this Act, the applicant may, in the proceedings on that application, apply to the court for an order under this section.

(2) Where on an application under subsection (1) above the court is satisfied—

(*a*) that the deceased made a contract by which he agreed to leave by his will a sum of money or other property to any person or by which he agreed that a sum of money or other property would be paid or transferred to any person out of his estate, and

(*b*) that the deceased made that contract with the intention of defeating an application for financial provision under this Act, and

(*c*) that when the contract was made full valuable consideration for that contract was not given or promised by the person with whom or for the benefit of whom the contract was made (in this section referred to as 'the donee') or by any other person, and

(*d*) that the exercise of the powers conferred by this section would facilitate the making of financial provision for the applicant under this Act,

then, subject to the provisions of this section and of sections 12 and 13 of this Act, the court may make any one or more of the following orders, that is to say—

(i) if any money has been paid or any other property has been transferred to or for the benefit of the donee in accordance with the contract, an order directing the donee to provide, for the purpose of the making of that financial provision, such sum of money or other property as may be specified in the order;

(ii) if the money or all the money has not been paid or the property or all the property has not been transferred in accordance with the contract, an order directing the personal representatives not to make any payment or transfer any property, or not to make any further payment or transfer any further property, as the case may be, in accordance therewith or directing the personal representatives only to make such payment or transfer such property as may be specified in the order.

(3) Notwithstanding anything in subsection (2) above, the court may exercise its powers thereunder in relation to any contract made by the deceased only to the extent that the court considers that the amount of any sum of money paid or to be paid or the value of any property transferred or to be transferred in accordance with the contract exceeds the value of any valuable consideration given or to be given for that contract, and for this purpose the court shall have regard to the value of property at the date of the hearing.

(4) In determining whether and in what manner to exercise its powers

under this section, the court shall have regard to the circumstances in which the contract was made, the relationship, if any, of the donee to the deceased, the conduct and financial resources of the donee and all other circumstances of the case.

(5) Where an order has been made under subsection (2) above in relation to any contract, the rights of any person to enforce that contract or to recover damages or to obtain other relief for the breach thereof shall be subject to any adjustment made by the court under section 12(3) of this Act and shall survive to such extent only as is consistent with giving effect to the terms of that order.

(6) The provisions of this section do not apply to a contract made before the commencement of this Act.

**12. Provisions supplementary to ss 10 and 11**

(1) Where the exercise of any of the powers conferred by section 10 or 11 of this Act is conditional on the court being satisfied that a disposition or contract was made by a deceased person with the intention of defeating an application for financial provision under this Act, that condition shall be fulfilled if the court is of the opinion that, on a balance of probabilities, the intention of the deceased (though not necessarily his sole intention) in making the disposition or contract was to prevent an order for financial provision being made under this Act or to reduce the amount of the provision which might otherwise be granted by an order thereunder.

(2) Where an application is made under section 11 of this Act with respect to any contract made by the deceased and no valuable consideration was given or promised by any person for that contract then, notwithstanding anything in subsection (1) above, it shall be presumed, unless the contrary is shown, that the deceased made that contract with the intention of defeating an application for financial provision under this Act.

(3) Where the court makes an order under section 10 or 11 of this Act it may give such consequential directions as it thinks fit (including directions requiring the making of any payment or the transfer of any property) for giving effect to the order or for securing a fair adjustment of the rights of the persons affected thereby.

(4) Any power conferred on the court by the said section 10 or 11 to order the donee, in relation to any disposition or contract, to provide any sum of money or other property shall be exercisable in like manner in relation to the personal representative of the donee, and—

(*a*) any reference in section 10(4) to the disposal of property by the donee shall include a reference to disposal by the personal representative of the donee, and

(*b*) any reference in section 10(5) to an application by the donee under that subsection shall include a reference to an application by the personal representative of the donee;

but the court shall not have power under the said section 10 or 11 to make an order in respect of any property forming part of the estate of the donee which has been distributed by the personal representative; and the personal representative shall not be liable for having distributed any such property before he has notice of the making of an application under the said section 10 or 11 on the ground that he ought to have taken into account the possibility that such an application would be made.

**13. Provisions as to trustees in relation to ss 10 and 11**

(1) Where an application is made for—

(*a*) an order under section 10 of this Act in respect of a disposition made by the deceased to any person as a trustee, or

(*b*) an order under section 11 of this Act in respect of any payment made or property transferred, in accordance with a contract made by the deceased, to any person as a trustee,

the powers of the court under the said section 10 or 11 to order that trustee to provide a sum of money or other property shall be subject to the following limitation (in addition, in a case of an application under section 10, to any provision regarding the deduction of inheritance tax) namely, that the amount of any sum of money or the value of any property ordered to be provided—

(i) in the case of an application in respect of a disposition which consisted of the payment of money or an application in respect of the payment of money in accordance with a contract, shall not exceed the aggregate of so much of that money as is at the date of the order in the hands of the trustee and the value at that date of any property which represents that money or is derived therefrom and is at that date in the hands of the trustee;

(ii) in the case of an application in respect of a disposition which consisted of the transfer of property (other than a sum of money) or an application in respect of the transfer of property (other than a sum of money) in accordance with a contract, shall not exceed the aggregate of the value at the date of the order of so much of that property as is at that date in the hands of the trustee and the value at that date of any property which represents the first-mentioned property or is derived therefrom and is at that date in the hands of the trustee.

(2) Where any such application is made in respect of a disposition made to any person as a trustee or in respect of any payment made or property transferred in pursuance of a contract to any person as a trustee, the trustee shall not be liable for having distributed any money or other property on the ground that he ought to have taken into account the possibility that such an application would be made.

(3) Where any such application is made in respect of a disposition made

to any person as a trustee or in respect of any payment made or property transferred in accordance with a contract to any person as a trustee, any reference in the said section 10 or 11 to the donee shall be construed as including a reference to the trustee or trustees for the time being of the trust in question and any reference in subsection (1) or (2) above to a trustee shall be construed in the same way.

*Special provisions relating to cases of divorce, separation etc*

**14. Provision as to cases where no financial relief was granted in divorce proceedings etc**

(1) Where, within twelve months from the date on which a decree of divorce or nullity of marriage has been made absolute or a decree of judicial separation has been granted, a party to the marriage dies and—

(*a*) an application for a financial provision order under section 23 of the Matrimonial Causes Act 1973 or a property adjustment order under section 24 of that Act has not been made by the other party to that marriage, or

(*b*) such an application has been made but the proceedings thereon have not been determined at the time of the death of the deceased,

then, if an application for an order under section 2 of this Act is made by that other party, the court shall, notwithstanding anything in section 1 or section 3 of this Act, have power, if it thinks it just to do so, to treat that party for the purposes of that application as if the decree of divorce or nullity of marriage had not been made absolute or the decree of judicial separation had not been granted, as the case may be.

(2) This section shall not apply in relation to a decree of judicial separation unless at the date of the death of the deceased the decree was in force and the separation was continuing.

**15. Restriction imposed in divorce proceedings etc on application under this Act**

(1) On the grant of a decree of divorce, a decree of nullity of marriage or a decree of judicial separation or at any time thereafter the court, if it considers it just to do so, may, on the application of either party to the marriage, order that the other party to the marriage shall not on the death of the applicant be entitled to apply for an order under section 2 of this Act.

In this subsection 'the court' means the High Court or, where a county court has jurisdiction by virtue of Part V of the Matrimonial and Family Proceedings Act 1984, a county court.

(2) In the case of a decree of divorce or nullity of marriage an order may be made under subsection (1) above before or after the decree is made

absolute, but if it is made before the decree is made absolute it shall not take effect unless the decree is made absolute.

(3) Where an order made under subsection (1) above on the grant of a decree of divorce or nullilty of marriage has come into force with respect to a party to a marriage, then, on the death of the other party to that marriage, the court shall not entertain any application for an order under section 2 of this Act made by the first-mentioned party.

(4) Where an order made under subsection (1) above on the grant of a decree of a judicial separation has come into force with respect to any party to a marriage, then, if the other party to that marriage dies while the decree is in force and the separation is continuing, the court shall not entertain any application for an order under section 2 of this Act made by the first-mentioned party.

**15A. Restriction imposed in proceedings under Matrimonial and Family Proceedings Act 1984 on application under this Act**

(1) On making an order under section 17 of the Matrimonial and Family Proceedings Act 1984 (orders for financial provision and property adjustment following overseas divorces, etc) the court, if it considers it just to do so, may, on the application of either party to the marriage, order that the other party to the marriage shall not on the death of the applicant be entitled to apply for an order under section 2 of this Act.

In this subsection 'the court' means the High Court or, where a county court has jurisdiction by virtue of Part V of the Matrimonial and Family Proceedings Act 1984, a county court.

(2) Where an order under subsection (1) above has been made with respect to a party to a marriage which has been dissolved or annulled, then, on the death of the other party to that marriage, the court shall not entertain an application under section 2 of this Act made by the first-mentioned party.

(3) Where an order under subsection (1) above has been made with respect to a party to a marriage the parties to which have been legally separated, then, if the other party to the marriage dies while the legal separation is in force, the court shall not entertain an application under section 2 of this Act made by the first-mentioned party.

**16. Variation and discharge of secured periodical payments orders made under Matrimonial Causes Act 1973**

(1) Where an application for an order under section 2 of this Act is made to the court by any person who was at the time of the death of the deceased entitled to payments from the deceased under a secured periodical payments order made under the Matrimonial Causes Act 1973, then, in the

proceedings on that application, the court shall have power, if an application is made under this section by that person or by the personal representative of the deceased, to vary or discharge that periodical payments order or to revive the operation of any provision thereof which has been suspended under section 31 of that Act.

(2) In exercising the powers conferred by this section the court shall have regard to all the circumstances of the case, including any order which the court proposes to make under section 2 or section 5 of this Act and any change (whether resulting from the death of the deceased or otherwise) in any of the matters to which the court was required to have regard when making the secured periodical payments order.

(3) The powers exercisable by the court under this section in relation to an order shall be exercisable also in relation to any instrument executed in pursuance of the order.

**17. Variation and revocation of maintenance agreements**

(1) Where an application for an order under section 2 of this Act is made to the court by any person who was at the time of the death of the deceased entitled to payments from the deceased under a maintenance agreement which provided for the continuation of payments under the agreement after the death of the deceased, then, in the proceedings on that application, the court shall have power, if an application is made under this section by that person or by the personal representative of the deceased, to vary or revoke that agreement.

(2) In exercising the powers conferred by this section the court shall have regard to all the circumstances of the case, including any order which the court proposes to make under section 2 or section 5 of this Act and any change (whether resulting from the death of the deceased or otherwise) in any of the circumstances in the light of which the agreement was made.

(3) If a maintenance agreement is varied by the court under this section the like consequences shall ensue as if the variation had been made immediately before the death of the deceased by agreement between the parties and for valuable consideration.

(4) In this section 'maintenance agreement', in relation to a deceased person, means any agreement made, whether in writing or not and whether before or after the commencement of this Act, by the deceased with any person with whom he entered into a marriage, being an agreement which contained provisions governing the rights and liabilities towards one another when living separately of the parties to that marriage (whether or not the marriage has been dissolved or annulled) in respect of the making or securing of payments or the disposition or use of any property, including such rights and liabilities with respect to the maintenance or education of any child, whether or not a child of the deceased or a person who was treated by the deceased as a child of the family in relation to that marriage.

### 18. Availability of court's powers under this Act in applications under ss 31 and 36 of the Matrimonial Causes Act 1973

(1) Where—

(*a*) a person against whom a secured periodical payments order was made under the Matrimonial Causes Act 1973 has died and an application is made under section 31(6) of that Act for the variation or discharge of that order or for the revival of the operation of any provision thereof which has been suspended, or

(*b*) a party to a maintenance agreement within the meaning of section 34 of that Act has died, the agreement being one which provides for the continuation of payments thereunder after the death of one of the parties, and an application is made under section 36(1) of that Act for the alteration of the agreement under section 35 thereof,

the court shall have power to direct that the application made under the said section 31(6) or 36(1) shall be deemed to have been accompanied by an application for an order under section 2 of this Act.

(2) Where the court gives a direction under subsection (1) above it shall have power, in the proceedings on the application under the said section 31(6) or 36(1), to make any order which the court would have had power to make under the provisions of this Act if the application under the said section 31(6) or 36(1), as the case may be, had been made jointly with an application for an order under the said section 2; and the court shall have power to give such consequential directions as may be necessary for enabling the court to exercise any of the powers available to the court under this Act in the case of an application for an order under section 2.

(3) Where an order made under section 15(1) of this Act is in force with respect to a party to a marriage, the court shall not give a direction under subsection (1) above with respect to any application made under the said section 31(6) or 36(1) by that party on the death of the other party.

*Miscellaneous and supplementary provisions*

### 19. Effect, duration and form of orders

(1) Where an order is made under section 2 of this Act then for all purposes, including the purposes of the enactments relating to inheritance tax, the will or the law relating to intestacy, or both the will and the law relating to intestacy, as the case may be, shall have effect and be deemed to have had effect as from the deceased's death subject to the provisions of the order.

(2) Any order made under section 2 or 5 of this Act in favour of—

(*a*) an applicant who was the former husband or former wife of the deceased, or

(*b*) an applicant who was the husband or wife of the deceased in a case where the marriage with the deceased was the subject of a decree of judicial separation and at the date of death the decree was in force and the separation was continuing,

shall, in so far as it provides for the making of periodical payments, cease to have effect on the remarriage of the applicant, except in relation to any arrears due under the order on the date of the marriage.

(3) A copy of every order made under this Act other than an order made under section 15(1) of this Act shall be sent to the principal registry of the Family Division for entry and filing, and a memorandum of the order shall be endorsed on, or permanently annexed to, the probate or letters of administration under which the estate is being administered.

**20. Provisions as to personal representatives**

(1) The provisions of this Act shall not render the personal representative of a deceased person liable for having distributed any part of the estate of the deceased, after the end of the period of six months from the date on which representation with respect to the estate of the deceased is first taken out, on the ground that he ought to have taken into account the possibility—

(*a*) that the court might permit the making of an application for an order under section 2 of this Act after the end of that period, or

(*b*) that, where an order has been made under the said section 2, the court might exercise in relation thereto the powers conferred on it by section 6 of this Act,

but this subsection shall not prejudice any power to recover, by reason of the making of an order under this Act, any part of the estate so distributed.

(2) Where the personal representative of a deceased person pays any sum directed by an order under section 5 of this Act to be paid out of the deceased's net estate, he shall not be under any liability by reason of that estate not being sufficient to make the payment, unless at the time of making the payment he has reasonable cause to believe that the estate is not sufficient.

(3) Where a deceased person entered into a contract by which he agreed to leave by his will any sum of money or other property to any person or by which he agreed that a sum of money or other property would be paid or transferred to any person out of his estate, then, if the personal representative of the deceased has reason to believe that the deceased entered into the contract with the intention of defeating an application for financial provision under this Act, he may, notwithstanding anything in that contract, postpone the payment of that sum of money or the transfer of that property until the expiration of the period of six months from the date on which representation with respect to the estate of the deceased is first taken out or, if during that period an application is made for an order under section 2 of this Act, until the determination of the proceedings on that application.

**21. Admissibility as evidence of statements made by deceased**

In any proceedings under this Act a statement made by the deceased, whether orally or in a document or otherwise, shall be admissible under section 2 of the Civil Evidence Act 1968 as evidence of any fact stated therein in like manner as if the statement were a statement falling within section 2(1) of that Act; and any reference in that Act to a statement admissible, or given or proposed to be given, in evidence under section 2 thereof or to the admissibility or the giving in evidence of a statement by virtue of that section or to any statement falling within section 2(1) of that Act shall be construed accordingly.

***

**23. Determination of date on which representation was first taken out**

In considering for the purposes of this Act when representation with respect to the estate of a deceased person was first taken out, a grant limited to settled land or to trust property shall be left out of account, and a grant limited to real estate or to personal estate shall be left out of account unless a grant limited to the remainder of the estate has previously been made or is made at the same time.

**24. Effect of this Act on s 46(1)(vi) of Administration of Estates Act 1925**

Section 46(1)(vi) of the Administration of Estates Act 1925, in so far as it provides for the devolution of property on the Crown, the Duchy of Lancaster or the Duke of Cornwall as bona vacantia, shall have effect subject to the provisions of this Act.

**25. Interpretation**

(1) In this Act—

'beneficiary', in relation to the estate of a deceased person, means—

(*a*) a person who under the will of the deceased or under the law relating to intestacy is beneficially interested in the estate or would be so interested if an order had not been made under this Act, and

(*b*) a person who has received any sum of money or other property which by virtue of section 8(1) or 8(2) of this Act is treated as part of the net estate of the deceased or would have received that sum or other property if an order had not been made under this Act;

'child' includes an illegitimate child and a child en ventre sa mère at the death of the deceased;

'the court' unless the context otherwise requires means the High Court, or where a county court has jurisdiction by virtue of section 22 of this Act, a county court;

'former wife' or 'former husband' means a person whose marriage with the deceased was during the lifetime of the deceased either—

(*a*) dissolved or annulled by a decree of divorce or a decree of nullity of marriage granted under the law of any part of the British Islands, or

(*b*) dissolved or annulled in any country or territory outside the British Islands by a divorce or annulment which is entitled to be recognised as valid by the law of England and Wales;

'net estate', in relation to a deceased person, means—

(*a*) all property of which the deceased had power to dispose by his will (otherwise than by virtue of a special power of appointment) less the amount of his funeral, testamentary and administration expenses, debts and liabilities, including any inheritance tax payable out of his estate on his death;

(*b*) any property in respect of which the deceased held a general power of appointment (not being a power exercisable by will) which has not been exercised;

(*c*) any sum of money or other property which is treated for the purposes of this Act as part of the net estate of the deceased by virtue of section 8(1) or (2) of this Act;

(*d*) any property which is treated for the purposes of this Act as part of the net estate of the deceased by virtue of an order made under section 9 of the Act;

(*e*) any sum of money or other property which is, by reason of a disposition or contract made by the deceased, ordered under section 10 or 11 of this Act to be provided for the purpose of the making of financial provision under this Act;

'property' includes any chose in action;

'reasonable financial provision' has the meaning assigned to it by section 1 of this Act;

'valuable consideration' does not include marriage or a promise of marriage;

'will' includes codicil.

(2) For the purposes of paragraph (*a*) of the definition of 'net estate' in subsection (1) above a person who is not of full age and capacity shall be treated as having power to dispose by will of all property of which he would have had power to dispose by will if he had been of full age and capacity.

(3) Any reference in this Act to provision out of the net estate of a deceased person includes a reference to provision extending to the whole of that estate.

(4) For the purposes of this Act any reference to a wife or husband shall be treated as including a reference to a person who in good faith entered into a void marriage with the deceased unless either—

(*a*) the marriage of the deceased and that person was dissolved or annulled during the lifetime of the deceased and the dissolution or annulment is recognised by the law of England and Wales, or

(*b*) that person has during the lifetime of the deceased entered into a later marriage.

(5) Any reference in this Act to remarriage or to a person who has remarried includes a reference to a marriage which is by law void or voidable or to a person who has entered into such a marriage, as the case may be, and a marriage shall be treated for the purposes of this Act as a remarriage, in relation to any party thereto, notwithstanding that the previous marriage of that party was void or voidable.

(6) Any reference in this Act to an order or decree made under the Matrimonial Causes Act 1973 or under any section of that Act shall be construed as including a reference to an order or decree which is deemed to have been made under that Act or under that section thereof, as the case may be.

(7) Any reference in this Act to any enactment is a reference to that enactment as amended by or under any subsequent enactment.

**26. Consequential amendments, repeals and transitional provisions**

(1) Section 36 of the Matrimonial Causes Act 1973 (which provides for the alteration of maintenance agreements by the High Court or a county court after the death of one of the parties) shall have effect subject to the following amendments (being amendments consequential on this Act), that is to say—

(*a*) in subsection (3) for the words 'section 7 of the Family Provision Act 1966' there shall be substituted the words 'section 22 of the Inheritance (Provision for Family and Dependants) Act 1975', for the words from 'the Inheritance (Family Provision) Act' to 'net estate' there shall be substituted the words 'that Act if the value of the property mentioned in that section' and for the words 'section 26 of the Matrimonial Causes Act 1965 (application for maintenance out of the deceased's estate by former spouse)' there shall be substituted the words 'section 2 of that Act';

(*b*) in subsection (7) for the words from 'section 7' to 'subsection (5)' there shall be substituted the words 'section 22 of the Inheritance (Provision for Family and Dependants) Act 1975 (which enables rules of court to provide for the transfer from a county court to the High Court or from the High Court to a county court of proceedings for an order under section 2 of that Act) and paragraphs (*a*) and (*b*) of subsection (4)' and for the words 'any such proceedings as are referred to in subsection (1) of that section' there shall be substituted the words 'proceedings for an order under section 2 of that Act'.

(2) Subject to the provisions of this section, the enactments specified in the Schedule to this Act are hereby repealed to the extent specified in the third column of the Schedule; and in paragraph 5(2) of Schedule 2 to the

Matrimonial Causes Act 1973 for the words 'that Act' there shall be substituted the words 'the Matrimonial Causes Act 1965'.

(3) The repeal of the said enactments shall not affect their operation in relation to any application made thereunder (whether before or after the commencement of this Act) with reference to the death of any person who died before the commencement of this Act.

(4) Without prejudice to the provisions of section 38 of the Interpretation Act 1889 (which relates to the effect of repeals) nothing in any repeal made by this Act shall affect any order made or direction given under any enactment repealed by this Act, and, subject to the provisions of this Act, every such order or direction (other than an order made under section 4A of the Inheritance (Family Provision) Act 1938 or section 28A of the Matrimonial Causes Act 1965) shall, if it is in force at the commencement of this Act or is made by virtue of subsection (3) above, continue in force as if it had been made under section 2(1)(*a*) of this Act, and for the purposes of section 6(7) of this Act the court in exercising its powers under that section in relation to an order continued in force by this subsection shall be required to have regard to any change in any of the circumstances to which the court would have been required to have regard when making that order if the order had been made with reference to the death of any person who died after the commencement of this Act.

**27. Short title, commencement and extent**

(1) This Act may be cited as the Inheritance (Provision for Family and Dependants) Act 1975.

(2) This Act does not extend to Scotland or Northern Ireland.

(3) This Act shall come into force on 1st April 1976.

SCHEDULE

ENACTMENTS REPEALED

| Chapter | Short Title | Extent of Repeal |
|---|---|---|
| 1938 c 72 | The Inheritance (Family Provision) Act 1938 | The whole Act |
| 1952 c 64 | The Intestates' Estates Act 1952 | Section 7 and Schedule 3 |
| 1965 c 72 | The Matrimonial Causes Act 1965 | Sections 26 to 28A and section 24(4) and (5) as applied by section 28(2) |
| 1966 c 35 | The Family Provision Act 1966 | The whole Act, except section 1 and subsections (1) and (3) of section 10 |
| 1969 c 46 | The Family Law Reform Act 1969 | Sections 5(1) and 18 |
| 1970 c 31 | The Administration of Justice Act 1970 | In Schedule 2, paragraph 16 |

| Chapter | Short Title | Extent of Repeal |
|---|---|---|
| 1970 c 33 | The Law Reform (Miscellaneous Provisions) Act 1970 | Section 6 |
| 1970 c 45 | The Matrimonial Proceedings and Property Act 1970 | Section 36 |
| 1971 c 23 | The Courts Act 1971 | Section 45(1)(*a*) |
| 1973 c 18 | The Matrimonial Causes Act 1973 | In section 50, in subsection (1)(*a*) the words from 'and sections 26' to the end of the paragraph, in subsection (1)(*d*) the words 'or sections 26 to 28A of the Matrimonial Causes Act 1965' and in subsection (2)(*a*) the words 'or under section 26 or 27 of the Matrimonial Causes Act 1965'<br>In Schedule 2, paragraph 5(1) and in paragraph 12 the words '(*a*) sections 26 to 28A of the Matrimonial Causes Act 1985' |
| 1975 c 7 | The Finances Act 1975 | In Schedule 12, paragraph 6 |

## INHERITANCE TAX ACT 1984, s 146

### 146. Inheritance (Provision for Family and Dependants) Act 1975

(1) Where an order is made under section 2 of the Inheritance (Provision for Family and Dependants) Act 1975 ('the 1975 Act') in relation to any property forming part of the net estate of a deceased person, then, without prejudice to section 19(1) of that Act, the property shall for the purposes of this Act be treated as if it had on his death devolved subject to the provisions of the order.

(2) Where an order is made under section 10 of the 1975 Act requiring a person to provide any money or other property by reason of a disposition made by the deceased, then—

(*a*) if that disposition was a chargeable transfer and the personal representatives of the deceased make a claim for the purpose—

(i) tax paid or payable on the value transferred by that chargeable transfer (whether or not by the claimants) shall be repaid to them by the Board or, as the case may be, shall not be payable, and

(ii) the rate or rates of tax applicable to the transfer of value made by the deceased on his death shall be determined as if the values previously trasnferred by chargeable transfers made by him were reduced by that value;

(*b*) the money or property shall be included in the deceased's estate for the purpose of the transfer of value made by him on his death.

(3) Where the money or other property ordered to be provided under section 10 of the 1975 Act is less than the maximum permitted by that section, subsection (2)(*a*) above shall have effect in relation to such part of the value there mentioned as is appropriate.

(4) The adjustment in consequence of the provisions of this section or of section 19(1) of the 1975 Act of the tax payable in respect of the transfer of value made by the deceased on his death shall not affect—

(*a*) the amount of any deduction to be made under section 8 of that Act in respect of tax borne by the person mentioned in subsection (3) of that section, or

(*b*) the amount of tax to which regard is to be had under section 9(2) of that Act;

and where a person is ordered under that Act to make a payment or transfer property by reason of his holding property treated as part of the deceased's net estate under section 8 or 9 and tax borne by him is taken into account for the purposes of the order, any repayment of that tax shall be made to the personal representatives of the deceased and not to that person.

(5) Tax repaid under paragraph (*a*)(i) of subsection (2) above shall be included in the deceased's estate for the purposes of the transfer of value made by him on his death; and tax repaid under that paragraph or under subsection (4) above shall form part of the deceased's net estate for the purposes of the 1975 Act.

(6) Anything which is done in compliance with an order under the 1975 Act or occurs on the coming into force of such an order, and which would (apart from this subsection) constitute an occasion on which tax is chargeable under any provision, other than section 79, of Chapter III of Part III of this Act, shall not constitute such an occasion; and where an order under the 1975 Act provides for property to be settled or for the variation of a settlement, and (apart from this subsection) tax would be charged under section 52(1) above on the coming into force of the order, section 52(1) shall not apply.

(7) In subsections (2)(*a*) and (5) above references to tax include references to interest on tax.

(8) Where an order is made staying or dismissing proceedings under the 1975 Act on terms set out in or scheduled to the order, this section shall have effect as if any of those terms which would have been included in an order under section 2 or 10 of that Act were provisions of such an order.

(9) In this section any reference to, or to any provision of, the 1975 Act includes a reference to, or to the corresponding provision of, the Inheritance (Provision for Family and Dependants) (Northern Ireland) Order 1979.

*Appendix 3*

# Statutory Provisions relating to Variations and Disclaimers

INHERITANCE TAX ACT 1984, ss 17, 142–5

**17. Changes in distribution of deceased's estate, etc**

None of the following is a transfer of value—

(*a*) a variation or disclaimer to which section 142(1) below applies;

(*b*) a transfer to which section 143 below applies;

(*c*) an election by a surviving spouse under section 47A of the Administration of Estates Act 1925;

(*d*) [*Applies to Scotland*]

*Changes in distribution of deceased's estate, etc*

**142. Alteration of dispositions taking effect on death**

(1) Where within the period of two years after a person's death—

(*a*) any of the dispositions (whether effected by will, under the law relating to intestacy or otherwise) of the property comprised in his estate immediately before his death are varied, or

(*b*) the benefit conferred by any of those dispositions is disclaimed,

by an instrument in writing made by the persons or any of the persons who benefit or would benefit under the dispositions, this Act shall apply as if the variation had been effected by the deceased or, as the case may be, the disclaimed benefit had never been conferred.

(2) Subsection (1) above shall not apply to a variation unless an election to that effect is made by written notice given to the Board within six months after the date of the instrument, or such longer time as the Board may allow, by—

(*a*) the person or persons making the instrument, and

(*b*) where the variation results in additional tax being payable, the personal representatives;

but personal representatives may decline to join in an election only if no, or no sufficient, assets are held by them in that capacity for discharging the additional tax.

(3) Subsection (1) above shall not apply to a variation or disclaimer made for any consideration in money or money's worth other than consideration consisting of the making, in respect of another of the dispositions, of a variation or disclaimer to which that subsection applies.

(4) Where a variation to which subsection (1) above applies results in property being held in trust for a person for a period which ends not more than two years after the death, this Act shall apply as if the disposition of the property that takes effect at the end of the period had had effect from the beginning of the period; but this subsection shall not affect the application of this Act in relation to any distribution or application of property occurring before that disposition takes effect.

(5) For the purposes of subsection (1) above the property comprised in a person's estate includes any excluded property but not any property to which he is treated as entitled by virtue of section 49(1) above or section 102 of the Finance Act 1986.

(6) Subsection (1) above applies whether or not the administration of the estate is complete or the property concerned has been distributed in accordance with the original dispositions.

(7) [*Applies to Scotland*]

**143. Compliance with testator's request**

Where a testator expresses a wish that property bequeathed by his will should be transferred by the legatee to other persons, and the legatee transfers any of the property in accordance with that wish within the period of two years after the death of the testator, this Act shall have effect as if the property transferred had been bequeathed by the will to the transferee.

**144. Distribution etc from property settled by will**

(1) This section applies where property comprised in a person's estate immediately before his death is settled by his will and, within the period of two years after his death and before any interest in possession has subsisted in the property, there occurs—

(*a*) an event on which tax would (apart from this section) be chargeable under any provision, other than section 64 or 79, of Chapter III of Part III of this Act, or

(*b*) an event on which tax would be so chargeable but for section 75 or 76 above or paragraph 16(1) of Schedule 4 to this Act.

(2) Where this section applies by virtue of an event within paragraph (*a*) of subsection (1) above, tax shall not be charged under the provision in question on that event; and in every case in which this section applies in relation to an event, this Act shall have effect as if the will had provided that on the testator's death the property should be held as it is held after the event.

**145. Redemption of surviving spouse's life interest**

Where an election is made by a surviving spouse under section 47A of the Administration of Estates Act 1925, this Act shall have effect as if the surviving spouse, instead of being entitled to the life interest, had been entitled to a sum equal to the capital value mentioned in that section.

## CAPITAL GAINS TAX ACT 1979, s 49(6)–(10)

**49. Death: general provisions**

(6) Subject to subsections (7) and (8) below, where within the period of two years after a person's death any of the dispositions (whether effected by will, under the law relating to intestacy or otherwise) of the property of which he was competent to dispose are varied, or the benefit conferred by any one of those dispositions is disclaimed, by an instrument in writing made by the persons or any of the persons who benefit or would benefit under the dispositions—

- (*a*) the variation or disclaimer shall not constitute a disposal for the purposes of this Act, and
- (*b*) this section shall apply as if the variation had been effected by the deceased or, as the case may be, the disclaimed benefit had never been conferred.

(7) Subsection (6) above does not apply to a variation unless the person or persons making the instrument so elect by written notice given to the Board within six months after the date of the instrument or such longer time as the Board may allow.

(8) Subsection (6) above does not apply to a variation or disclaimer made for any consideration in money or money's worth other than consideration consisting of the making of a variation or disclaimer in respect of another of the dispositions.

(9) Subsection (6) above applies whether or not the administration of the estate is complete or the property has been distributed in accordance with the original dispositions.

(10) In this section references to assets of which a deceased person was competent to dispose are references to assets of the deceased which (otherwise than in right of a power of appointment or of the testamentary power conferred by statute to dispose of entailed interests) he could, if of full age and capacity, have disposed of by his will, assuming that all the assets were situated in England and, if he was not domiciled in the United Kingdom, that he was domiciled in England, and include references to his severable share in any assets to which, immediately before his death, he was beneficially entitled as a joint tenant.

*Appendix 4*

# Statutory Provisions relating to Powers of Trustees

## TRUSTEE ACT 1925, ss 19, 31, 32

**19. Power to insure**

(1) A trustee may insure against loss or damage by fire any building or other insurable property to any amount, including the amount of any insurance already on foot, not exceeding three fourth parts of the full value of the building or property, and pay the premiums for such insurance out of the income thereof or out of the income of any other property subject to the same trusts without obtaining the consent of any person who may be entitled wholly or partly to such income.

(2) This section does not apply to any building or property which a trustee is bound forthwith to convey absolutely to any beneficiary upon being requested to do so.

**31. Power to apply income for maintenance and to accumulate surplus income during a minority**

(1) Where any property is held by trustees in trust for any person for any interest whatsoever, whether vested or contingent, then, subject to any prior interests or charges affecting that property—

(i) during the infancy of any such person, if his interest so long continues, the trustees may, at their sole discretion, pay to his parent or guardian, if any, or otherwise apply for or towards his maintenance, education, or benefit, the whole or such part, if any, of the income of that property as may, in all the circumstances, be reasonable, whether or not there is—

  (*a*) any other fund applicable to the same purpose; or

  (*b*) any person bound by law to provide for his maintenance or education; and

(ii) if such person on attaining the age of eighteen years has not a vested interest in such income, the trustees shall thenceforth pay the income of that property and of any accretion thereto under subsection (2) of this section to him, until he either attains a vested interest therein or dies, or until failure of his interest:

Provided that, in deciding whether the whole or any part of the income of the property is during a minority to be paid or applied for the purposes aforesaid, the trustees shall have regard to the age of the infant and his requirements and generally to the circumstances of the case, and in particular to what other income, if any, is applicable for the same purposes; and where trustees have notice that the income of more than one fund is applicable for those purposes, then, so far as practicable, unless the entire income of the funds is paid or applied as aforesaid or the court otherwise directs, a proportionate part only of the income of each fund shall be so paid or applied.

(2) During the infancy of any such person, if his interest so long continues, the trustees shall accumulate all the residue of that income in the way of compound interest by investing the same and the resulting income thereof from time to time in authorised investments, and shall hold those accumulations as follows:

(i) If any such person—

(*a*) attains the age of eighteen years, or marries under that age, and his interest in such income during his infancy or until his marriage is a vested interest; or

(*b*) on attaining the age of eighteen years or on marriage under that age becomes entitled to the property from which such income arose in fee simple, absolute or determinable, or absolutely, or for an entailed interest;

the trustees shall hold the accumulations in trust for such person absolutely, but without prejudice to any provision with respect thereto contained in any settlement by him made under any statutory powers during his infancy, and so that the receipt of such person after marriage, and though still an infant, shall be a good discharge; and

(ii) In any other case the trustees shall, notwithstanding that such person had a vested interest in such income, hold the accumulations as an accretion to the capital of the property from which such accumulation arose, and as one fund with such capital for all purposes, and so that, if such property is settled land, such accumulations shall be held upon the same trusts as if the same were capital money arising therefrom;

but the trustees may, at any time during the infancy of such person if his interest so long continues, apply those accumulations, or any part thereof, as if they were income arising in the then current year.

(3) This section applies in the case of a contingent interest only if the limitation or trust carries the intermediate income of the property, but it applies to a future or contingent legacy by the parent of, or a person standing in loco parentis to, the legatee, if and for such period as, under the

general law, the legacy carries interest for the maintenance of the legatee, and in any such case as last aforesaid the rate of interest shall (if the income available is sufficient, and subject to any rules ofcourt to the contrary) be five pounds per centum per annum.

(4) This section applies to a vested annuity in like manner as if the annuity were the income of property held by trustees in trust to pay the income thereof to the annuitant for the same period for which the annuity is payable, save that in any case accumulations made during the infancy of the annuitant shall be held in trust for the annuitant or his personal representatives absolutely.

(5) This section does not apply where the instrument, if any, under which the interest arises came into operation before the commencement of this Act.

**32. Power of advancement**

(1) Trustees may at any time or times pay or apply any capital money subject to a trust, for the advancement or benefit, in such manner as they may, in their absolute discretion, think fit, of any person entitled to the capital of the trust property or of any share thereof, whether absolutely or contingently on his attaining any specified age or on the occurrence of any other event, or subject to a gift over on his death under any specified age or on the occurrence of any other event, and whether in possession or in remainder or reversion, and such payment or application may be made notwithstanding that the interest of such person is liable to be defeated by the exercise of a power of appointment or revocation, or to be diminished by the increase of the class to which he belongs:

Provided that—

(*a*) the money so paid or applied for the advancement or benefit of any person shall not exceed altogether in amount one-half of the presumptive or vested share or interest of that person in the trust property; and

(*b*) if that person is or becomes absolutely and indefeasibly entitled to a share in the trust property the money so paid or applied shall be brought into account as part of such share; and

(*c*) no such payment or application shall be made so as to prejudice any person entitled to any prior life or other interest, whether vested or contingent, in the money paid or applied unless such person is in existence and of full age and consents in writing to such payment or application.

(2) This section applies only where the trust property consists of money or securities or of property held upon trust for sale calling in and conversion, and such money or securities, or the proceeds of such sale calling in and conversion are not by statute or in equity considered as land,

or applicable as capital money for the purposes of the Settled Land Act 1925.

(3) This section does not apply to trusts constituted or created before the commencement of this Act.

*Appendix 5*

# Statutory Provisions relating to Accumulation and Maintenance Settlements

INHERITANCE TAX ACT 1984, s 71

**71. Accumulation and maintenance trusts**

(1) Subject to subsection (2) below, this section applies to settled property if—

(*a*) one or more persons (in this section referred to as beneficiaries) will, on or before attaining a specified age not exceeding twenty-five, become beneficially entitled to it or to an interest in possession in it, and

(*b*) no interest in possession subsists in it and the income from it is to be accumulated so far as not applied for the maintenance, education or benefit of a beneficiary.

(2) This section does not apply to settled property unless either—

(*a*) not more than twenty-five years have elapsed since the commencement of the settlement or, if it was later, since the time (or latest time) when the conditions stated in paragraphs (*a*) and (*b*) of subsection (1) above became satisfied with respect to the property, or

(*b*) all the persons who are or have been beneficiaries are or were either—

(i) grandchildren of a common grandparent, or

(ii) children, widows or widowers of such grandchildren who were themselves beneficiaries but died before the time when, had they survived, they would have become entitled as mentioned in subsection (1)(*a*) above.

(3) Subject to subsections (4) and (5) below, there shall be a charge to tax under this section—

(*a*) where settled property ceases to be property to which this section applies, and

(*b*) in a case in which paragraph (*a*) above does not apply, where the trustees make a disposition as a result of which the value of settled property to which this section applies is less than it would be but for the disposition.

(4) Tax shall not be charged under this section—

(*a*) on a beneficiary's becoming beneficially entitled to, or to an interest in possession in, settled property on or before attaining the specified age, or

(*b*) on the death of a beneficiary before attaining the specified age.

(5) Subsections (3) to (8) and (10) of section 70 above shall apply for the purposes of this section as they apply for the purposes of that section (with the substitution of a reference to subsection (3)(*b*) above for the reference in section 70(4) to section 70(2)(*b*)).

(6) Where the conditions stated in paragraphs (*a*) and (*b*) of subsection (1) above were satisfied on 15th April 1976 with respect to property comprised in a settlement which commenced before that day, subsection (2)(*a*) above shall have effect with the substitution of a reference to that day for the reference to the commencement of the settlement, and the condition stated in subsection (2)(*b*) above shall be treated as satisfied if—

(*a*) it is satisfied in respect of the period beginning with 15th April 1976, or

(*b*) it is satisfied in respect of the period beginning with 1st April 1977 and either there was no beneficiary living on 15th April 1976 or the beneficiaries on 1st April 1977 included a living beneficiary, or

(*c*) there is no power under the terms of the settlement whereby it could have become satisfied in respect of the period beginning with 1st April 1977, and the trusts of the settlement have not been varied at any time after 15th April 1976.

(7) In subsection (1) above 'persons' includes unborn persons; but the conditions stated in that subsection shall be treated as not satisfied unless there is or has been a living beneficiary.

(8) For the purposes of this section a person's children shall be taken to include his illegitimate children, his adopted children and his stepchildren.

*Appendix 6*

# Amendments to Wills Act 1837 and other Provisions as to Rectification, Interpretation and Execution of Wills

ADMINISTRATION OF JUSTICE ACT 1982, ss 17–22

**17. Relaxation of formal requirements for making wills**

The following section shall be substituted for section 9 of the Wills Act 1837—

'Signing and attestation of wills.

**9.** No will shall be valid unless—

(*a*) it is in writing, and signed by the testator, or by some other person in his presence and by his direction; and

(*b*) it appears that the testator intended by his signature to give effect to the will; and

(*c*) the signature is made or acknowledged by the testator in the presence of two or more witnesses present at the same time; and

(*d*) each witness either—

(i) attests and signs the will; or

(ii) acknowledges his signature,

in the presence of the testator (but not necessarily in the presence of any other witness),

but no form of attestation shall be necessary.'

**18. Effect of marriage or its termination on wills**

(1) The following section shall be substituted for section 18 of the Wills Act 1837—

'Wills to be revoked by marriage except in certain cases.

**18.**—(1) Subject to subsections (2) to (4) below, a will shall be revoked by the testator's marriage.

(2) A disposition in a will in exercise of a power of appointment shall take effect notwithstanding the testator's subsequent marriage unless the property so

appointed would in default of appointment pass to his personal representatives.

(3) Where it appears from a will that at the time it was made the testator was expecting to be married to a particular person and that he intended that the will should not be revoked by the marriage, the will shall not be revoked by his marriage to that person.

(4) Where it appears from a will that at the time it was made the testator was expecting to be married to a particular person and that he intended that a disposition in the will should not be revoked by his marriage to that person,—

(*a*) that disposition shall take effect notwithstanding the marriage; and

(*b*) any other disposition in the will shall take effect also, unless it appears from the will that the testator intended the disposition to be revoked by the marriage.'

(2) The following section shall be inserted after that section—

'Effect of dissolution or annulment of marriage on wills.

**18A.**—(1) Where, after a testator has made a will, a decree of a court dissolves or annuls his marriage or declares it void,—

(*a*) the will shall take effect as if any appointment of the former spouse as an executor or as the executor and trustee of the will were omitted; and

(*b*) any devise or bequest to the former spouse shall lapse,

except in so far as a contrary intention appears by the will.

(2) Subsection (1)(*b*) above is without prejudice to any right of the former spouse to apply for financial provision under the Inheritance (Provision for Family and Dependants) Act 1975.

(3) Where—

(*a*) by the terms of a will an interest in remainder is subject to a life interest; and

(*b*) the life interest lapses by virtue of subsection (1)(*b*) above,

the interest in remainder shall be treated as if it had not been subject to the life interest and, if it was contingent upon the termination of the life interest, as if it had not been so contingent.'

**19. Gifts to children etc who predecease testator**

The following section shall be substituted for section 33 of the Wills Act 1837—

'Gifts to children or other issue who leave issue living at the testator's death shall not lapse.

**33.**—(1) Where—

(*a*) a will contains a devise or bequest to a child or remoter descendant of the testator; and

(*b*) the intended beneficiary dies before the testator, leaving issue; and

(*c*) issue of the intended beneficiary are living at the testator's death,

then, unless a contrary intention appears by the will, the devise or bequest shall take effect as a devise or bequest to the issue living at the testator's death.

(2) Where—

(*a*) a will contains a devise or bequest to a class of persons consisting of children or remoter descendants of the testator; and

(*b*) a member of the class dies before the testator, leaving issue; and

(*c*) issue of that member are living at the testator's death,

then, unless a contrary intention appears by the will, the devise or bequest shall take effect as if the class included the issue of its deceased member living at the testator's death.

(3) Issue shall take under this section through all degrees, according to their stock, in equal shares if more than one, any gift or share which their parent would have taken and so that no issue shall take whose parent is living at the testator's death and so capable of taking.

(4) For the purposes of this section—

(*a*) the illegitimacy of any person is to be disregarded; and

(*b*) a person conceived before the testator's death and born living thereafter is to be taken to have been living at the testator's death.'

*Rectification and interpretation of wills*

**20. Rectification**

(1) If a court is satisfied that a will is so expressed that it fails to carry out the testator's intentions, in consequence—

(*a*) of a clerical error; or

(*b*) of a failure to understand his instructions.
it may order that the will shall be rectified so as to carry out his intentions.

(2) An application for an order under this section shall not, except with the permission of the court, be made after the end of the period of six months from the date on which representation with respect to the estate of the deceased is first taken out.

(3) The provisions of this section shall not render the personal representatives of a deceased person liable for having distributed any part of the estate of the deceased, after the end of the period of six months from the date on which representation with respect to the estate of the deceased is first taken out, on the ground that they ought to have taken into account the possibility that the court might permit the making of an application for an order under this section after the end of that period; but this subsection shall not prejudice any power to recover, by reason of the making of an order under this section, any part of the estate so distributed.

(4) In considering for the purposes of this section when representation with respect to the estate of a deceased person was first taken out, a grant limited to settled land or to trust property shall be left out of account, and a grant limited to real estate or to personal estate shall be left out of account unless a grant limited to the remainder of the estate has previously been made or is made at the same time.

**21. Interpretation of wills—general rules as to evidence**

(1) This section applies to a will—

(*a*) in so far as any part of it is meaningless;

(*b*) in so far as the language used in any part of it is ambiguous on the face of it;

(*c*) in so far as evidence, other than evidence of the testator's intention, shows that the language used in any part of it is ambiguous in the light of surrounding circumstances.

(2) In so far as this section applies to a will extrinsic evidence, including evidence of the testator's intention, may be admitted to assist in its interpretation.

**22. Presumption as to effect of gifts to spouses**

Except where a contrary intention is shown it shall be presumed that if a testator devises or bequeaths property to his spouse in terms which in themselves would give an absolute interest to the spouse, but by the same instrument purports to give his issue an interest in the same property, the gift to the spouse is absolute notwithstanding the purported gift to the issue.

NON-CONTENTIOUS PROBATE RULES 1987, R 12

**12. Evidence as to due execution of will**

(1) Subject to paragraphs (2) and (3) below, where a will contains no attestation clause or the attestation clause is insufficient, or where it appears to the registrar that there is doubt about the due execution of the will, he shall before admitting it to proof require an affidavit as to due execution from one or more of the attesting witnesses or, if no attesting witness is conveniently available, from any other person who was present when the will was executed; and if the registrar, after considering the evidence, is satisfied that the will was not duly executed, he shall refuse probate and mark the will accordingly.

(2) If no affidavit can be obtained in accordance with paragraph (1) above, the registrar may accept evidence on affidavit from any person he may think fit to show that the signature on the will is in the handwriting of the deceased, or of any other matter which may raise a presumption in favour of due execution of the will, and may if he thinks fit require that notice of the application be given to any person who may be prejudiced by the will.

(3) A registrar may accept a will for proof without evidence as aforesaid if he is satisfied that the distribution of the estate is not thereby affected.

*Appendix 7*

# Statutory Provisions relating to Potentially Exempt Transfers

## FINANCE ACT 1986, s 101 AND SCHEDULE 19

### 101. Lifetime transfers potentially exempt etc

(1) The 1984 Act shall have effect subject to the amendments in Part I of Schedule 19 to this Act, being amendments—

(*a*) removing liability for tax on certain transfers of value where the transfer occurs at least seven years before the transferor's death;

(*b*) providing for one Table of rates of tax;

(*c*) abolishing exemptions for mutual transfers;

(*d*) making provision with respect to the amounts of tax to be charged on transfers occurring before the death of the transferor;

(*e*) making provision with respect to the application of relief under Chapter I (business property) and Chapter II (agricultural property) of Part V of the 1984 Act to such transfers; and

(*f*) reducing the period during which the values transferred by chargeable transfers are aggregated from ten years to seven;

and amendments making provisions consequential on or incidental to the matters referred to above and to sections 102 and 103 below.

(2) In consequence of the amendments effected by Part I of Schedule 19 to this Act, section 79 of the Finance Act 1980 (capital gains tax: general relief for gifts). . . .[1]

(3) Part I of Schedule 19 to this Act has effect subject to Part II of that Schedule with respect to transfers of value made, and other events occurring, on or after 18th March 1986.

(4) The transitional provisions in Part II of Schedule 19 to this Act shall have effect.

1 FA 1980, s 79 repealed by FA 1989, s 124.

Section 101

# SCHEDULE 19

## INHERITANCE TAX

### PART I
### AMENDMENTS OF 1984 ACT

1. After section 3 there shall be inserted the following section—

**'3A. Potentially exempt transfers**

(1) Any reference in this Act to a potentially exempt transfer is a reference to a transfer of value—

(*a*) which is made by an individual on or after 18th March 1986; and

(*b*) which, apart from this section, would be a chargeable transfer (or to the extent to which, apart from this section, it would be such a transfer); and

(*c*) to the extent that it constitutes either a gift to another individual or a gift into an accumulation and maintenance trust or a disabled trust;

but this subsection has effect subject to any provision of this Act which provides that a disposition (or transfer of value) of a particular description is not a potentially exempt transfer.

(2) Subject to subsection (6) below, a transfer of value falls within subsection (1)(*c*) above, as a gift to another individual—

(*a*) to the extent that the value transferred is attributable to property which, by virtue of the transfer, becomes comprised in the estate of that other individual, ...[1] or

(*b*) so far as that value is not attributable to property which becomes comprised in the estate of another person, to the extent that, by virtue of the transfer, the estate of that other individual is increased ...[1]

(3) Subject to subsection (6) below, a transfer of value falls within subsection (1)(*c*) above, as a gift into an accumulation and maintenance trust or a disabled trust, to the extent that the value transferred is attributable to property which, by virtue of the transfer, becomes settled property to which section 71 or 89 of this Act applies.

(4) A potentially exempt transfer which is made seven years or more before the death of the transferor is an exempt transfer and any other potentially exempt transfer is a chargeable transfer.

(5) During the period beginning on the date of a potentially exempt transfer and ending immediately before—

(*a*) the seventh anniversary of that date, or

(*b*) if it is earlier, the death of the transferor,

it shall be assumed for the purposes of this Act that the transfer will prove to be an exempt transfer.

(6) Where, under any provision of this Act other than section 52[2], tax is in any circumstances to be charged as if a transfer of value had been made, that transfer shall be taken to be a transfer which is not a potentially exempt transfer.

(7) In the application of this section to an event on the happening of which tax is chargeable under section 52 below, the reference in subsection (1)(*a*) above to the individual by whom the transfer of value is made is a reference to the person who, by virtue of section 3(4) above, is treated as the transferor.'[3]

---

1 Words omitted by F(No 2)A 1987, s 96(2)(*a*) and (*b*).
2 Words inserted by F(No 2)A 1987, s 96(2)(*c*).
3 Subsection (7) added by F(No 2)A 1987, s 96(3).

2.—(1) In section 7 (rates of tax), in subsection (1)—

(*a*) at the beginning there shall be inserted the words 'Subject to subsections (2), (4) and (5) below';
(*b*) for the words 'ten years' there shall be substituted 'seven years'; and
(*c*) the word 'appropriate' shall be omitted.

(2) For subsection (2) of that section there shall be substituted the following subsection—

> '(2) Except as provided by subsection (4) below, the tax charged on the value transferred by a chargeable transfer made before the death of the transferor shall be charged at one-half of the rate or rates referred to in subsection (1) above.'

(3) In subsection (3) of that section for the words 'each of the Tables' there shall be substituted 'the Table'.

(4) After subsection (3) of that section there shall be inserted the following subsections—

> '(4) Subject to subsection (5) below, subsection (2) above does not apply in the case of a chargeable transfer made at any time within the period of seven years ending with the death of the transferor but, in the case of a chargeable transfer made within that period but more than three years before the death, the tax charged on the value transferred shall be charged at the following percentage of the rate or rates referred to in subsection (1) above—
>
> (*a*) where the transfer is made more than three but not more than four years before the death, 80 per cent;
> (*b*) where the transfer is made more than four but not more than five years before the death, 60 per cent;
> (*c*) where the transfer is made more than five but not more than six years before the death, 40 per cent; and

(*d*) where the transfer is made more than six but not more than seven years before the death, 20 per cent.

(5) If, in the case of a chargeable transfer made before the death of the transferor, the tax which would fall to be charged in accordance with subsection (4) above is less than the tax which would have been chargeable (in accordance with subsection (2) above) if the transferor had not died within the period of seven years beginning with the date of the transfer, subsection (4) above shall not apply in the case of that transfer.'

3.—(1) In section 8 (indexation) in subsection (1) for the words 'new Tables for the Tables' there shall be substituted 'a new Table for the Table'.

(2) After subsection (1) of that section there shall be inserted the following subsection—[1]

(3) In subsection (2) of that section for the word 'Tables', in each place where it occurs, there shall be substituted 'Table' and for the words 'they replace' there shall be substituted 'it replaces'.

(4) In subsection (4) of that section, for the word 'Tables' there shall be substituted 'Table'.

---

1 Subsection 1(A) repealed by FA 1988, s 136(3) in relation to transfers of value made after 14 March 1988.

4. In section 9 (transitional provisions on reduction of tax) for the words 'new Tables' there shall be substituted 'a new Table'.

5. In section 19 (annual exemption), after subsection (3) there shall be inserted the following subsection—

'(3A) A transfer of value which is potentially exempt transfer—

(*a*) shall in the first instance be left out of account for the purposes of subsections (1) to (3) above; and

(*b*) if it proves to be a chargeable transfer, shall for the purposes of those subsections be taken into account as if, in the year in which it was made, it was made later than any transfer of value which was not a potentially exempt transfer.'

6. After section 26 there shall be inserted the following section—

**'26A. Potentially exempt transfer of property subsequently held for national purposes etc**

A potentially exempt transfer which would (apart from this section) have proved to be a chargeable transfer shall be an exempt transfer to the extent that the value transferred by it is attributable to property which has been or could be designated under section 31(1) below and which, during the period beginning with the date of the transfer and ending with the death of the transferor,—

(*a*) has been disposed of by sale by private treaty to a body mentioned in Schedule 3 to this Act or has been disposed of to such a body otherwise than by sale, or

(*b*) has been disposed of in pursuance of section 230 below.'

7. In section 30 (conditionally exempt transfers) after subsection (3) there shall be inserted the following subsections—

'(3A) The provisions of this section shall be disregarded in determining under section 3A above whether a transfer of value is a potentially exempt transfer.

(3B) No claim may be made under subsection (1) above with respect to a potentially exempt transfer until the transferor has died.

(3C) Subsection (1) above shall not apply to a potentially exempt transfer to the extent that the value transferred by it is attributable to property which has been disposed of by sale during the period beginning with the date of the transfer and ending with the death of the transferor.'

8.—(1) In section 31 (designation and undertakings) after subsection (1) there shall be inserted the following subsection—

'(1A) Where the transfer of value in relation to which the claim for designation is made is a potentially exempt transfer which (apart from section 30 above) has proved to be a chargeable transfer, the question whether any property is appropriate for designation under this section shall be determined by reference to circumstances existing after the death of the transferor.'

(2) After subsection (4F) of that section there shall be inserted the following subsection—

'(4G) In a case where—

(*a*) the transfer of value in question is a potentially exempt transfer which (apart from section 30 above) has proved to be a chargeable transfer, and

(*b*) at the time of the transferor's death an undertaking by such a person as is mentioned in section 30(1)(*b*) above given under paragraph 3(3) of Schedule 4 to this Act or under section 147 of the Capital Gains Tax Act 1979 is in force with respect to any property to which the value transferred by the transfer is attributable,

that undertaking shall be treated for the purposes of this Chapter as an undertaking given under section 30 above.'

9. In section 32 (chargeable events) in subsection (1) after the words 'after the transfer' there shall be inserted '(or, if the transfer was a potentially exempt transfer, after the death of the transferor)'.

10. In section 32A (associated properties) in subsection (2) after the words 'after the transfer' there shall be inserted '(or, if the transfer was a potentially exempt transfer, after the death of the transferor)'.

11.—(1) In section 33 (amount of charge in relation to conditionally exempt transfers) in subsection (1)(*b*)—

(*a*) in sub-paragraph (i) for the words 'under the second Table in Schedule 1 to this Act' there shall be substituted 'in accordance with section 7(2) above'; and

(*b*) in sub-paragraph (ii) for the words 'under the appropriate Table' there shall be substituted 'in accordance with the appropriate provision of section 7 above'.

(2) For subsection (2) of that section there shall be substituted the following subsections—

'(2) For the purposes of subsection (1)(*b*)(ii) above the appropriate provision of section 7 above is—

(*a*) if the conditionally exempt transfer by the relevant person was made on death (but the property was not treated as forming part of his estate immediately before his death only by virtue of section 102(3) of the Finance Act 1986), subsection (1) of section 7; and

(*b*) in any other case, subsection (2) of section 7.

(2A) The rate or rates of tax determined under subsection (1)(*b*)(i) above in respect of any chargeable event shall not be affected by the death of the relevant person after that event.'.

(3) In subsection (7) of that section at the beginning there shall be inserted the words 'Subject to subsection (8) below'.

(4) After that subsection there shall be added the following subsection—

'(8) Where after a conditionally exempt transfer of any property there is a potentially exempt transfer the value transferred by which is wholly or partly attributable to that property and either—

(*a*) the potentially exempt transfer is a chargeable event with respect to the property, or

(*b*) after the potentially exempt transfer, but before the death of the person who is the transferor in relation to the potentially exempt transfer, a chargeable event occurs with respect to the property,

the tax charged in accordance with this section by reference to that chargeable event shall be allowed as a credit against any tax which may become chargeable, by reason of the potentially exempt transfer proving to be a chargeable transfer, on so much of the value transferred by that transfer as is attributable to the property; and subsection (7) above shall not apply with respect to any tax so becoming chargeable.'

12. In section 35 (conditional exemption on death before 7th April 1976) in subsection (3) for the words 'section 33(7) above, the reference' there shall be substituted 'section 33(7) and (8) above, references', and for the words 'includes a reference' there shall be substituted 'include references'.

13. In section 38 (attribution of value to specific gifts) in subsection (6) after the words 'section 5(5) above' there shall be inserted 'or by virtue of section 103 of the Finance Act 1986' and at the end of that subsection there shall be added 'and, to the extent that any liability of the transferor is abated under the said section 103, that liability shall be treated as a specific gift'.

14. ...[1]

15. ...[1]

---

1 Words added by paras 14 and 15 have been omitted by F(No 2)A 1987, s 96(4) and (5).

16.—(1) In section 66 (rate of ten-yearly charge) in subsection (3)(*b*) for the words 'preceding ten years' there shall be substituted 'preceding seven years'.

(2) For paragraph (*c*) of subsection (3) of that section there shall be substituted—

> '(*c*) on which tax is charged in accordance with section 7(2) of this Act'.

(3) In subsection (5)(*a*) of that section for the word 'ten' there shall be substituted 'seven'.

17. In section 67 (added property etc.) in subsections (3)(*b*) and (4) for the words 'ten' there shall be substituted 'seven'.

18.—(1) In section 68 (rate before first ten-year anniversary) in subsection (4)(*b*) for the word 'ten', in both places where it occurs, there shall be substituted 'seven'.

(2) For paragraph (*c*) of subsection (4) and for paragraph (*c*) of subsection (6) of that section there shall be substituted—

> '(*c*) on which tax is charged in accordance with section 7(2) of this Act'.

(3) In subsection (6)(*b*) of that section—

(*a*) for the word 'ten', in the first place where it occurs, there shall be substituted 'seven'; and

(*b*) in sub-paragraph (i) for the words 'that period of ten years' there shall be substituted 'the period of ten years ending with that day'.

19.—(1) In section 78 (conditionally exempt occasions) in subsection (4) for the words from 'and the appropriate Table' to the end there shall be substituted 'and the appropriate provision of section 7 for the purposes of section 33(1)(*b*)(ii) is, if the settlement was created on his death, subsection (1) and, if not, subsection (2).'

(2) In subsection (5) of that section, in the substituted sub-paragraph (ii) for section 33(1)(*b*), for the words 'under the appropriate Table' there shall be substituted 'in accordance with the appropriate provision of section 7 above.'

20. At the end of section 98 (effect of alteration of capital of close company etc.) there shall be added the following subsection—

'(3) The disposition referred to in subsection (1) above shall be taken to be one which is not a potentially exempt transfer.'

21. After section 113 there shall be inserted the following sections—

**'113A. Transfers within seven years before death of transferor**

(1) Where any part of the value transferred by a potentially exempt transfer which proves to be a chargeable transfer would (apart from this section) be reduced in accordance with the preceding provisions of this Chapter, it shall not be so reduced unless the conditions in subsection (3) below are satisfied.

(2) Where—

(*a*) any part of the value transferred by any chargeable transfer, other than a potentially exempt transfer, is reduced in accordance with the preceding provisions of this Chapter, and

(*b*) the transfer is made within seven years of the death of the transferor,

then, unless the conditions in subsection (3) below are satisfied, the additional tax chargeable by reason of the death shall be calculated as if the value transferred had not been so reduced.

(3) The conditions referred to in subsections (1) and (2) above are—

(*a*) that the original property was owned by the transferee throughout the period beginning with the date of the chargeable transfer and ending with the death of the transferor; and

(*b*) except to the extent that the original property consists of shares or securities to which subsection (3A) below applies[1] that, in relation to a notional transfer of value made by the transferee immediately before the death, the original property would (apart from section 106 above) be relevant business property.

(3A) This subsection applies to shares or securities—

(*a*) which were quoted at the time of the chargeable transfer referred to in subsection (1) or subsection (2) above; or

(*b*) which fell within paragraph (*b*) of section 105(1) above in relation to that transfer and were unquoted throughout the period referred to in subsection (3)(*a*) above.[1]

(4) If the transferee has died before the transferor, the reference in subsection (3) above to the death of the transferor shall have effect as a reference to the death of the transferee.

(5) If the conditions in subsection (3) above are satisfied only with respect to part of the original property, then,—

(*a*) in a case falling within subsection (1) above, only a proportionate part of so much of the value transferred as is attributable to the original property shall be reduced in accordance with the preceding provisions of this Chapter, and

(*b*) in a case falling within subsection (2) above, the additional tax shall be calculated as if only a proportionate part of so much of the value transferred as was attributable to the original property had been so reduced.

(6) Where any shares owned by the transferee immediately before the death in question—

(*a*) would under any of the provisions of sections 77 to 86 of the Capital Gains Tax Act 1979 be identified with the original property (or part of it), or

(*b*) were issued to him in consideration of the transfer of a business or interest in a business consisting of the original property (or part of it),

they shall be treated for the purposes of this section as if they were the original property (or that part of it).

(7) This section has effect subject to section 113B below.

(8) In this section—

'the original property' means the property which was relevant business property in relation to the chargeable transfer referred to in subsection (1) or subsection (2) above; and

'the transferee' means the person whose property the original property became on that chargeable transfer or, where on the transfer the original property became or remained settled property in which no qualifying interest in possession (within the meaning of Chapter III of Part III of this Act) subsists, the trustees of the settlement.

---

1 Words inserted into subsection (3)(*b*) and subsection (3A) added by FA 1987, Sched 8, para 8(1) and (2).

**113B. Application of section 113A to replacement property**

(1) Subject to subsection (2) below, this section applies where—

(*a*) the transferee has disposed of all or part of the original property before the death of the transferor; and

(*b*) the whole of the consideration received by him for the disposal has been applied by him in acquiring other property (in this section referred to as 'the replacement property').

(2) This section does not apply unless—

(*a*) the replacement property is acquired, or a binding contract for its acquisition is entered into, within twelve months after the disposal of the original property (or, as the case may be, the part concerned); and

(*b*) the disposal and acquisition are both made in transactions at arm's length or on terms such as might be expected to be included in a transaction at arm's length.

(3) Where this section applies, the conditions in section 113A(3) above shall be taken to be satisfied in relation to the original property (or, as the case may be, the part concerned) if—

(*a*) the replacement property is owned by the transferee immediately before the death of the transferor; and

(*b*) throughout the period beginning with the date of the chargeable transfer and ending with the death (disregarding any period between the disposal and acquisition) either the original property or the replacement property was owned by the transferee; and

(*c*) in relation to a notional transfer of value made by the transferee immediately before the death, the replacement property would (apart from section 106 above) be relevant business property.

(4) If the transferee has died before the transferor, any reference in subsections (1) to (3) above to the death of the transferor shall have effect as a reference to the death of the transferee.

(5) In any case where—

(*a*) all or part of the original property has been disposed of before the death of the transferor or is excluded by section 113 above from being relevant business property in relation to the notional transfer of value referred to in section 113A(3)(*b*) above, and

(*b*) the replacement property is acquired, or a binding contract for its acquisition is entered into, after the death of the transferor but within twelve months after the disposal of the original property or part, and

(*c*) the transferor dies before the transferee,

subsection (3) above shall have effect with the omission of paragraph (*a*), and as if any reference to a time immediately before the death of the transferor or to the death were a reference to the time when the replacement property is acquired.

(6) Section 113A(6) above shall have effect in relation to the replacement property as it has effect in relation to the original property.

(7) Where a binding contract for the disposal of any property is entered into at any time before the disposal of the property, the disposal shall be regarded for the purposes of subsections (2)(*a*) and (5)(*b*) above as taking place at that time.

(8) In this section 'the original property' and 'the transferee' have the same meaning as in section 113A above.'

22. After section 124 there shall be inserted the following sections—

**'124A. Transfers within seven years before death of transferor**

(1) Where any part of the value transferred by a potentially exempt transfer which proves to be a chargeable transfer would (apart from this section) be reduced in accordance with the preceding provisions of this Chapter, it shall not be so reduced unless the conditions in subsection (3) below are satisfied.

(2) Where—

(*a*) any part of the value transferred by any chargeable transfer, other than a potentially exempt transfer, is reduced in accordance with the preceding provisions of this Chapter, and

(*b*) the transfer is made within seven years of the death of the transferor,

then, unless the conditions in subsection (3) below are satisfied, the additional tax chargeable by reason of the death shall be calculated as if the value transferred had not been so reduced.

(3) The conditions referred to in subsections (1) and (2) above are—

(*a*) that the original property was owned by the transferee throughout the period beginning with the date of the chargeable transfer and ending with the death of the transferor (in this subsection referred to as 'the relevant period') and it is not at the time of the death subject to a binding contract for sale; and

(*b*) except in a case falling within paragraph (*c*) below, that the original property is agricultural property immediately before the death and has been occupied (by the transferee or another) for the purposes of agriculture throughout the relevant period; and

(*c*) where the original property consists of shares in or securities of a company, that throughout the relevant period the agricultural property to which section 116 above applied by virtue of section 122(1) above on the chargeable transfer was owned by the company and occupied (by the company or another) for the purposes of agriculture.

(4) If the transferee has died before the transferor, the reference in subsection (3) above to the death of the transferor shall have effect as a reference to the death of the transferee.

(5) If the conditions in subsection (3) above are satisfied only with respect to part of the original property, then—

(*a*) in a case falling within subsection (1) above, only a proportionate part of so much of the value transferred as is attributable to the original property shall be reduced in accordance with the preceding provisions of this Chapter, and

(*b*) in a case falling within subsection (2) above, the additional tax shall be calculated as if only a proportionate part of so much of the value transferred as was attributable to the original property had been so reduced.

(6) Where any shares owned by the transferee immediately before the death in question—

(*a*) would under any of the provisions of sections 77 to 86 of the Capital Gains Tax Act 1979 be identified with the original property (or part of it), or

(*b*) were issued to him in consideration of the transfer of agricultural property consisting of the original property (or part of it),

his period of ownership of the original property shall be treated as including his period of ownership of the shares.[1]

(7) This section has effect subject to section 124B below.

(8) In this section—

'the original property' means the property which, in relation to the chargeable transfer referred to in subsection (1) or subsection (2) above, was either agricultural property to which section 116 above applied or shares or securities of a company owning agricultural property to which that section applied by virtue of section 122(1) above; and

'the transferee' means the person whose property the original property became on that chargeable transfer or, where on the transfer the original property became or remained settled property in which no qualifying interest in possession (within the meaning of Chapter III of Part III of this Act) subsists, the trustees of the settlement.

1 Words in subsection (6) substituted by FA 1987, Sched 8, para 9.

**124B. Application of section 124A to replacement property**

(1) Subject to subsection (2) below, this section applies where—

(*a*) the transferee has disposed of all or part of the original property before the death of the transferor; and

(*b*) the whole of the consideration received by him for the disposal has been applied by him in acquiring other property (in this section referred to as 'the replacement property').

(2) This section does not apply unless—

(*a*) the replacement property is acquired, or a binding contract for its acquisition is entered into, within twelve months after the disposal of the original property or, as the case may be, the part concerned); and

(*b*) the disposal and acquisition are both made in transactions at arm's length or on terms such as might be expected to be included in a transaction at arm's length.

(3) Where this section applies, the conditions in section 124A(3) above shall be taken to be satisfied in relation to the original property (or, as the case may be, the part concerned) if—

(*a*) the replacement property is owned by the transferee immediately before the death of the transferor and is not at that time subject to a binding contract for sale; and

(*b*) throughout the period beginning with the date of the chargeable transfer and ending with the disposal, the original property was owned by the transferee and occupied (by the transferee or another) for the purposes of agriculture; and

(*c*) throughout the period beginning with the date when the transferee acquired the replacement property and ending with the death, the replacement property was owned by the transferee and occupied (by the transferee or another) for the purposes of agriculture; and

(*d*) the replacement property is agricultural property immediately before the death.

(4) If the transferee has died before the transferor, any reference in subsections (1) to (3) above to the death of the transferor shall have effect as a reference to the death of the transferee.

(5) In any case where—

(*a*) all or part of the original property has been disposed of before the death of the transferor or is subject to a binding contract for sale at the time of the death, and

(*b*) the replacement property is acquired, or a binding contract for its acquisition is entered into, after the death of the transferor but within twelve months after the disposal of the original property or part, and

(*c*) the transferor dies before the transferee,

subsection (3) above shall have effect with the omission of paragraphs (*a*) and (*c*), and as if any reference to a time immediately before the death of the transferor were a reference to the time when the replacement property is acquired.

(6) Section 124A(6) above shall have effect in relation to the replacement property as it has effect in relation to the original property.

(7) Where a binding contract for the disposal of any property is entered into at any time before the disposal of the property, the disposal shall be regarded for the purposes of subsections (2)(*a*) and (5)(*b*) above as taking place at that time.

(8) In this section 'the original property' and 'the transferee' have the same meaning as in section 124A above.'

23.—(1) In section 131 (relief in respect of additional tax payable on transfers within three years of death), in subsection (1) for the words from 'by virtue' to 'transfer and' there shall be substituted 'because of the transferor's death within seven years of the transfer, tax becomes chargeable in respect of the value transferred by a potentially exempt transfer or (by virtue of section 7(4) above) additional tax becomes chargeable in respect of the value transferred by any other chargeable transfer and (in either case)'.

(2) In subsection (2) of that section for the words 'the additional tax', in each place where they occur, there shall be substituted 'the tax or, as the case may be, additional tax'.

(3) After that subsection there shall be inserted the following subsection—

'(2A) Where so much of the value transferred as is attributable to the value, or agricultural value, of the transferred property is reduced by any percentage (in this subsection referred to as 'the appropriate percentage'), in accordance with Chapter I or Chapter II of this Part of this Act, references in subsection (2) above to the market value of the transferred property at any time shall have effect—

(*a*) in a case within Chapter I, as references to that market value reduced by the appropriate percentage; and

(*b*) in a case within Chapter II, as references to that market value less the appropriate percentage of the agricultural value of the transferred property at that time.'

24. In section 142 (alteration of dispositions taking effect on death) at the end of subsection (5) there shall be added 'or section 102 of the Finance Act 1986'.

25. Sections 148 and 149 (exemptions for mutual transfers) shall not apply if the donee's transfer (as defined in section 148) is made on or after 18th March 1986.

26. In section 199 (liability for tax etc. on dispositions by transferor) for subsection (2) there shall be substituted the following subsection—

'(2) Subsection (1)(*a*) above shall apply in relation to—

(*a*) the tax on the value transferred by a potentially exempt transfer; and

(*b*) so much of the tax on the value transferred by any other chargeable transfer made within seven years of the transferor's death as exceeds what it would have been had the transferor died more than seven years after the transfer,

with the substitution for the reference to the transferor of a reference to his personal representatives.'

27. In section 201 (liability for tax in respect of settled property), in subsection (2) for the words 'three years', in each place where they occur, there shall be substituted 'seven years'.

28.—(1) In section 204 (limitation of liability), subsection (4) shall be omitted.

(2) In subsection (6)(*a*) of that section, after the word 'transferor' there shall be inserted 'or personal representative of the transferor'.

(3) For subsection (7) of that section there shall be substituted the following subsections—

'(7) Where the tax exceeds what it would have been had the

transferor died more than seven years after the transfer, subsection (6) above shall not apply in relation to the excess.

(8) A person liable by virtue of section 199(2) above for any tax as personal representative of the transferor shall be liable only to the extent that either—

(*a*) in consequence of subsections (2), (3) and (5) above, no person falling within paragraphs (*b*) to (*d*) of section 199(1) above is liable for the tax, or

(*b*) the tax remains unpaid twelve months after the end of the month in which the death of the transferor occurs,

and, subject to that, shall be liable only to the extent of the assets mentioned in subsection (1) above.

(9) Where by virtue of subsection (3) of section 102 of the Finance Act 1986 the estate of a deceased person is treated as including property which would not apart from that subsection form part of his estate, a person shall be liable under section 200(1)(*a*) above as personal representative for tax attributable to the value of that property only if the tax remains unpaid twelve months after the end of the month in which the death occurs and, subject to that, only to the extent of the assets mentioned in subsections (1) above.'

29.—(1) In section 216 (delivery of accounts) in subsection (1) after paragraph (*b*) there shall be inserted the following paragraphs—

'(*bb*) is liable under section 199(1)(*b*) above for tax on the value transferred by a potentially exempt transfer which proves to be a chargeable transfer, or would be so liable if tax were chargeable on that value, or

(*bc*) is liable under section 200(1)(*c*) above for tax on the value transferred by a chargeable transfer made on death, so far as the tax is attributable to the value of property which, apart from section 102(3) of the Finance Act 1986, would not form part of the deceased's estate, or would be so liable if tax were chargeable on the value transferred on the death, or'.

(2) In subsection (3) of that section after the words 'his death' there shall be inserted 'other than property which would not, apart from section 102(3) of the Finance Act 1986, form part of his estate'.

(3) In subsection (6) of that section after paragraph (*a*) there shall be inserted the following paragraphs—

'(*aa*) in the case of an account to be delivered by a person within subsection (1)(*bb*) above, before the expiration of the period of twelve months from the end of the month in which the death of the transferor occurs;

(*ab*) in the case of an account to be delivered by a person within subsection (1)(*bc*) above, before the expiration of the period of twelve months from the end of the month in which the death occurs'.

30.—(1) In section 226 (payment: general rules), in subsection (3) for the words 'three years', in each place where they occur, there shall be substituted 'seven years'.

(2) After subsection (3) of that subsection there shall be inserted the following subsections—

'(3A) Without prejudice to subsection (3) above, the tax chargeable on the value transferred by a potentially exempt transfer which proves to be a chargeable transfer shall be due six months after the end of the month in which the transferor's death occurs.

(3B) So much (if any) of the tax chargeable on the value transferred by a chargeable transfer made under Chapter III of Part III of this Act within the period of seven years ending with the settlor's death as exceeds what it would have been had the settlor died more than seven years after the date of the transfer shall be due six months after the end of the month in which the death occurs.'

31.—(1) In section 227 (payment by instalments) after subsection (1) there shall be inserted the following subsections—

'(1A) Subsection (1) above does not apply to—

(*a*) tax payable on the value transferred by a potentially exempt transfer which proves to be a chargeable transfer, or

(*b*) additional tax becoming payable on the value transferred by any chargeable transfer by reason of the transferor's death within seven years of the transfer,

except to the extent that the tax is attributable to the value of property which satisfies one of the conditions specified in subsection (1C) below and, in the case of property consisting of unquoted shares or unquoted securities, the further condition specified in section 228(3A) below.'[1]

(1B) In this section[2] 'the transferee' means the person whose property the qualifying property became on the transfer or, where on the transfer the qualifying property became comprised in a settlement in which no qualifying interest in possession (within the meaning of Chapter III of Part III of this Act) subsists, the trustees of the settlement.'

'(1C) The conditions referred to in subsection (1A) above are—

(*a*) that the property was owned by the transferee throughout the period beginning with the date of the chargeable transfer and ending with the death of the transferor (or, if earlier, the death of the transferee), or

(*b*) that for the purposes of determining the tax, or additional tax, due by reason of the death of the transferor, the value of the property is reduced in accordance with the provisions of Chapter I or Chapter II of Part V of this Act by virtue of section 113B or section 124B above.'[2]

(2) In subsection (5) of that section after the words 'subsection (1)(*b*) above' there shall be inserted 'other than a case within subsection (1A) above where the transferee dies before the transferor'.

---

[1] Subsection (1A) substituted by FA 1987, Sched 8, para 15(1).
[2] Words in subsection (1B) substituted and subsection (1C) inserted by FA 1987 Sched 8, para 15(2) and (3).

32. In section 233 (interest on unpaid tax) in subsection (2) . . .[1]

---

[1] Subsection (2) repealed by FA 1989, Sched 17; for interest rates, see FA 1989, s 178 and the Taxes (Interest Rate) Regulations 1989 (SI 1989 No 1297).

33.—(1) In section 236 (application of section 233 in special cases etc), in subsection (1)(*a*), for the words 'three years', in each place where they occur, there shall be substituted 'seven years'.

(2) After subsection (1) of that section there shall be inserted the following subsection—

'(1A) Section 233 above shall apply in relation to the amount (if any) by which—

(*a*) the tax chargeable on the value transferred by a chargeable transfer made under Chapter III of Part III of this Act within the period of seven years ending with the settlor's death,

exceeds

(*b*) what that tax would have been had the settlor died more than seven years after the date of the transfer,

as if the chargeable transfer had been made on the death of the settlor.'

34. In section 237 (imposition of charge) after subsection (3) there shall be inserted the following subsection—

'(3A) In the case of a potentially exempt transfer which proves to be a chargeable transfer—

(*a*) property concerned, or an interest in property concerned, which has been disposed of to a purchaser before the transferor's death is not subject to the Inland Revenue charge, but

(*b*) property concerned which has been otherwise disposed of before the death and property which at the death represents any property or interest falling within paragraph (*a*) above shall be subject to the charge;

and in this subsection 'property concerned' means property to the value of which the value transferred by the transfer is wholly or partly attributable.'

35. In section 239 (certificates of discharge) after subsection (2) there shall be inserted the following subsection—

'(2A) An application under subsection (1) or (2) above with respect to tax which is or may become chargeable on the value transferred by a potentially exempt transfer may not be made before the expiration of two years from the death of the transferor (except where the Board think fit to entertain the application at an earlier time after the death).'

36. For Schedule 1 (rates of tax) there shall be substituted—

'SCHEDULE 1

TABLE OF RATES OF TAX

| *Portion of value* | | *Rate of tax* |
|---|---|---|
| *Lower limit* | *Upper limit* | *Per cent* |
| £ | £ | |
| 0 | 128,000 | Nil |
| 128,000 | — | 40. |

[*Note*—Rate applies to chargeable transfers made after 5 April 1990.]

37.—(1) In Schedule 2 (provisions applying on reduction of tax),—

(*a*) for the words 'new Tables', wherever occurring, there shall be substituted 'a new Table'; and

(*b*) for the words 'the Tables', wherever occurring, there shall be substituted 'the Table'.

(2) In paragraph (1)(*b*) of that Schedule for the word 'come' there shall be substituted 'comes'.

(3) After paragraph 1 of that Schedule there shall be inserted the following paragraph—

'*Death within seven years of potentially exempt transfer*

1A. Where a person who has made a potentially exempt transfer before a reduction dies after that reduction (or after that and one or more subsequent reductions) and within the period of seven years beginning with the date of the transfer, tax shall be chargeable by reason of the transfer proving to be a chargeable transfer only if, and to the extent that, it would have been so chargeable if the Table in Schedule 1 as substituted by that reduction (or by the most recent of those reductions) had applied to that transfer.'

(4) In paragraph 2 of that Schedule,—

(*a*) for the words 'three years', wherever occurring, there shall be substituted 'seven years'; and

(*b*) after the words 'chargeable transfer' there shall be inserted '(other than a potentially exempt transfer)'; and

(*c*) the words 'the first of' shall be omitted.

(5) In paragraph 3 of that Schedule, the words 'the second of' shall be omitted.

(6) In paragraph 4 of that Schedule, the words 'the first of' shall be omitted.

38.—(1) In Schedule 4 (maintenance funds for historic buildings etc) in paragraph 14 (rate of charge) in sub-paragraphs (1) to (3), for the words 'under the appropriate Table', wherever occurring, there shall be substituted 'in accordance with the appropriate provision of section 7 of this Act'.

(2) After sub-paragraph (1) of that paragraph there shall be inserted the following sub-paragraph—

> '(1A) The rate or rates of tax determined under sub-paragraph (1) above in respect of any occasion shall not be affected by the death of the settlor after that occasion.'

(3) In sub-paragraph (6) of that paragraph for the words 'ten years' there shall be substituted 'seven years'.

(4) For sub-paragraph (9) of that paragraph there shall be substituted the following sub-paragraph—

> '(9) For the purposes of sub-paragraph (1) above the appropriate provision of section 7 of this Act is subsection (2), and for the purposes of sub-paragraphs (2) and (3) above it is (if the settlement was made on death) subsection (1) and (if not) subsection (2).'

39. In Schedule 6 (transition from estate duty) in paragraph 4(3) after the words 'sections 33(7)' there shall be inserted the words 'and (8).'

## PART II
## TRANSITIONAL PROVISIONS

40.—(1) Notwithstanding that Part I of this Schedule has effect with respect to events occurring on or after 18th March 1986, where a death or other event occurs on or after that date, nothing in that Part shall affect the tax chargeable on a transfer of value occurring before that date.

(2) Sub-paragraph (1) above does not authorise the making of a claim under section 149 of the 1984 Act where the donee's transfer, as defined in section 148 of that Act, occurs on or after 18th March 1986.

41. Where tax is chargeable under section 32 or section 32A of the 1984 Act by reason of a chargeable event occurring on or after 18th March 1986

and the rate or rates at which it is charged fall to be determined under the provisions of section 33(1)(*b*)(ii) of the 1984 Act by reference to a death which occurred before that date, those provisions shall apply (subject to paragraph 5 of Schedule 2 to that Act) as if the amendments of section 7 of, and Schedule 1 to, that Act contained in Part I of this Schedule had been in force at the time of the death.

42. Where tax is chargeable under paragraph 8 of Schedule 4 to the 1984 Act on any occasion on or after 18th March 1986 and the rate at which it is charged falls to be determined under paragraph 14 of that Schedule by reference to a death which occurred before that date, that paragraph shall apply (subject to paragraph 6 of Schedule 2 to the 1984 Act) as if the amendments of section 7 of, and Schedule 1 to, the 1984 Act contained in Part I of this Schedule had been in force at the time of the death.

43.—(1) This paragraph applies if, in the case of a settlement,—

(*a*) tax is charged under section 65 of the 1984 Act on an occasion falling on or after 18th March 1986; and

(*b*) the rate at which tax is so charged falls to be determined under section 69 of that Act (rate between ten-year anniversaries) by reference to the rate (in this paragraph referred to as 'the last ten-year rate') at which tax was last charged under section 64 of that Act (or would have been charged apart from section 66(2) thereof); and

(*c*) the most recent ten-year anniversary fell before 18th March 1986.

(2) For the purpose of determining the rate at which tax is charged on the occasion referred to in sub-paragraph (1)(*a*) above, it shall be assumed that the last ten-year rate was what that rate would have been if, immediately before the ten-year anniversary referred to in sub-paragraph (1)(*c*) above, the amendments of sections 66 and 67 of the 1984 Act contained in Part I of this Schedule had been in force.

(3) Where this paragraph applies, paragraph 3 of Schedule 2 to the 1984 Act shall have effect as if—

(*a*) references to a reduction included references to a reduction by the substitution of a new Table in Schedule 1 to the 1984 Act; and

(*b*) in relation to a reduction resulting from the substitution of such a new Table, the reference to the second of the Tables in Schedule 1 to the 1984 Act were a reference to a Table in which the rates of tax were one-half of those specified in the new Table.

(4) In this paragraph 'ten-year anniversary' has the same meaning as in Chapter III of Part III of the 1984 Act.

44. In relation to a death on or after 18th March 1986, paragraph 2 of Schedule 2 to the 1984 Act (provisions applying on reduction of tax) shall have effect, in a case where the chargeable transfer in question was made before 18th March 1986, as if—

(*a*) references to a reduction included references to a reduction by the substitution of a new Table in Schedule 1 to the 1984 Act; and (*b*) the Table in Schedule 1 to the Act was the first Table in that Schedule.

45. In relation to a disposal of trees or underwood on or after 18th March 1986, paragraph 4 of Schedule 2 to the 1984 Act shall have effect, in a case where the death in question occurred before 18th March 1986, as mentioned in paragraphs (*a*) and (*b*) of paragraph 44 above.

46. Notwithstanding anything in section 3A of the 1984 Act, a transfer of value which is made on or after 1st July 1986 and which, by virtue of subsection (4) of section 49 of the Finance Act 1975 (transitional provision relating to estate duty deferment in respect of timber etc), brings to an end the period during which estate duty is payable on the net moneys received from the sale of timber etc is not a potentially exempt transfer.

## FINANCE (NO 2) ACT 1987, SCHEDULE 7

### SCHEDULE 7

Section 96

### INHERITANCE TAX: INTERESTS IN POSSESSION

1. After section 54 of the Inheritance Tax Act 1984 (in this Schedule referred to as 'the 1984 Act') there shall be inserted the following sections—

**'54A. Special rate of charge where settled property affected by potentially exempt transfer**

(1) If the circumstances fall within subsection (2) below, this section applies to any chargeable transfer made—

(*a*) under section 52 above, on the coming to an end of an interest in possession in settled property during the life of the person beneficially entitled to it, or

(*b*) on the death of a person beneficially entitled to an interest in possession in settled property;

and in the following provisions of this section the interest in possession mentioned in paragraph (*a*) or paragraph (*b*) above is referred to as 'the relevant interest'.

(2) The circumstances referred to in subsection (1) above are—

(*a*) that the whole or part of the value transferred by the transfer is attributable to property in which the relevant interest subsisted and which became settled property in which there subsisted an interest in possession (whether the relevant interest or any previous interest) on the making by the settlor of a potentially exempt transfer at any time on or after 17th March 1987 and within the period of seven years ending with the date of the chargeable transfer; and

(*b*) that the settlor is alive at the time when the relevant interest comes to an end; and (*c*) that, on the coming to an end of the relevant interest, any of the property in which that interest subsisted becomes settled property in which no qualifying interest in possession (as defined in section 59 below) subsists, other than property to which section 71 below applies; and

(*d*) that, within six months of the coming to an end of the relevant interest, any of the property in which that interest subsisted has neither—

(i) become settled property in which a qualifying interest in possession subsists or to which section 71 below applies, nor

(ii) become property to which an individual is beneficially entitled.

(3) In the following provisions of this section 'the special rate property', in relation to a chargeable transfer to which this section applies, means the property in which the relevant interest subsisted or, in a case where—

(*a*) any part of that property does not fall within subsection (2)(*a*) above, or

(*b*) any part of that property does not become settled property of the kind mentioned in subsection (2)(*c*) above,

so much of that property as appears to the Board or, on appeal, to the Special Commissioners to be just and reasonable.

(4) Where this section applies to a chargeable transfer (in this section referred to as 'the relevant transfer'), the tax chargeable on the value transferred by the transfer shall be whichever is the greater of the tax that would have been chargeable apart from this section and the tax determined in accordance with subsection (5) below.

(5) The tax determined in accordance with this subsection is the aggregate of—

(*a*) the tax that would be chargeable on a chargeable transfer of the description specified in subsection (6) below, and

(*b*) so much (if any) of the tax that would, apart from this section, have been chargeable on the value transferred by the relevant transfer as is attributable to the value of property other than the special rate property.

(6) The chargeable transfer postulated in subsection (5)(*a*) above is one—

(*a*) the value transferred by which is equal to the value transferred by the relevant transfer or, where only part of that value is attributable to the special rate property, that part of that value;

(*b*) which is made at the time of the relevant transfer by a transferor who has in the preceding seven years made chargeable transfers having an aggregate value equal to the aggregate of the values transferred by any chargeable transfers made by the settlor in the period of seven years ending with the date of the potentially exempt transfer; and

(*c*) for which the applicable rate or rates are one-half of the rate or rates referred to in section 7(1) above.

(7) This section has effect subject to section 54B below.

**54B. Provisions supplementary to section 54A**

(1) The death of the settlor, at any time after a chargeable transfer to which section 54A above applies, shall not increase the tax chargeable on the value transferred by the transfer unless, at the time of the transfer, the tax determined in accordance with subsection (5) of that section is greater than the tax that would be chargeable apart from that section.

(2) The death of the person who was beneficially entitled to the relevant interest, at any time after a chargeable transfer to which section 54A above applies, shall not increase the tax chargeable on the value transferred by the transfer unless, at the time of the transfer, the tax that would be chargeable apart from that section is greater than the tax determined in accordance with subsection (5) of that section.

(3) Where the tax chargeable on the value transferred by a chargeable transfer to which section 54A above applies falls to be determined in accordance with subsection (5) of that section, the amount referred to in paragraph (*a*) of that subsection shall be treated for the purposes of this Act as tax attributable to the value of the property in which the relevant interest subsisted.

(4) Subsection (5) below shall apply if—

(*a*) during the period of seven years preceding the date on which a chargeable transfer to which section 54A above applies ('the current transfer') is made, there has been another chargeable transfer to which that section applied, and

(*b*) the person who is for the purposes of the current transfer the settlor mentioned in subsection (2)(*a*) of that section is the settlor for the purposes of the other transfer (whether or not the settlements are the same);

and in subsections (5) and (6) below the other transfer is referred to as the 'previous transfer'.

(5) Where this subsection applies, the appropriate amount in relation to the previous transfer (or, if there has been more than one previous transfer, the aggregate of the appropriate amounts in relation to each) shall, for the purposes of calculating the tax chargeable on the current transfer, be taken to be the value transferred by a chargeable transfer made by the settlor immediately before the potentially exempt transfer was made.

(6) In subsection (5) above 'the appropriate amount', in relation to a previous transfer, means so much of the value transferred by the previous transfer as was attributable to the value of property which was the special rate property in relation to that transfer.

(7) In this section—

'the relevant interest' has the meaning given by subsection (1) of section 54A above; and 'the special rate property' has the meaning given by subsection (3) of that section.'.

2. In section 56 of the 1984 Act (exclusion of certain exemptions) in subsection (5) after the word 'disposition' there shall be inserted 'for such consideration'.

3.—(1) Section 201 of the 1984 Act (liability for tax relating to settled property) shall be amended as follows.

(2) In subsection (2) after the word 'death' there shall be inserted 'but is not a potentially exempt transfer'.

(3) After subsection (3) there shall be inserted the following subsection—

> '(3A) Subsection (1)(*d*) above shall not apply in relation to the tax chargeable on the value transferred by a potentially exempt transfer which proves to be a chargeable transfer in a case where the settlement was made before 17th March 1987 if the trustees were resident in the United Kingdom when the settlement was made, but have not been resident there at any time between 16th March 1987 and the death of the transferor.'

4.—(1) Section 216 of the 1984 Act (delivery of accounts) shall be amended as follows.

(2) In subsection (1) after paragraph (*bc*) there shall be inserted the following paragraph—

> '(*bd*) is liable under section 201(1)(*b*), (*c*) or (*d*) above for tax on the value transferred by a potentially exempt transfer which is made under section 52 above and which proves to be a chargeable transfer, or would be so liable if tax were chargeable on that value, or'

(3) In subsection (6)(*aa*) of that section after the words 'subsection (1)(*bb*)' there shall be inserted 'or (*bd*)'.

5. In section 265 of the 1984 Act (chargeable transfers affecting more than one property) after the words 'subject to' there shall be inserted 'section 54B(3) above and to'.

[*Note*—Amendments made by F(No 2)A 1987 relate to transactions on or after 17 March 1987.]

*Appendix 8*

# Statutory Provisions relating to Gifts with Reservations

FINANCE ACT 1986, S 102 AND SCHEDULE 20

**102. Gifts with reservation**

(1) Subject to subsections (5) and (6) below, this section applies where, on or after 18th March 1986, an individual disposes of any property by way of gift and either—

(*a*) possession and enjoyment of the property is not bona fide assumed by the donee at or before the beginning of the relevant period; or

(*b*) at any time in the relevant period the property is not enjoyed to the entire exclusion, or virtually to the entire exclusion, of the donor and of any benefit to him by contract or otherwise;

and in this section 'the relevant period' means a period ending on the date of the donor's death and beginning seven years before that date or, if it is later, on the date of the gift.

(2) If and so long as—

(*a*) possession and enjoyment of any property is not bona fide assumed as mentioned in subsection (1)(*a*) above, or

(*b*) any property is not enjoyed as mentioned in subsection (1)(*b*) above,

the property is referred to (in relation to the gift and the donor) as property subject to a reservation.

(3) If, immediately before the death of the donor, there is any property which, in relation to him, is property subject to a reservation then, to the extent that the property would not, apart from this section, form part of the donor's estate immediately before his death, that property shall be treated for the purposes of the 1984 Act as property to which he was beneficially entitled immediately before his death.

(4) If, at a time before the end of the relevant period, any property ceases to be property subject to a reservation, the donor shall be treated for the purposes of the 1984 Act as having at that time made a disposition of the property by a disposition which is a potentially exempt transfer.

(5) This section does not apply if or, as the case may be, to the extent that the disposal of property by way of gift is an exempt transfer by virtue of any of the following provisions of Part II of the 1984 Act,—

(*a*) section 18 (transfers between spouses);
(*b*) section 20 (small gifts);
(*c*) section 22 (gifts in consideration of marriage);
(*d*) section 23 (gifts to charities);
(*e*) section 24 (gifts to political parties);
(*ee*) section 24A (gifts to housing associations);[1]
(*f*) section 25 (gifts for national purposes, etc.);
(*g*) section 26 (gifts for public benefit);
(*h*) section 27 (maintenance funds for historic buildings); and
(*i*) section 28 (employee trusts).

(6) This section does not apply if the disposal of property by way of gift is made under the terms of a policy issued in respect of an insurance made before 18th March 1986 unless the policy is varied on or after that date so as to increase the benefits secured or to extend the term of the insurance; and, for this purpose, any change in the terms of the policy which is made in pursuance of an option or other power conferred by the policy shall be deemed to be a variation of the policy.

(7) If a policy issued as mentioned in subsection (6) above confers an option or other power under which benefits and premiums may be increased to take account of increases in the retail prices index (as defined in section 8(3) of the 1984 Act) or any similar index specified in the policy, then, to the extent that the right to exercise that option or power would have been lost if it had not been exercised on or before 1st August 1986, the exercise of that option or power before that date shall be disregarded for the purposes of subsection (6) above.

(8) Schedule 20 to this Act has effect for supplementing this section.

---

1 Subsection (5)(*ee*) added by FA 1989, s 171(5), (6).

## SCHEDULE 20 — Section 102

### Gifts with Reservation

*Interpretation and application*

1.—(1) In this Schedule—

'the material date', in relation to any property means, in the case of property falling within subsection (3) of the principal section, the date of the donor's death and, in the case of property falling within subsection (4) of that section, the date on which the property ceases to be property subject to a reservation;

'the principal section' means section 102 of this Act; and

'property subject to a reservation' has the same meaning as in the principal section.

(2) Any reference in this Schedule to a disposal by way of gift is a reference to such a disposal which is made on or after 18th March 1986.

(3) This Schedule has effect for the purposes of the principal section and the 1984 Act.

*Substitutions and accretions*

(2).—(1) Where there is a disposal by way of gift and, at any time before the material date, the donee ceases to have the possession and enjoyment of any of the property comprised in the gift, then on and after that time the principal section and the following provisions of this Schedule shall apply as if the property, if any, received by the donee in substitution for that property had been comprised in the gift instead of that property (but in addition to any other property comprised in the gift).

(2) This paragraph does not apply if the property disposed of by the gift—

(*a*) becomes settled property by virtue of the gift; or
(*b*) is a sum of money in sterling or any other currency.

(3) In sub-paragraph (1) above the reference to property received by the donee in substitution for property comprised in the gift includes in particular—

(*a*) in relation to property sold, exchanged or otherwise disposed of by the donee, any benefit received by him by way of consideration for the sale, exchange or other disposition; and
(*b*) in relation to a debt or security, any benefit received by the donee in or towards the satisfaction or redemption thereof; and
(*c*) in relation to any right to acquire property, any property acquired in pursuance of that right.

(4) Where, at a time before the material date, the donee makes a gift of property comprised in the gift to him, or otherwise voluntarily divests himself of any such property otherwise than for a consideration in money or money's worth not less than the value of the property at that time, then, unless he does so in favour of the donor, he shall be treated for the purposes of the principal section and sub-paragraph (1) above as continuing to have the possession and enjoyment of that property.

(5) For the purposes of sub-paragraph (4) above—

(*a*) a disposition made by the donee by agreement shall not be deemed to be made voluntarily if it is made to any authority who, when the agreement is made, is authorised by, or is or can be authorised under, any enactment to acquire the property compulsorily; and
(*b*) a donee shall be treated as divesting himself, voluntarily and without consideration, of any interest in property which merges

or is extinguished in another interest held or acquired by him in the same property.

(6) Where any shares in or debentures of a body corporate are comprised in a gift and the donee is, as the holder of those shares or debentures, issued with shares in or debentures of the same or any other body corporate, or granted any right to acquire any such shares or debentures, then, unless the issue or grant is made by way of exchange for the first-mentioned shares or debentures, the shares or debentures so issued, or the right granted, shall be treated for the purposes of the principal section and this Schedule as having been comprised in the gift in addition to any other property so comprised.

(7) In sub-paragraph (6) above the reference to an issue being made or right being granted to the donee as the holder of shares or debentures shall be taken to include any case in which an issue or grant is made to him as having been the holder of those shares or debentures, or is made to him in pursuance of an offer or invitation made to him as being or having been the holder of those shares or debentures, or of an offer or invitation in connection with which any preference is given to him as being or having been the holder thereof.

3.—(1) Where either sub-paragraph (3)(*c*) or sub-paragraph (6) of paragraph 2 above applies to determine, for the purposes of the principal section, the property comprised in a gift made by a donor—

(*a*) the value of any consideration in money or money's worth given by the donee for the acquisition in pursuance of the right referred to in the said sub-paragraph (3)(*c*) or for the issue or grant referred to in the said sub-paragraph (6), as the case may be, shall be allowed as a deduction in valuing the property comprised in the gift at any time after the consideration is given, but

(*b*) if any part (not being a sum of money) of that consideration consists of property comprised in the same or another gift from the donor and treated for the purposes of the 1984 Act as forming part of the donor's estate immediately before his death or as being attributable to the value transferred by a potentially exempt transfer made by him, no deduction shall be made in respect of it under this sub-paragraph.

(2) For the purposes of sub-paragraph (1) above, there shall be left out of account so much (if any) of the consideration for any shares in or debentures of a body corporate, or for the grant of any right to be issued with any such shares or debentures, as consists in the capitalisation of reserves of that body corporate, or in the retention by that body corporate, by way of set-off or otherwise, of any property distributable by it, or is otherwise provided directly or indirectly out of the assets or at the expense of that or any associated body corporate.

(3) For the purposes of sub-paragraph (2) above, two bodies corporate shall be deemed to be associated if one has control of the other or if another person has control of both.

*Donee predeceasing the material date*

4. Where there is a disposal by way of gift and the donee dies before the date which is the material date in relation to any property comprised in the gift, paragraphs 2 and 3 above shall apply as if—

(*a*) he had not died and the acts of his personal representatives were his acts; and

(*b*) property taken by any person under his testamentary dispositions or his intestacy (or partial intestacy) were taken under a gift made by him at the time of his death.

*Settled gifts*

5.—(1) Where there is a disposal by way of gift and the property comprised in the gift becomes settled property by virtue of the gift, paragraphs 2 to 4 above shall not apply but, subject to the following provisions of this paragraph, the principal section and the following provisions of this Schedule shall apply as if the property comprised in the gift consisted of the property comprised in the settlement on the material date, except in so far as that property neither is, nor represents, nor is derived from,property originally comprised in the gift.

(2) If the settlement comes to an end at some time before the material date as respects all or any of the property which, if the donor had died immediately before that time, would be treated as comprised in the gift,—

(*a*) the property in question, other than property to which the donor then becomes absolutely and beneficially entitled in possession, and

(*b*) any consideration (not consisting of rights under the settlement) given by the donor for any of the property to which he so becomes entitled,

shall be treated as comprised in the gift (in addition to any other property so comprised).

(3) Where property comprised in a gift does not become settled property by virtue of the gift, but is before the material date settled by the donee, sub-paragraphs (1) and (2) above shall apply in relation to property comprised in the settlement as if the settlement had been made by the gift; and for this purpose property which becomes settled property under any testamentary disposition of the donee or on his intestacy (or partial intestacy) shall be treated as settled by him.

(4) Where property comprised in a gift becomes settled property either by virtue of the gift or as mentioned in sub-paragraph (3) above, any property which—

(*a*) on the material date is comprised in the settlement, and

(*b*) is derived, directly or indirectly, from a loan made by the donor to the trustees of the settlement, shall be treated for the purposes of sub-paragraph (1) above as derived from property originally comprised in the gift.

(5) Where, under any trust or power relating to settled property, income arising from that property after the material date is accumulated, the accumulation shall not be treated for the purposes of sub-paragraph (1) above as derived from that property.

*Exclusion of benefit*

6.—(1) In determining whether any property which is disposed of by way of gift is enjoyed to the entire exclusion, or virtually to the entire exclusion, of the donor and of any benefit to him by contract or otherwise—

(*a*) in the case of property which is an interest in land or a chattel, retention or assumption by the donor of actual occupation of the land or actual enjoyment of an incorporeal right over the land, or actual possession of the chattel shall be disregarded if it is for full consideration in money or money's worth;

(*b*) in the case of property which is an interest in land, any occupation by the donor of the whole or any part of the land shall be disregarded if—

(i) it results from a change in the circumstances of the donor since the time of the gift, being a change which was unforeseen at that time and was not brought about by the donor to receive the benefit of this provision; and

(ii) it occurs at a time when the donor has become unable to maintain himself through old age, infirmity or otherwise; and

(iii) it represents a reasonable provision by the donee for the care and maintenance of the donor; and

(iv) the donee is a relative of the donor or his spouse;

(*c*) a benefit which the donor obtained by virtue of any associated operations (as defined in section 268 of the 1984 Act) of which the disposal by way of gift is one shall be treated as a benefit to him by contract or otherwise.

(2) Any question whether any property comprised in a gift was at any time enjoyed to the entire exclusion, or virtually to the entire exclusion, of the donor and of any benefit to him shall (so far as that question depends upon the identity of the property) be determined by reference to the property which is at that time treated as property comprised in the gift.

(3) In the application of this paragraph to Scotland, references to a chattel shall be construed as references to a corporeal moveable.

7.—(1) Where arrangements are entered into under which—

(*a*) there is a disposal by way of gift which consists of or includes, or is made in connection with, a policy of insurance on the life of the donor or his spouse or on their joint lives, and (*b*) the benefits which will or may accrue to the donee as a result of the gift vary by reference to benefits accruing to the donor or his spouse (or both of them) under that policy or under another policy (whether issued before, at the same time as or after that referred to in paragraph (*a*) above),

the property comprised in the gift shall be treated for the purposes of the principal section as not enjoyed to the entire exclusion, or virtually to the entire exclusion, of the donor.

(2) In sub-paragraph (1) above—

(*a*) the reference in paragraph (*a*) to a policy on the joint lives of the donor and his spouse includes a reference to a policy on their joint lives and on the life of the survivor; and

(*b*) the reference in paragraph (*b*) to benefits accruing to the donor or his spouse (or both of them) includes a reference to benefits which accrue by virtue of the exercise of rights conferred on either or both of them.

*Agricultural property and business property*

8.—(1) This paragraph applies where[1] there is a disposal by way of gift of property which, in relation to the donor, is at that time—

(*a*) relevant business property within the meaning of Chapter I of Part V of the 1984 Act, or

(*b*) agricultural property, within the meaning of Chapter II of that Part, to which section 116 of that Act applies, or

(*c*) shares or securities to which section 122(1) of that Act applies (agricultural property of companies),

and that property is property subject to a reservation.[2]

(1A) Where this paragraph applies—

(*a*) any question whether, on the material transfer of value, any shares or securities fall within paragraph (*b*) or paragraph (*bb*) of section 105(1) of the 1984 Act (which specify shares and securities qualifying for 50 per cent relief) shall be determined, subject to the following provisions of this paragraph, as if the shares or securities were owned by the donor and had been owned by him since the disposal by way of gift; and

(*b*) subject to paragraph (*a*) above, any question whether, on the material transfer of value, relief is available by virtue of Chapter I or Chapter II of Part V of the 1984 Act and, if relief is available by virtue of Chapter II, what is the appropriate percentage for that relief, shall be determined, subject to the following provisions of this paragraph, as if, so far as it is attributable to the property comprised in the gift, that transfer were a transfer of value by the donee.[3]

(2) For the purpose only of determining whether, on the transfer of value which, by virtue of sub-paragraph (1A)(*b*)[4] above, the donee is assumed to make, the requirement of section 106 or, as the case may be, section 117 of the 1984 Act (minimum period of ownership or occupation) is fulfilled,—

(*a*) ownership by the donor prior to the disposal by way of gift shall be treated as ownership by the donee; and

(*b*) occupation by the donor prior to the disposal and any occupation by him after that disposal shall be treated as occupation by the donee.

(3) Where the property disposed of by the gift consists of shares or securities falling within paragraph (*c*) of sub-paragraph (1) above, relief shall not be available by virtue of Chapter II of Part V of the 1984 Act on the material transfer of value[5] unless—

(*a*) section 116 of the 1984 Act applied in relation to the value transferred by the disposal, and

(*b*) throughout the period beginning with the disposal and ending on the material date, the shares or securities are owned by the donee,

and for the purpose only of determining whether, on the transfer of value which, by virtue of sub-paragraph (1A)(*b*)[4] above, the donee is assumed to make, the requirements of subsection (1) of section 123 of the 1984 Act are fulfilled, it shall be assumed that the requirement in paragraph (*b*) of that subsection (as to the ownership of the shares or securities) is fulfilled.

(4) In this paragraph, 'the material transfer of value' means, as the case may require,—

(*a*) the transfer of value under section 4 of the 1984 Act on the death of the donor; or

(*b*) the transfer of value under subsection (4) of the principal section on the property concerned ceasing to be subject to a reservation.

(5) If the donee dies before the material transfer of value, then, as respects any time after his death, any reference in the preceding provisions of this paragraph to the donee shall be construed as a reference to his personal representatives or, as the case may require, the person (if any) by whom the property, shares or securities concerned were taken under a testamentary disposition made by the donee or under his intestacy (or partial intestacy).

---

1 Words substituted by FA 1987, Sched 8, para 18(2).
2 Words omitted by FA 1987, Sched 8, para 18(2).
3 Subpara (1A) inserted by FA 1987, Sched 8, para 18(3)
4 Words substituted by FA 1987, Sched 8, para 18(4) and (5)(*b*).
5 Words substituted by FA 1987, Sched 8, para 18(5)(*a*).

# *Appendix 9*

# Will Forms

It is the policy of this book to offer a collection of particular precedent clauses from which, by selection, a complete draft may readily be compiled to meet the individual circumstances of any particular case. This is still considered to be the most economical presentation; and also the most convenient format for the storage of material on a database.

However the following three complete will forms are also included, to supplement the precedent clauses. Although there should never be any such thing as a 'standard' will form, these forms may be found acceptable for generalised use in a number of straightforward cases, with or without modification; and may conveniently be stored as 'common form' material, for that purpose.

**Will 1 Absolute gift to widow, if she survives by 28 days; failing which, upon trust for children; solicitor trustees being appointed in that event**

THIS IS THE LAST WILL AND TESTAMENT

Of me      of

in the County of

1 I HEREBY REVOKE all former wills and testamentary dispositions made by me.

2 IF and only if my wife      survives me by twenty-eight clear days I DEVISE AND BEQUEATH all my real and personal property whatsoever and wheresoever unto my said Wife absolutely and appoint her sole Executrix hereof

3 IF my said wife fails to attain a vested interest hereunder (but not otherwise) the following clauses shall have effect in substitution for Clause 2 above

4 I APPOINT      and      of      Solicitors (hereinafter called 'my Trustees' which expression where the context admits includes any trustee hereof for the time being) to be the Executors and Trustees hereof

5 (1) I GIVE DEVISE AND BEQUEATH to my Trustees all my real and personal property not otherwise specifically disposed of upon trust for sale with full power to postpone sale

(2) MY TRUSTEES shall pay and discharge therefrom all my debts and funeral testamentary and administration expenses
(3) MY TRUSTEES shall hold the balance of my said real and personal property remaining after such payments (hereinafter called 'my residuary estate') upon the beneficial trusts and with and subject to the powers and provisions hereinafter contained

6 MY TRUSTEES shall hold my residuary estate UPON TRUST for such of my children as shall be living at my death and shall attain the age of twenty-one years and if more than one in equal shares absolutely Provided Always that if any child of mine shall die without having attained a vested interest hereunder leaving a child or children living at my death then any such child or children (meaning in either case a grandchild or grandchildren of mine) as shall attain the age of eighteen years shall take by substitution and in equal shares if more than one per stirpes the share of my residuary estate which such deceased child of mine would have taken had he or she survived and attained a vested interest

7 MY TRUSTEES shall have power to invest trust money and to vary and transpose investments from time to time with the same full and unrestricted freedom in their choice of investments as if they were a sole absolute beneficial owner

8 BY WAY OF EXTENSION of the powers conferred upon them by law:
(1) My Trustees may exercise the powers as to application of income conferred by section 31 of the Trustee Act 1925 without regard to the restrictions in the proviso to subsection (1) of that section
(2) My Trustees may exercise the power of advancement conferred by section 32 of the Trustee Act 1925 without regard to the restriction in paragraph (a) of subsection (1) of that section

9 I DECLARE that any Executor or Trustee of this my Will who is or shall be a Solicitor or engaged in any other profession or business shall be entitled to charge and be paid his usual professional or other charges for work done by him or his firm in the execution or otherwise in relation to the trusts hereof including any work or business which he might be as a Trustee required to do or transact in person

AS WITNESS my hand this day of 199

SIGNED by the above-named in our joint presence and then by us in his:

**Will 2 Tax-saving will of married woman, leaving bulk of estate in trust for children in any event**

THIS IS THE LAST WILL AND TESTAMENT

of me of in the County of Wife of

1 I HEREBY REVOKE all former wills and testamentary dispositions

2 I APPOINT and of in the County of (hereinafter called 'my Trustees' which expression where the context admits includes any trustees hereof for the time being) to be the executors and trustees hereof

3 I GIVE to my husband absolutely all my personal chattels as defined by section 55(1)(x) of the Administration of Estates Act 1925

4 SUBJECT TO payment thereout of my debts and funeral and testamentary expenses and all legacies given hereby or by any codicil hereto I give to my Trustees all my real and personal property not otherwise specifically disposed of upon trust for sale with full power to postpone sale and my Trustees shall hold the same and the net proceeds of sale thereof (subject as aforesaid) UPON TRUST for such of my children as shall be living at my death and if more than one in equal shares absolutely PROVIDED ALWAYS that if any child of mine shall die in my lifetime leaving a child or children living at my death who shall attain the age of twenty-five years such last-mentioned child or children shall take by substitution and if more than one in equal shares per stirpes the share of my estate which his her or their parent would have taken if he or she had survived to attain a vested interest

5 The following powers and discretions shall be exercisable by my trustees in addition to their powers and discretions under the general law:–

(1) Power to invest money and to vary and transpose investments from time to time with the same full and unrestricted freedom in their choice of investments as if my Trustees were a sole absolute beneficial owner

(2) Power to exercise the statutory powers as to application of income conferred by section 31 of the Trustee Act 1925 without regard to the restrictions in the proviso to subsection (1) of that section

(3) Power to exercise the statutory power of advancement conferred by section 32 of the Trustee Act 1925 without regard to the restriction in paragraph (a) of subsection (1) of that section

(4) Power in any case where my Trustees have any obligation or discretion under the provisions of my will or under the general law to pay or apply income or capital to or for the benefit of any person who is a minor to discharge that obligation or to exercise that discretion if and whenever they think fit to do so by making payment either to the parent or guardian of the minor or else to the minor personally if of the

age of sixteen years at least and so that their respective receipts shall be a full discharge to my Trustees who shall not be required to see to the application of any income or capital so paid

(5) Power for any of my Trustees who is a Solicitor or other person engaged in any profession or business to be so employed or act and to charge and be paid all usual professional and other charges for any business transacted or work done by him or his firm in connection with the administration and distribution of my estate or the trusts of my will whether or not of a professional nature and whether or not any person could have done the same personally.

IN WITNESS whereof I have hereunto set my hand this day of 199

SIGNED by the above-named
in
our joint presence and then
by us in hers:

**Will 3 Tax-saving will, creating trust fund by way of settled legacy for children, within the nil rate of IHT; residue to widow for life and, subject thereto, in trust for children**

THIS IS THE LAST WILL AND TESTAMENT
Of me of in the County of

1 I HEREBY REVOKE all former wills and testamentary dispositions

2 I APPOINT and of in the County of (hereinafter called 'my Trustees' which expression where the context admits includes any trustee hereof for the time being) to be the executors and trustees hereof

3 I GIVE to my wife absolutely all my personal chattels as defined by section 55(1)(x) of the Administration of Estates Act 1925

4 (1) I GIVE to my Trustees such a sum as can be transferred on my death without being chargeable to Inheritance Tax (disregarding any exemption or relief) at any rate above the nil rate of tax UPON such and the like TRUSTS for the benefit of my children and issue as are declared in respect of my residuary estate by Clause 6(2) below but as if my said wife had predeceased me

(2) In relation to the trusts of this gift my Trustees shall have all such and the like powers and discretions hereinafter conferred upon them or otherwise applicable in relation to my residuary estate as are for the time being capable of being exercised in relation to this gift

5 (1) I GIVE to my Trustees all my real and personal property not otherwise specifically disposed of UPON TRUST for sale with full power to postpone sale

(2) My Trustees shall pay and discharge therefrom all my debts (including any debt which is a charge on any property in which at the time of my death I have a beneficial interest) and funeral and testamentary expenses and all tax payable by reason of my death

(3) My Trustees shall hold the balance of my said real and personal property remaining after such payments (herinafter called 'my residuary estate') Upon the beneficial trusts and with and subject to the powers and provisions hereinafter declared and contained

6 MY TRUSTEES shall hold my residuary estate UPON the following TRUSTS:

(1) UPON TRUST to pay the income thereof to my said wife during her life and subject thereto

(2) UPON TRUST for such of my children as shall be living at my death and who shall have attained or shall attain the age of eighteen years and if more than one in equal shares absolutely PROVIDED ALWAYS that if any child of mine shall die in my lifetime leaving a child or children living at my death who shall attain the age of twenty-five years such last-mentioned child or children shall take by substitution and if more than one in equal shares per stirpes the share of my residuary estate which his or her or their parent would have taken if he or she had survived to attain a vested interest / and PROVIDED FURTHER that if any child of mine shall die in my lifetime leaving no child who shall attain a vested interest under the foregoing proviso but such deceased child of mine shall leave a widow or widower living at my death then such widow or widower shall take by substitution the share of my residuary estate which such deceased child of mine would have taken if he or she had survived to attain a vested interest

7 The following powers and discretions shall be exercisable by my Trustees in addition to their powers and discretions under the general law:–

(1) Power to treat all income from any part of my estate which is actually received after my death or after the time when any person becomes or ceases to be entitled or prospectively entitled to any beneficial interest in my residuary estate as accruing wholly after my death or after that time as the case may be without apportionment whatever the period in respect of which it is actually payable to the intent that the Apportionment Act 1870 and the rules of equity relating to apportionments including those known as the rules in Howe v Dartmouth and Allhusen v Whittell in all their branches shall for all purposes be wholly excluded in the administration of my estate and of the trusts of this my will

(2) Power in the administration and execution of any of the trusts hereof to make any such appropriation as is authorised by section 41 of the Administration of Estates Act 1925 but without being required to obtain any such consents as are referred to in that section

(3) Power to insure against loss or damage by fire or from any other insurable risk any property for the time being comprised in my residuary estate to any amount and to pay all premiums for any such insurance at their discretion out of the income or capital of my residuary estate and so that any money received under any such insurance shall be applicable at their discretion either in or towards making good the loss or damage in respect of which it was received or otherwise as if it were proceeds of sale of the property insured

(4) Power to invest trust money and to vary and transpose investments from time to time with the same full and unrestricted freedom in their choice of investments as if my Trustees were a sole absolute beneficial owner

(5) Power to apply trust money at any time and from time to time in the purchase (upon trust for sale but with full power to postpone sale) or in the improvement of any freehold or leasehold dwelling-house within the United Kingdom and to permit any such dwelling-house to be used as a residence by my said wife upon such terms and conditions as in their absolute discretion my Trustees from time to time think fit to require

(6) Power at any time to effect any policy of insurance of whatever nature upon the lives of any of the beneficiaries and to pay or apply any part of the capital or income (including accumulations of income) of my residuary estate in or towards the payment of any premium for effecting or maintaining any such policy or to borrow from any person or corporation (including any one or more of themselves) the whole or any part of the moneys required for the payment of any such premium whether or not the loan is secured upon the whole or any part of my residuary estate and upon such terms as to interest repayment and otherwise as my Trustees shall see fit to agree to the intent that my Trustees shall hold any such policy and the proceeds thereof and all moneys arising therefrom as an accretion to the capital of my residuary estate

(7) Power at any time and from time to time to pay or apply capital money from my residuary estate to any extent up to a maximum of one half to my said wife or for her benefit as my Trustees in their absolute discretion may think fit

(8) Power to exercise the statutory powers as to application of income conferred by section 31 of the Trustee Act 1925 without regard to the restrictions in the proviso to subsection (1) of that section

(9) Power to exercise the statutory power of advancement conferred by section 32 of the Trustee Act 1925 without regard to the restriction in paragraph (a) of subsection (1) of that section

(10) Power in any case where my Trustees have any obligation or discretion under the provisions of my will or under the general law to pay or apply income or capital to or for the benefit of any person who is

a minor to discharge that obligation or to exercise that discretion if and whenever they think fit to do so by making payment either to the parent or guardian of the minor or else to the minor personally if of the age of sixteen years at least and so that their respective receipts shall be a full discharge to my Trustees who shall not be required to see to the application of any income or capital so paid

(11) Power for any of my Trustees who is a Solicitor or other person engaged in any profession or business to be so employed or act and to charge and be paid all usual professional and other charges for any business transacted or work by him or his firm in connection with the administration and distribution of my estate or the trusts of my will whether or not of a professional nature and whether or not any person could have done the same personally

8 None of the powers and discretions conferred upon or vested in my Trustees (whether by virtue of any of the provisions of this my will or by operation of law) shall be capable of exercise in any way such as will or may directly or indirectly prevent section 71 of the Inheritance Act 1984 (or any re-enactment or replacement thereof for the time being) from applying or continuing to apply to any property given or held from time to time under the trusts of this my will for the benefit of any of my said children or their children widows or widowers which is for the time being settled property for the purposes of Inheritance Tax and in which for the time being no interest in possession subsists

9 The power of appointing from time to time a new or additional trustee or trustees of this my will shall be vested in my said wife during her life

10 I DECLARE that the foregoing provisions of my will are made and the dispositions of my estate therein contained shall have effect only (if at all) subject to the overriding powers and discretions which I hereby confer upon my Trustees but so that all such powers and discretions shall be exercisable only (if at all) with the consent of my said wife that is to say:

(1) During the period of twenty-three months following my death (or so much of that period during which any part of my estate continues to be subject to the trusts and powers of my will) my Trustees shall accumulate the income of my residuary estate (or so much thereof as is not from time to time applied for the maintenance education or benefit of any person pursuant to the provisions of paragraph (2) of this Clause) and shall hold such accumulations by way of addition to the capital of my residuary estate

(2) During the period aforesaid by Trustees shall have power at any time and from time to time and whenever they may in their absolute and uncontrolled discretion think fit to pay or apply the whole or any part or parts of the income or of the capital or of the income and the capital of my residuary estate to or for the benefit of all or any one or more exclusively of the others or other of the following persons that is

to say my said wife and any of my children and any widow widower or child born during the lifetime of the survivor of myself and my said wife of any child of mine who may predecease such survivor

(3) If any of my Trustees is or may become personally interested as a beneficiary in the exercise of (or omission to exercise) any or all of the powers and discretions hereby conferred upon my Trustees generally he may from time to time join in exercising that power or any such discretion as if he were not so interested and may nevertheless retain for his own use any benefit which in good faith he may derive in consequence thereof as if he were not a trustee

(4) My Trustees may exercise any or all of the powers and discretions hereby conferred upon them at any time after my death and in particular whether or not probate of my will has been granted and whether or not the administration of my estate has (subject to any exercise of any of the said powers and discretions) been completed

(5) Notwithstanding the fiduciary nature of the powers and discretions hereby conferred on my Trustees I further DECLARE that my Trustees may at any time wholly or in part release the same but without prejudice to any payment or application of capital or income previously made by them thereunder

IN WITNESS whereof I have hereunto set my hand this day of 199

SIGNED by the above-named
in
our joint presence and then
by us in his: }

# *Appendix 10*

# Statutory Provisions relating to Family Law

## FAMILY LAW REFORM ACT 1987, ss 1, 6, 18–21

### 1. General principle

(1) In this Act and enactments passed and instruments made after the coming into force of this section, references (however expressed) to any relationship between two persons shall, unless the contrary intention appears, be construed without regard to whether or not the father and mother of either of them, or the father and mother of any person through whom the relationship is deduced, have or had been married to each other at any time.

(2) In this Act and enactments passed after the coming into force of this section, unless the contrary intention appears—

(*a*) references to a person whose father and mother were married to each other at the time of his birth include; and

(*b*) references to a person whose father and mother were not married to each other at the time of his birth do not include,

references to any person to whom subsection (3) below applies, and cognate references shall be construed accordingly.

(3) This subsection applies to any person who—

(*a*) is treated as legitimate by virtue of section 1 of the Legitimacy Act 1976;

(*b*) is a legitimated person within the meaning of section 10 of that Act;

(*c*) is an adopted child within the meaning of Part IV of the Adoption Act 1976; or

(*d*) is otherwise treated in law as legitimate.

(4) For the purposes of construing references falling within subsection (2) above, the time of a person's birth shall be taken to include any time during the period beginning with—

(*a*) the insemination resulting in his birth; or

(*b*) where there was no such insemination, his conception,

and (in either case) ending with his birth.

**6. Appointment of guardians**

(1) At the end of section 3 of the 1971 Act (rights of surviving parent as to guardianship) there shall be added the following subsections—

'(3) Where the father and mother of a child were not married to each other at the time of his birth, this section does not apply unless the father satisfies the requirements of subsection (4) of this section.

(4) The father of a child satisfies the requirements of this subsection if—

(*a*) an order is in force under section 4 of the Family Law Reform Act 1987 giving him all the parental rights and duties with respect to the child; or

(*b*) he has a right to custody, legal or actual custody or care and control of the child by virtue of an order made under any other enactment.'

(2) At the end of section 4 of that Act (power of father and mother to appoint testamentary guardians) there shall be added the following subsection—

'(7) Where the father and mother of a child were not married to each other at the time of his birth—

(*a*) subsection (1) of this section does not apply, and subsection (3) of this section does not apply in relation to a guardian appointed by the mother, unless the father satisfies the requirements of section 3(4) of this Act; and

(*b*) any appointment under subsection (1) of this section shall be of no effect unless the father satisfies those requirements immediately before his death.'

(3) At the end of section 5 of the Act (power of court to appoint guardian for child having no parent etc) there shall be added the following subsection—

'(3) Where the father and mother of a child were not married to each other at the time of his birth, subsection (1) of this section shall have effect as if for the words 'no parent' there were substituted the words 'no mother, no father satisfying the requirements of section 3(4) of this Act'.'

## PART III
## PROPERTY RIGHTS

**18. Succession on intestacy**

(1) In Part IV of the Administration of Estates Act 1925 (which deals with the distribution of the estate of an intestate), references (however expressed) to any relationship between two persons shall be construed in accordance with section 1 above.

(2) For the purpose of subsection (1) above and that Part of that Act, a person whose father and mother were not married to each other at the time of his birth shall be presumed not to have been survived by his father, or by any person related to him only through his father, unless the contrary is shown.

(3) In section 50(1) of that Act (which relates to the construction of documents), the reference to Part IV of that Act, or to the foregoing provisions of that Part, shall in relation to an instrument inter vivos made, or a will or codicil coming into operation, after the coming into force of this section (but not in relation to instruments inter vivos made or wills or codicils coming into operation earlier) be construed as including references to this section.

(4) This section does not affect any rights under the intestacy of a person dying before the coming into force of this section.

**19. Dispositions of property**

(1) In the following dispositions, namely—

(*a*) dispositions inter vivos made on or after the date on which this section comes into force; and

(*b*) dispositions by will or codicil where the will or codicil is made on or after that date,

references (whether express or implied) to any relationship between two persons shall be construed in accordance with section 1 above.

(2) It is hereby declared that the use, without more, of the word 'heir' or 'heirs' or any expression which is used to create an entailed interest in real or personal property does not show a contrary intention for the purposes of section 1 as applied by subsection (1) above.

(3) In relation to the dispositions mentioned in subsection (1) above, section 33 of the Trustee Act 1925 (which specifies the trust implied by a direction that income is to be held on protective trusts for the benefit of any person) shall have effect as if any reference (however expressed) to any relationship between two persons were construed in accordance with section 1 above.

(4) Where under any disposition of real or personal property, any interest in such property is limited (whether subject to any preceding limitation or charge or not) in such a way that it would, apart from this section, devolve (as nearly as the law permits) along with a dignity or title of honour, then—

(*a*) whether or not the disposition contains an express reference to the dignity or title of honour; and

(*b*) whether or not the property or some interest in the property may in some event become severed from it,

nothing in this section shall operate to sever the property or any interest in it from the dignity or title, but the property or interest shall devolve in all respects as if this section had not been enacted.

(5) This section is without prejudice to section 42 of the Adoption Act 1976 (construction of dispositions in cases of adoption).

(6) In this section 'disposition' means a disposition, including an oral disposition, of real or personal property whether inter vivos or by will or codicil.

(7) Notwithstanding any rule of law, a disposition made by will or codicil executed before the date on which this section comes into force shall not be treated for the purposes of this section as made on or after that date by reason only that the will or codicil is confirmed by a codicil executed on or after that date.

**20. No special protection for trustees and personal representatives**

Section 17 of the Family Law Reform Act 1969 (which enables trustees and personal representatives to distribute property without having ascertained that no person whose parents were not married to each other at the time of his birth, or who claims through such a person, is or may be entitled to an interest in the property) shall cease to have effect.

**21. Entitlement to grant of probate etc**

(1) For the purpose of determining the person or persons who would in accordance with probate rules be entitled to a grant of probate or administration in respect of the estate of a deceased person, the deceased shall be presumed, unless the contrary is shown, not to have been survived—

(*a*) by any person related to him whose father and mother were not married to each other at the time of his birth; or

(*b*) by any person whose relationship with him is deduced through such a person as is mentioned in paragraph (*a*) above.

(2) In this section 'probate rules' means rules of court made under section 127 of the Supreme Court Act 1981.

(3) This section does not apply in relation to the estate of a person dying before the coming into force of this section.

*Appendix 11*

# Statutory Provisions relating to Recognition of Trusts

## Recognition of Trusts Act 1987

### SCHEDULE

Section 1

### Convention on the Law Applicable to Trusts and on Their Recognition

#### Chapter I—Scope

*Article 1*

This Convention specifies the law applicable to trusts and governs their recognition.

*Article 2*

For the purpose of this Convention, the term 'trust' refers to the legal relationship created—inter vivos or on death—by a person, the settlor, when assets have been placed under the control of a trustee for the benefit of a beneficiary or for a specified purpose.

A trust has the following characteristics—

(*a*) the assets constitute a separate fund and are not a part of the trustee's own estate;

(*b*) title to the trust assets stands in the name of the trustees or in the name of another person on behalf of the trustee;

(*c*) the trustee has the power and the duty, in respect of which he is accountable, to manage, employ or dispose of the assets in accordance with the terms of the trust and the special duties imposed upon him by law.

The reservation by the settlor of certain rights and powers, and the fact that the trustee may himself have rights as a beneficiary, are not necessarily inconsistent with the existence of a trust.

*Article 3*

The Convention applies only to trusts created voluntarily and evidenced in writing.

### *Article 4*

The Convention does not apply to preliminary issues relating to the validity of wills or of other acts by virtue of which assets are transferred to the trustee.

### *Article 5*

The Convention does not apply to the extent that the law specified by Chapter II does not provide for trusts or the category of trusts involved.

## CHAPTER II—APPLICABLE LAW

### *Article 6*

A trust shall be governed by the law chosen by the settlor. The choice must be express or be implied in the terms of the instrument creating or the writing evidencing the trust, interpreted, if necessary, in the light of the circumstances of the case.

Where the law chosen under the previous paragraph does not provide for trusts or the category of trust involved, the choice shall not be effective and the law specified in Article 7 shall apply.

### *Article 7*

Where no applicable law has been chosen, a trust shall be governed by the law with which it is most closely connected.

In ascertaining the law with which a trust is most closely connected reference shall be made in particular to—

(*a*) the place of administration of the trust designated by the settlor;
(*b*) the situs of the assets of the trust;
(*c*) the place of residence or business of the trustee;
(*d*) the objects of the trust and the places where they are to be fulfilled.

### *Article 8*

The law specified by Article 6 or 7 shall govern the validity of the trust, its construction, its effects and the administration of the trust. In particular that law shall govern—

(*a*) the appointment, resignation and removal of trustees, the capacity to act as a trustee, and the devolution of the office of trustee;
(*b*) the rights and duties of trustees among themselves;
(*c*) the right of trustees to delegate in whole or in part the discharge of their duties or the exercise of their powers;
(*d*) the power of trustees to administer or to dispose of trust assets, to create security interests in the trust assets, or to acquire new assets;
(*e*) the powers of investment of trustees;

(*f*) restrictions upon the duration of the trust, and upon the power to accumulate the income of the trust;
(*g*) the relationships between the trustees and the beneficiaries including the personal liability of the trustees to the beneficiaries;
(*h*) the variation or termination of the trust;
(*i*) the distribution of the trust assets;
(*j*) the duty of trustees to account for their administration.

*Article 9*

In applying this Chapter a severable aspect of the trust, particularly matters of administration, may be governed by a different law.

*Article 10*

The law applicable to the validity of the trust shall determine whether that law or the law governing a severable aspect of the trust may be replaced by another law.

## Chapter III—Recognition

*Article 11*

A trust created in accordance with the law specified by the preceding Chapter shall be recognised as a trust.

Such recognition shall imply, as a minimum, that the trust property constitutes a separate fund, that the trustee may sue and be sued in his capacity as trustee, and that he may appear or act in this capacity before a notary or any person acting in an official capacity.

In so far as the law applicable to the trust requires or provides, such recognition shall imply in particular—
(*a*) that personal creditors of the trustees shall have no recourse against the trust assets;
(*b*) that the trust assets shall not form part of the trustee's estate upon his insolvency or bankruptcy;
(*c*) that the trust assets shall not form part of the matrimonial property of the trustee or his spouse nor part of the trustee's estate upon his death;
(*d*) that the trust assets may be recovered when the trustee, in breach of trust, has mingled trust assets with his own property or has alienated trust assets. However, the rights and obligations of any third party holder of the assets shall remain subject to the law determined by the choice of law rules of the forum.

*Article 12*

Where the trustee desires to register assets, movable or immovable, or documents of title to them, he shall be entitled, in so far as this is not prohibited by or inconsistent with the law of the State where registration is sought, to do so in his capacity as trustee or in such other way that the existence of the trust is disclosed.

*Article 14*

The Convention shall not prevent the application of rules of law more favourable to the recognition of trusts.

## CHAPTER IV—GENERAL CLAUSES

*Article 15*

The Convention does not prevent the application of provisions of the law designated by the conflicts rules of the forum, in so far as those provisions cannot be derogated from by voluntary act, relating in particular to the following matters—

(*a*) the protection of minors and incapable parties;
(*b*) the personal and proprietary effects of marriage;
(*c*) succession rights, testate and intestate, especially the indefeasible shares of spouses and relatives;
(*d*) the transfer of title to property and security interests in property;
(*e*) the protection of creditors in matters of insolvency;
(*f*) the protection, in other respects, of third parties acting in good faith.

If recognition of a trust is prevented by application of the preceding paragraph, the court shall try to give effect to the objects of the trust by other means.

*Article 16*

The Convention does not prevent the application of those provisions of the law of the forum which must be applied even to international situations, irrespective of rules of conflict of laws.

*Article 17*

In the Convention the word 'law' means the rules of law in force in a State other than its rules of conflict of laws.

*Article 18*

The provisions of the Convention may be disregarded when their application would be manifestly incompatible with public policy.

*Article 22*

The Convention applies to trusts regardless of the date on which they were created.

# Index

The figures in ordinary type refer to page numbers. The figures in bold type refer to form numbers.

SURVIVORSHIP CONDITIONS P. 28
30 DAY RULE